"An important contribution to remembering the brave men and women who gave their lives to defending India's freedom and continuity of her civilization."

—Sanjeev Sanyal
Author and Principal Economic Adviser to Govt. of India

"In India, since times immemorial, we have sung the praises and celebrated the valorous deeds of our Dharmic warriors. Of many thousands of these heroes, Manoshi Sinha selects fifty-two — almost one for each week of the year — whose stories she re-tells with eloquent aplomb. Especially noteworthy in these pages are our forgotten, almost unsung braves, Svarajya soldiers I would call them, whose inspiring feats will fill us will pride and gratitude."

—Makarand R. Paranjape
Poet, Literary Critic, Academic, Professor at JNU

"India's history is a history of warriors. But only a handful are known to most Indians. Manoshi Sinha's book should be celebrated, and read, by everyone who is interested in the past or future of India."

—Hindol Sengupta
Journalist, Entrepreneur and Author

"Down the tumultuous centuries, when our forbearers faced one onslaught after another, there were not many who faced the challenge in a manner which could inspire us today. Of those who did, some had a degree of success, others did not. Yet they all symbolized the valour and undying spirit of India-the nation which despite hundreds of years of foreign rule could not be fully conquered. It is a pity that still not much attention is paid to the valiant warriors of past in India today. Manoshi Sinha Rawal's attempt in this context is seminal. Though clichéd, American president Calvin Coolidge's words are so apt for India. "A nation that forgets its heroes will itself soon be forgotten."

—Anuj Dhar
Former Journalist and Bestselling Author of India's Biggest Cover-Up

SAFFRON SWORDS

Centuries of Indic Resistance to Invaders

Manoshi Sinha Rawal
Yogaditya Singh Rawal

गरुड

First published in India 2019

Copyright © 2019
Manoshi Sinha Rawal
Yogaditya Singh Rawal

ISBN: 978-1-942426-10-3
Cover Design: Rakesh Chaudhary

Garuda Prakashan Private Limited
Gurugram, Bharat
www.garudaprakashan.com
www.garudabooks.com

Printed in India

ॐ

सरस्वति नमस्तुभ्यं वरदे कामरूपिणि ।
विद्यारम्भं करिष्यामि सिद्धिर्भवतु मे सदा ॥

Dedicated to

Hari Kiran Vadlamani Sir, my mentor, who further gave wings to my dreams.

Smt. Sudha Verma, my mother-in-law and Author Saiswaroopa Iyer Ji, two great souls, who were the first to advise me to compile the stories of the unsung warriors of India into a book.

Foreword

This is a book of brave heroes and heroines of India down the ages. India is one of the oldest civilizations with the *Vedas* as one of the oldest written records. We have historical records of our ancient times recorded in the *Ramayana* and the *Mahabharata*. Various dynasties ruled the country with golden periods witnessed during the Magadhas, Mauryas, Vijaynagara, to name a few. During Islamic and colonial rule, hundreds and thousands of our warriors gave a stiff resistance. But their saga of blood and glory, their tales of valor have not been highlighted in our History text books. Few tales that find a place in the history text books are not well described.

Manoshi Sinha Rawal and Yogaditya Singh Rawal have highlighted those neglected, unknown, and hidden tales of valor from the last 1300 years in this book *Saffron Swords*. There are 52 tales of valor, which encompass the brave exploits of warriors from across the country, from east to the west, north to the south. These include Nag Bhat I, Suhal Dev, Raja Prithu, Mula Gabharu, Raja Narasimhadeva, Rani Velu Nacchiyar, Kuyili, Hemchandra Vikramaditya, Saraswathi Rajamani, Shivdevi Tomar, Alluri Sitarama Raju, Uda Devi, Mahabiri Devi, Matmur Jamoh, Paona Brajabasi, Pasaltha Khaungchera, Rani Roipulliani, and more warriors.

One of the chapters delves on Nag Bhat I, a Gurjar Pratihar king, who with an alliance of Chalukyas, Rashtrakutas, Guhils, and more forces decimated the combined Arab army led by Emir Junaid of Sind in 738 AD. In the words of Suleiman, an Arab chronicler, the Arab forces in this battle 'were scattered like hay by the hoofs of the horses of the Gurjar king and his alliances'. Inscriptions about this great victory have been found at various places including Gwalior in Madhya Pradesh.

The book has described the valorous saga of many unknown warriors. Narasimhadeva I of Orissa defeated Tughan Khan, the Turkish Muslim Nawab of Bengal in 1244 AD. He was the first king of Orissa to give a strong defence against Muslim invasion during his reign. He was one of the greatest rulers of the imperial Ganga family, of the Eastern Ganga dynasty.

There is one tale of valor of Mula Gabharu, the wife of Ahom commander Phrasengmung Borgohain. She fought like Goddess Shakti in battlefield in 1533 AD against Mohammedan forces of the Bengal Sultanate commanded by Turbak Khan, an Afghan. Khan treacherously killed Phrasengmung Borgohain in battle. The death of the commander demoralized the Ahom forces. Mula Gabharu immediately set to action, marching towards the battlefield on a horse with a flashing sword in hand. She killed two Lieutenants of the enemy including several soldiers before attaining martyrdom in the battlefield. The Ahoms won this battle.

In one tale, the book describes how Kapaya Nayaka led a confederation of Telugu nobles to liberate the South Indian kingdom of Warangal from the Delhi Sultanate. Delhi was then under the Tughlaqs. He drove the Tughlaqs out of the Warangal territory in 1336.

The British established their supremacy in parts of the northeastern states after the Treaty of Yandaboo signed in 1826 with Burma. It was in the 1900s that the British moved inwards towards the hill regions of Arunachal Pradesh. There is a tale of valor of Matmur Jamoh and a group of Adi warriors from Pasighat, Arunachal Pradesh. They collectively killed two British officers and their attendants in 1911.

Then there is description of the valorous tale of Roipulliani, an 84 year old village chief from Mizoram. The book describes how she defended her people from British aggression. Roipulliani never paid any tax to the British nor gave in to any of their demands. The following was her declaration, which she followed till the end of her rule: "My subjects and I have never paid any tax to anyone, neither have we done any forced labor. We are the owners of this land. We must evict and chase out any and everyone who is an alien."

Today, India is a youthful country with almost 50% of her population below the age of 25. It needs role models to inspire and motivate. This book therefore fulfills a very great need of our times. I commend the authors for this pioneering effort.

—Maj Gen (Dr.) GD Bakshi

Preface

Indian History text books hardly glorify the real warriors of the soil. Select few warriors find a place in the text books. We grow up reading more about the glories of invaders rather than the brave feats of our ancestors from the east to west, north to south. When our history books blank several great heroes and heroines and glorify a select few, and when we read only about defeats and no resistance by our ancestors, we end up deviating ourselves from a sense of belongingness for the nation. We do not know about our own historical roots. History needs to be retold. Our objective behind writing this book is presenting to the citizens of the country and the world about the brave exploits of our warriors from the last 1300 plus years.

In this context, my husband Yogaditya Singh Rawal, co-author of this book says, "History, especially Military History being my favorite subject, I was often left wondering: were we always defeated? Were we on the losing side always? So I started reading whatever I could find anywhere beyond the NCERT books. I, like countless others, was influenced much by the defeats and routs. Such portrayal creates a feeling that we were inferior to the invaders, thus sowing the seeds of inferiority complex. This happens to such an extent that one robotically tends to think that all that is from foreign lands is better than what we have here."

Rawal further says, "Let us trace the path of finding and knowing about the battles which we have never read before, about heroes we never knew existed. Let us read about the stratagems, the pure valor and strength of our brave warriors who decimated the invaders."

There are 52 tales of Indian valor in this book. Many of these warriors are unheard of. Few names are Matmur Jamoh, Pasaltha

Khaungchera, Kapaya Nayaka, Alluri Sitarama Raju, Kaneganti Hanumanthu, Narasimhadeva, Roipulliani, Suhaldev, Rana Hammir Singh, Rani Velu Nacchiyar, Chain Singh, Kuyili, Avantibai, Suhungmung, Mula Gabharu, Kanhoji Angre, Naiki Devi. All of these warriors put up a brave resistance against Muslim rulers and British supremacy. Few of these warriors won battles against Mughals, Turks, Lodhis, and the Sultanate.

A friend Govind Raj, a doctor from Kochi, Kerala says, "We Indians are the most shameless, pride-less and gutless people with extreme deficiency of self respect. A community, a state or a nation that does not respect its history will never be taken seriously and will remain a third world country forever. We are utterly careless about our icons while we get insanely jingoistic about as trivial a thing as a Cricket match victory over Bangladesh. That is why we find it tough to find respect among ourselves and in the world community. When our history books blank several great heroes and glorify a select few, we as a nation become a joke."

There are hundreds and thousands of unsung warriors from the east to west, north to south, who put up a brave resistance against Muslim rulers in battle and against British oppression. They don't find a place in history text books. Hence the citizens of India do not get to read or know about the brave exploits of their own ancestors! When citizens of a nation are inspired by the exploits of warriors from the past, patriotism robotically evolves. This spirit is lacking in India. Because real history still remains hidden.

Tamal Sanyal, a friend from Varanasi, says, "The Nation which forgets its Heroes, is soon doomed, because it is their deeds only, which inspires the youth towards true patriotism and only true patriotism can inspire sacrifice and sacrifice is necessary for a Nation's survival. So it's necessary to see what kind of narrative we build - a true narrative, which demands only dedication and sacrifice or a rosy narrative which will surely ensure re-enslavement of the nation."

This book is an effort to bring to you the brave feats of our ancestors — those tales of valor, which we should feel proud of.

My Rakhi brother, Anjan Mitra Da says, "History is the strength and source of knowledge for a nation. The next generation when aware of it can know and avoid past mistakes. When that is doctored in a meticulous way, the fundamental fabric of the nation is torn apart."

A rich heritage and culture identifies India. Let's bask in the glory, the valor of our ancestors.

—*Manoshi Sinha Rawal*

Acknowledgement

I draw inspiration from the brave feats of our ancestors, from across the four corners of Bharat. As I read and write about them, I could feel their blessings. It is their blessings that resulted in the shaping of *Saffron Swords*. Few stories of valor gave me goose bumps as I wrote and few stories brought tears to my eyes. These were tears of pride, of glory, of valorous resistance to foreign rule, of sacrifice. These were tears of love for the motherland. There have been near and dear ones, friends and strangers, who directly and indirectly steered me, with their love, with their support, and with their motivation, helping me give shape to this book. I thank them all.

Foremost, I offer my gratitude to my *Maa* Anupoma and *Baba* Mahendra, who have brought me to this world, who have laid for me a strong foundation so that I work miracles in my life, weaving my life amid the many challenges I come across from time to time. *Maa* is no more, but I know, she is watching me from her world and blessing us. Her teachings and her sacrifices for us continue to inspire and motivate me at every step of my life. I inherited my interest in History and curiosity in knowing our ancient heritage and culture from my Baba since my childhood.

Maa Saraswati, my Goddess and the Goddess of millions, for blessing me and inciting me to type letters into words, words into sentences, sentences into paragraphs, which ultimately resulted in the creation of a book.

Maj Gen (Dr) GD Bakshi, combat veteran and author of 37 books for the Foreword. When he addresses me as *Bitia Rani* every time we interact, I could feel his blessings. He is a true son of the soil, for whom Nation always comes first.

Smt. Sudha Verma, my mother-in-law, who first advised me to compile the valorous stories of the great heroes and heroines of India into a book. Herself a postgraduate in Sanskrit and Hindi, she often acquainted me with the philosophies of life, depicted in the *Vedas* in the coffee-table at home and during the evening stroll. I offer my gratitude to her.

My husband Yogaditya Singh Rawal, who is the co-author of this book, for taking me to historical places across India, to the forts and fortresses where kings and queens once ruled, to ancient and medieval temples where devotees of yester years once offered their prayers, and to the sites of ancient and medieval glory.

Hari Kiran Vadlamani Sir, for further giving wings to my dreams. He has been working selflessly and devotedly towards bringing an intellectual, cultural and spiritual renaissance of Bharat through his organization Indic Academy. Indic Today, Indic Book Club, Creative India mag, Advaita, Indic Knowledge Systems, and Indic Festivals are all arms of Indic Academy, operational worldwide.

My *rakhi* brothers Sri Rameshwar Teli, member of the Bharatiya Janata Party and elected to the Lok Sabha from Dibrugarh, Assam (Lok Sabha constituency) in the general elections of 2014 and Sri G.D. Chelleng, Managing Director of M/S Security Agency for encouraging me throughout in my venture.

My sisters Manobi, Manomi, Millee, and Anamika, my brother Raja and my sister in law Sudeshna, my brother-in-law Pragyaditya, my *nanad* Sumedha Nidhi, my brothers-in-law Shibu, Bhaskar, Tapesh, and Manoj, for being by my side, in my heart, every moment. How can I miss my nephews Nishesh, Vishesh, Taksheel, and nieces Abhishree (Tia) and Mitakshi, who are always a source of bliss for me! Without them all, my world lacks.

Saiswaroopa Iyer, London-based bestselling author of *Abhaya*, *Avishi*, and *Mauri* for advising me to compile the stories and get them published as a book. My gratefulness to K Raghuraman from Chennai and Anjan Mitra Dada who gave me the same advice. Dev Mukerji from Vancouver, Devneet Lamba, my brother from Meerut, and my school teacher Renuka Sharma Mam, for always motivating me to unearth the hidden glory of the brave sons and daughters of the soil.

The publishing team at Garuda Publications, especially Sankrant Sanu and Ankur Pathak for translating our manuscript into a book.

I thank you, the readers, for the love you shower on us.

—Manoshi Sinha Rawal

Contents

Foreword ix

Preface xiii

Acknowledgement xvi

1. Rampyari Gurjar: How 40,000 Women Led by Rampyari
   Gurjar Attacked Taimur and His Forces 23

2. Prithu: Assam King Who Badly Defeated Bakhtiyar Khilji
   in 1206 AD 29

3. Saraswathi Rajamani: Youngest Spy to Work for Netaji
   Bose's INA 33

4. Jhalkaribai: Rani Laxmibai's Lookalike Who Defended
   Jhansi against British in 1857-58 36

5. Bajiprabhu Deshpande: Led 300 Soldiers against 12000
   Adilshahi Army, Defending Shivaji 40

6. Karnavati: Garhwal Queen who Defeated Mughal Army
   in 1640; Cut Noses of Surviving Invaders 45

7. Rana Sanga: Fiercely Defeated Delhi Sultan in Khatoli
   Battle 50

8. Battle of Haldighati: Who Won? Rana Pratap or Akbar?
   The Real Story! 53

9. Tonkham Borpatra Gohain: Ahom General Who
   Defeated and Killed Afghan Turbak Khan in 1533 AD 60

10. Veer Savarkar: Active Role in Assassination of British
    Officials; Coined 'Hindutva' 63

11. Chennamma: Rani of Keladi Who Fought Bravely against
    Mughals and Gave Shelter to Shivaji's Son   68

12. Kuyili: First Human Bomb of India against British   73

13. Unknown Hindu Yogi: How He Shot Dead a British
    Captain in Front of British Army in 1857!   77

14. Gurjars in Freedom Movement in 1824: 100s of Gurjars
    Martyred and 100s Hung in Single Tree   81

15. Naiki Devi: Gujarat Chalukyan Queen Who Defeated
    Mohammad Ghori in 1178 Battle   85

16. Tarabai Bhosale: Maratha Queen Who Successfully Led
    War against Aurangzeb's Forces   88

17. Baji Rout: Youngest Freedom Fighter Martyred at 12 Years   94

18. Tirot Sing: Meghalaya King, Who was Guerrilla Terror to
    British from 1829 to 1833   98

19. The Bishnois: 15th Century Legacy of Vaishnava
    Theology and Ecology Conservation   103

20. Kanaklata Barua: Freedom Fighter Martyred at 17 for
    Holding High the National Flag   107

21. Uda Devi: The Unsung Heroine Who Killed 32 British
    Soldiers in Sikandar Bagh in 1857   110

22. Roipulliani: 84 Year Old Mizoram Village Chief Who
    Defended her People from British Aggression   114

23. Kartar Singh Sarabha: Sikh Freedom Fighter Martyred at
    19; Bhagat Singh Regarded Him as Guru   117

24. Bhagat Singh, Rajguru, and Sukhdev: What You Must
    Know   121

25. Chandrashekhar Azad: The Journey for 'Swatantrata'   125

26. Khudiram Bose: An Orphan at 7 to Hanging by British at
    Age 18   129

27. Paona Brajabashi: Fearless Manipur General Who Led
    Fierce Battle against British in 1891   134

28. Shivdevi Tomar: 16 Year Old Jat Girl Who Killed 17
    British Soldiers during Revolt of 1857   138

29. Veerapandiya Kattabomman: Tamil Nadu Chieftain Who
    Opposed British Rule, Defeated Them Twice and Hanged
    at 39   141

30. Kanhoji Angre: 18th Century Maratha Navy Admiral
    Who Was Never Defeated by European Forces   146

31. Pasaltha Khuangchera And Brave Warriors of Mizoram
    Who Fought against Britishers   150

32. Lakshmi Bai: Motherless at 4 to Battlefield Warrior
    Against British Forces and Martyrdom at 30   155

33. Hemchandra Vikramaditya: From a Vegetable Seller to
    the Last Hindu Ruler of Delhi   161

34. Alluri Sitarama Raju: Freedom Fighter Who Killed
    Several British Officers and Martyred at 26   166

35. Rana Hammir Singh: Regained Mewar from Delhi
    Sultanate and Rajputana from Tughlaqs   169

36. Kakatiyas and Kapaya Nayaka: Telugu Chieftain Who
    Reconquered Warangal from Delhi Sultanate   174

37. Matmur Jamoh: Arunachal Pradesh Freedom Fighter
    Who Killed British Officer; Jailed at Kalapani   179

38. Kalyan Singh Gurjar: Terrorized the British by Killing
    Many Britishers in 1822-24   183

39. Sambhudhan Phonglo: Dimasa Freedom Fighter Who
    Raised an Army for War against British   188

40. Banda Singh: Sikh General Who Led 5 Battles to Victory
    against Mughals and Established Supremacy in Punjab   194

41. Mula Gabharu: Ahom Warrior Who Killed Two
    Lieutenants of Muslim Army in 1533 Battle   201

42. Chain Singh: 24 Year Old Rajput Who Led an Army of
    50 against Huge British Force in 1824   205

43. Kaneganti Hanumanthu: Revolted Against British Tax
    Policy Imposed on Farmers; Martyred at 30   210

44. Avantibai: Ramgarh Rani who Won 1st Battle against
    British and Martyred in 2nd at 27 Years   213

45. Mahabiri Devi: How Mahabiri Devi and 22 Village
    Women Killed Many British Soldiers in 1857   216

46. Suhaldev: Shravasti Raja who Defeated and Killed
    Ghaznavid General Salar Masud in 1034 AD   218

47. Durgadas Rathore: Protected Jodhpur Prince from
    Aurangzeb and Kept Marwar Flag Flying High   223

48. Prataprao Gurjar: Defeat of Mughal Army in Salher Battle
    and Encounter with Bahalol Khan   228

49. Narasimhadeva: Orissa King Who Defeated Turkic
    Afghan Tughan Khan in 1244 AD   233

50. Benoy Badal Dinesh: Bengal Freedom Fighters who Killed
    Col NS Simpson, British IG of Police   237

51. Nag Bhat I: This Gurjar Pratihar King Badly Defeated
    Arab Forces   242

52. Santi Ghosh and Suniti Choudhury: How the Two
    Teenage Freedom Fighters Assassinated British Magistrate 245

53. Bibliography   249

1

Rampyari Gurjar

How 40,000 Women Led by Rampyari Gurjar Attacked Taimur and His Forces

Rampyari Gurjar! She is an unknown name in Indian History. But her tale of valor is unmatched in the annals of our history books. Like thousands of other warriors who don't find a place in our historical records, she remains unsung. 20-year old Rampyari Gurjar, along with 40,000 women warriors, wreaked havoc on Taimur in Meerut and Haridwar in 1398, forcing him to flee India. Around 80,000 men from different communities, ranging from Jats, Gurjars, Rajputs, Brahmins to Ahirs, Valmikis, and hill tribes were part of the troop that attacked Taimur and slaughtered a major portion of his army. Meerut, Haridwar and neighboring areas were saved from being looted and plundered by Taimur. They saved the Hindus of the region from being massacred. Who doesn't know about Taimur Lang who massacred lakhs of Hindus, razed temples to the ground, and looted wealth of temples and civilians! All of this happened on his way from across the Indus River covering Attock towards Delhi. But he couldn't do this act of barbarism on his return route!

Rampyari Gurjar was born in Saharanpur in a Chauhan Gurjar family. During her childhood days, she loved listening to tales of valor of Indian warriors. She dressed up as a male as she grew up and took interests in exercises and wrestling. She was daring and fearless since her childhood. While in the farmland, she would quietly perform the daily exercises. She also practiced the art of warfare all by herself. She watched wrestling matches with great zest. She was known far and wide for her soldierly traits.

Much of the historical records available about the glories and victories of Indian warriors were destroyed by the British. This was to prove their superiority and show the later generations and the world that they were superior and that they civilized India. The Gurjars were very brutal against British. They slaughtered a great number of Britishers. In return, the British declared the Gurjars as a criminal tribe in records and wiped off whatever historical records they could come across about this community. Counted few Britishers left true accounts they saw. Through these accounts, true history of this community and accounts of heroism of other Indian warriors are exposed. Besides, historical ballads and folklores, passed down from one generation to another orally, glorify the warriors. Folklores and ballads in the UP, Haridwar, and Garhwal region glorify Rampyari Gurjar and all those warriors who fought against Taimur.

Most of the available historical records glorify Taimur's conquest of Delhi. These records don't mention the barbaric Turco-Mongol conqueror's failed expedition in Meerut, Haridwar, and the Garhwal region. The Hairdwar-Garhwal episode does find mention in 15th-century Persian historian Sharaf ad-Dīn'Alī Yazdī's book *Zafarnama*, a biography on Taimur. The same is quoted by Muhammad ibn Arabshah, an Arab writer and traveler, in a biography on the Turco-Mongol conqueror.

What actually happened to Taimur that hastened him to flee India without repeating the crimes he committed during his onward journey to Delhi? Historical records describe the barbarism committed by Taimur in Delhi. He had 100,000 Hindu captives by the time he reached Delhi. He executed all of them and created a pillar with the heads. He spared those who converted to Islam. Vincent A Smith in his book *The Oxford History of India: From the Earliest Times to the End of 1911* wrote how Taimur's attack was targeted on the Hindu population. His forces spared only Muslim neighbourhoods and massacred or enslaved the Hindus.

Henry Miers Elliot and John Dowson in their book *The History of India, as Told by Its Own Historians: The Muhammadan Period. Vol. III* finds mention of the following description about Taimur's barbarism in Delhi, quoted from Sharaf ad-Dīn'Alī Yazdī's book *Zafarnama:*

'(Timur's) soldiers grew more eager for plunder and destruction. On that Friday night, there were about 15,000 men in the city who were engaged from early eve till morning in plundering and burning the houses. In many places the impure infidel gabrs (of Delhi) made resistance. (...) Every soldier obtained more than twenty persons as slaves, and some brought as many as fifty or a hundred men, women and children as slaves of the city. The other plunder and spoils were immense, gems and jewels of all sorts, rubies, diamonds, stuffs and fabrics, vases and vessels of gold and silver. (...) On the 19th of the month Old Delhi was thought of, for many Hindus had fled thither. Amir Shah Malik and Ali Sultan Tawachi, with 500 trusty men, proceeded against them, and falling upon them with the sword despatched them to hell.'

Taimur's return journey was not by choice, but by compulsion. He was badly defeated in several battles in Meerut and Haridwar. He had to flee with a fatal wound that led to his death later.

During this time, Devpala, a Jat was the leader in the region comprising Meerut, Saharanpur, parts of Haryana, and Haridwar. The people were alerted of the atrocities and massacre of Hindus committed by Taimur. People of different communities, principally Jats, Gurjars, Ahirs, Valmikis, Rajputs, Brahmins, tribals, and more got united for a common cause — to save the region from being looted and plundered and to save the Hindus from being massacred. Panchayat system was prevalent during this time under Devpala.

A Mahapanchayat was organized in urgency under the instructions of Devpala. It was around the end of 1398 when Taimur was in Delhi. Leaders from adjoining regions attended the Mahapanchayat. It was decided that 500 young horsemen would spy on Taimur to know about his plans and future attacks. That all strong men and women of the region would take up arms, get trained, and join the Mahapanchayat army. That the elders and children would be shifted to safe places and few villages prone to attacks would be vacated.

At this Mahapanchayat, Mahabali Jograj Singh Gurjar was chosen as the Supreme General. Around 80,000 men joined the cause. Several generals were chosen by the panchayat. Among the generals were Mamchand Gurjar, Harbir Singh Gulia Jat, Dhula Valmiki, Durjanpal Ahir, Tuhiram Rajput, Umra Tyagi, Hula Nai, to name a few.

Rampyari Gurjar was made the Commander of the women wing. She was only 20 years old, but was strong and was trained in the art of warfare. She had leadership attributes. She was entrusted to expand her army by requesting more women to join. Other women who were appointed in similar rank were Hardai Jat, Devi Kaur Rajput, Chandro Brahmin, and Ramdai Tyagi. In a short period of time, around 40,000 young village women comprising of Jats, Gurjars, Rajputs, Brahmins, Ahirs, Valmikis, and more joined the cause under Rampyari Gurjar. These women never took part in a battle. But to save the motherland, to save the temples, to save the Hindus from being slaughtered, they were ready to sacrifice their lives. She trained the women on the various tactics of using weapons.

Meanwhile, the entrusted spies brought the news that Taimur would be advancing towards Meerut. This meant that he might take the route towards Saharanpur, Haridwar, and Garhwal. All the 80,000 men and 40,000 women warriors assembled to hear from their Supreme General Mahabali Jograj Singh Gurjar. They were armed with swords and chanted war cries. Jograj Singh Gurjar thundered thus,

'Veeroh, reflect on the discourse given by Lord Krishna to Arjun in the *Bhagavad Gita*. For us the door to heaven (*moksha*) has been opened. That *moksha*, which the Rishi Munis achieve by doing Yoga, the hero warriors achieve by sacrificing their lives on the battlefield. Save the nation, that is — sacrifice yourselves, the world will honor you. You have chosen me leader. To my last breath I will not withdraw. I salute the Panchayat, and take oath that until my last breath I will defend the soil of Bharat. Our nation has been shaken by the crimes and attacks of Taimur. Warriors arise and do not delay. Fight the enemy army and throw them out of the nation.'

Rampyari Gurjar kissed her sword, so did the other women warriors. The men and the women together took an oath that until their last breath they would obey the Supreme General and sacrifice their lives for the motherland. They pledged that they would never let Taimur and his army breathe freely until they were driven out of the country.

For reduced casualties of the Hindu army, it was decided that they would attack Taimur and his army following Guerilla warfare techniques and plan according to information given by the spies. The Guerrilla warfare involved involvement of a small group of combatants in ambushes, hit-and-run tactics, sabotage, raids, etc. using arms. They also decided to face the enemy forces in open battles.

Rampyari Gurjar instructed her troops how to act during Taimur's attack. It was decided that the women would accompany the men. While part of the group of women would take up arms and attack the enemy, few would prepare food for the entire unit. Few would also help deliver war materials to men and women warriors in action. Rampyari Gurjar also entrusted the brave women to attack and loot the supplies of the enemy. This would lead to food shortage of the enemy. Their starvation would only weaken their spirits and the Hindu army could wreak havoc in the enemy lines.

According to an account by Dalip Singh Ahlawat in *Jat History*, 20,000 Mahapanchayat warriors laid a surprise attack on Taimur's army in the middle of the night in Delhi. 9,000 of the enemy soldiers were slaughtered and their corpses thrown in river Yamuna. Before daylight, the Mahapanchayat warriors disappeared towards the outskirts of Delhi, far away from Taimur's forces. This continued for three nights. A frustrated Taimur Lang then left Delhi and advanced towards Meerut.

Taimur Lang's attempt of plundering Meerut failed. Following the information given by the Panchayat spies, the heavily populated areas in Meerut were emptied and precious belongings shifted to a safe place. Villages en route to Meerut from Delhi, especially the route taken by Taimur, were also vacated. Hence Taimur and his army felt restless. The Mahapanchayat warriors attacked Taimur's forces during the day.

At night Rampyari Gurjar and the women warriors laid surprise Guerrilla attacks in the enemy camps, butchering the Mohammedan forces and looting their food supplies. As the enemy soldiers were taken unawares, they could not retaliate fully. Many of them were killed. They remained alert the next night and retaliated. This continued for a couple of days. The Hindu army gave the enemy no chance to take rest or relax even at night. There were casualties from both sides, but it was higher on the enemy side.

Frustrated, Taimur and his forces marched towards Haridwar. The hill tribes, who were experts in archery, joined the Hindu forces. The Mahapanchayat followed the same strategy, as they followed in Meerut. Taimur was defeated thrice in Haridwar. In the last battle, 22 year old Harbir Singh Gulia Jat was able to hit Taimur on his chest with a spear. In retaliation, Taimur's soldiers badly wounded Harbir. Jograj Singh Gurjar took charge of the situation, at the same time facilitating the wounded Harbir to be taken to a safe place. The wounded Taimur, escorted by one his ablest soldiers, fled the battlefield.

It is said Taimur could not recover fully from this wound. Description about this wound in a Haridwar battle finds mention in one of Taimur's biographies. He died after 7 years. Taimur had come to India with an army of over 1 and half lakh men. He returned with only a few thousand soldiers. The rest were slain by the Hindu army. Around 40000 Mahapanchayat Hindu warriors, both men and women, attained martyrdom. But they saved the region from being looted and plundered. They saved the Hindus from being massacred.

Salute to Rampyari Gurjar and the Mahapanchayat warriors! Jai Hind!

2

Prithu

Assam King Who Badly Defeated Bakhtiyar Khilji in 1206 AD

The antiquity of Assam dates back to several thousand years. Assam finds mention as 'Pragjyotishpur' in the *Ramayana, Mahabharata, Puranas* and other ancient Indian scriptures. Later, the kingdom was named 'Kamrupa', which also finds mention in several scriptures. Nidhanpur and Doobi inscriptions tell about the kings of the dynasty of Naraka, Bhagadatta and Vajradatta and their descendants, who ruled for 3000 years. The Allahabad inscription of Samudragupta mentions Kamrupa as a frontier territory.

There is another connotation to the naming of this northeastern kingdom of Bharat as Kamrupa. Assam is home to the Peacock Island, a small hillock in the middle of the Brahmaputra River. It is the world's smallest inhabited river island. According to legend, it was at this hillock that Kamdev interrupted Mahadev's meditation. Mahadev burnt Kamdev to ashes. The hillock is also, thus, known as Bhasmacala. The Umananda Temple, built during the 17th century by the then Ahom king Gadadhar Singha, is located at Peacock Island.

Following Ahom rule, the area to the east of the Manas came to be known as Assam. Kamrupa, today, is a district in Assam. Do you know Muhammad bin Bakhtiyar Khilji invaded Kamrupa in 1206 AD? He attacked with a huge army of 12,000 horsemen. Prithu, who was then the king of Kamrupa, badly defeated Khilji. The Turkish general lost all of his army except a few in this battle. Khilji, who became a completely sick man in the Assam expedition after being badly defeated, somehow managed to save his life with the help of a local tribal chieftain and escaped out of Kamrupa.

13th century Persian historian Minhaj-i-Siraj in his book *Tabaqat-i Nasiri* recorded many of Bakhtiyar Khilji's battlefield exploits, loot, and plunder in India. *Tabaqat-i Nasiri* contains a detailed account of Khilji's attack of Kamrupa and his defeat. An inscription near Guwahati, dating back to this period, records the utter rout of the 'Turkish' or Muslim army in Kamrupa. This implies that Khilji penetrated to the interior regions of Kamrupa. Historian Edward Albert Gait in his book *History of Assam* writes that during Bakhtiyar Khilji's attack of Assam, 'the ruler of Kamrupa bore the title Kameswar, and his western boundary was the Karatoya River'.

Bakhtiyar Khilji was the first Islamic invader who attacked Kamrupa. Khilji was assigned two villages on the border of Bihar which had become a political no-man's land. Later, he began a series of successful plundering raids in Bihar. He was recognized and rewarded for his raids by his superiors. It was then that Khilji destroyed the ancient Nalanda University and set fire to the library that accommodated several million manuscripts! It was the year 1193 AD. *Tabaqat-i Nasiri* mentions how thousands of monks were burnt alive and thousands beheaded as Khilji tried his best to plant Islam by the sword. The book also mentions about the burning of the library that continued for several months and 'smoke from the burning manuscripts hung for days like a dark pall over the low hills.' He also destroyed the ancient Vikramshila University and burnt its library to ashes. Khilji started looting and plundering more kingdoms until he set on an expedition to Kamrupa towards the end of 1205 AD with an army of 12,000 horsemen. He actually set out to conquer Tibet besides attacking and plundering kingdoms on the way. His defeat of Lakshman Sena, the last Sena King of Bengal, further boosted his confidence to conquer more regions around and beyond the Himalayas.

Devkot (modem Gangarampur), ten miles south of Dinajpur, was the starting point for Bakhtiyar Khilji to attack Kamrupa. Few miles ahead of the border of Kamrupa, he succeeded in converting a local Mech chieftain to Islam. The convert took a new name 'Ali, the

Mej'. Ali and his followers guided Khilji in the expedition. Following his guidance, Khilji and his army entered the city of Burdhankot, in the east of Bengal. Ali marched along with the Turkish army for 10 days until they reached a giant stone bridge over a channel of river Barnadi in Hajo near Kamrupa. (Currently this ancient stone bridge is stranded in the middle of a small lake as Barnadi River changed its course over time).

Tabaqat-i Nasiri mentions that at this place where the giant stone bridge is located, Khilji's army 'built a bridge of hewn stone consisting of upwards, of twenty arches'. Before Khilji proceeded further, he entrusted two of his commanders along with a troop to keep guard of the bridge until he returned. After few more days of marching amid the hilly terrains and treacherous jungles, Khilji and his army reached the kingdom of Kamrupa, an open tract of land that was densely populated. There was a strong fort in the middle of the villages. Khilji's army immediately set to action — loot and plundering of the villages.

Kamrupa was then ruled by king Prithu from a dynasty that drew their lineage from Narakasura. They worshipped Kamatashwari, a form of Goddess Durga. Kanai Varasi rock inscription records the destruction of the Turks who invaded Kamrupa in 1206 A.D.

Koch Rajbongshi, Bodo and Keot tribes also resided in the region and surrounding areas. Knowing the gravity of the situation, the three tribes extended their support to Prithu. The combined Kamrupi forces attacked Khilji's army. Such was the valor of the tribal army that many Turkish soldiers were killed. Khilji's army could not advance further. Many of Khilji's soldiers were taken prisoners.

The first day of the first battle ended with a huge loss for Khilji. The battle was to resume the next day. Meanwhile, Khilji learnt that king Prithu would attack them with a larger army reinforced by a well-trained cavalry force from the neighboring city of Karampattan. The Turkish chieftain could foresee defeat. He thus broke up his camp the same night and began to retrace his steps.

But king Prithu attacked the Turkish Muslim army on the road. A fierce fight followed. Khilji lost more of his army. Many of his soldiers were captured. Khilji somehow managed to escape with few hundred soldiers until they reached the stone bridge. To their utter dismay, they found the middle arch of it broken off by the natives. With the Kamrupi forces behind, Khilji and his army were forced to swim to reach the other end of the river. The strong current of the river led hundreds of the Mohammedan soldiers to their watery grave. Only Khilji and few men could survive the disaster. At the other end of the river, the converted Ali and his tribe helped the now sick and discomfited Khilji reach Bengal.

Do you know after the failed Assam expedition, Khilji became a completely sick man? He could lead no further expeditions or plunders and loots. While he was lying ill at Devkot (Bengal), he was assassinated by Ali Mardan, a general, who then became the ruler of Bengal.

What happened to the prisoners of war in Kamrupa? Hundreds of Khilji's soldiers were captured by Prithu in battle. The imprisoned soldiers sought pardon and shelter. The kind king Prithu pardoned them, set them free, and made arrangements for their settlement. This was part of the rule of Dharma that Hindu kings followed in warfare and while dealing with prisoners of war. He gave them all essential commodities for a living. As they came from Gauda (Bengal), the king christened them as Gaudia. This marked the beginning of Islamic settlements in Assam.

3

Saraswathi Rajamani

Youngest Spy to Work for Netaji Bose's INA

How many of you have heard about Saraswathi Rajamani, one of the bravest freedom fighters of India? Do you know she was born with the golden spoon in Rangoon? Her father was the owner of a gold mine in Trichy. He was actively involved in activities against the British. To evade arrest by British forces, he settled down in Rangoon and continued supporting freedom fighters. He was counted as one of the richest Indians settled there. Yet, such was Saraswathi's love for the motherland that she decided to be part of the Indian freedom struggle from her childhood days. Her family strongly supported the Indian independence movement.

Saraswathi Rajamani was aged 10 when Mahatma Gandhi visited her home in Rangoon. While all family members were busy interacting with Gandhi, little Rajamani was practicing the art of shooting. She was against the concept of Gandhi's non-violence theory. Shocked to see her with the gun, Mahatma Gandhi asked her why she needed a gun and why she practiced. Without even looking at Gandhi she bluntly replied that looters should be killed and that the British had been looting India. Though Gandhi advocated non-violence to the little girl, the latter expressed her desire to shoot the British. She said that when she would grow up, she would shoot and kill at least one British officer.

The 1927 born Rajamani heard a lot about Netaji Bose and the INA. It was Netaji Subash Chandra Bose who christened her with the name Saraswathi. There is an interesting incident behind this. It was the year 1942. Netaji Bose was then in Rangoon to recruit volunteers and collect funds for the INA. 15-year old Rajamani attended his speech.

Bose, in his speech, urged Indians in Burma to take up arms to liberate India from the colonial British rule. She was so inspired by Netaji's speech that she donated all her gold and diamond jewellery to the INA. Besides, Rajamani's father had himself given massive donations to the INA. After knowing about the donor and about her age, Netaji thought that naivety must have let her do the act. He himself visited Rajamani's house to return the jewellery. But Rajamani refused to take it back. She was adamant on her decision saying it was her jewellery, not her parents'. Impressed by her resolve, he christened her Saraswathi. According to Bose, Lakshmi (wealth) comes and goes but not Saraswathi. He found in Rajamani the wisdom of Saraswathi. Thenceforth, she was called Saraswathi Rajamani.

Saraswathi Rajamani including four of her friends expressed their interest to join the INA. Netaji's powerful speech had kindled in them a passion to fight for the freedom of India. Rajamani's father did not stop her neither did the other parents. Moreover, there were no restrictions for girls in her family. Netaji Bose inducted all five into the Rani of Jhansi regiment of INA as covert spies. Their role was to smuggle secrets for the INA's intelligence wing.

These five girls disguised themselves as boys and started working as errand boys at British military camps and officers' houses. They intercepted government orders and military intelligence from the British officers and handed the same to the INA. Rajamani was then known as Mani. It continued for two years until one of her friends was caught by the British troops. The witty Saraswathi Rajamani planned a trick to rescue her. Dressed as a dancer, she entered the camp where her friend was kept captive.

She drugged the British officers and freed her. While the two were escaping, a bullet happened to hit Rajamani's leg. The wound did not deter her spirit and they continued running. With large number of British soldiers carrying out their search operation, the two girls, to evade arrest, climbed up a tree where they camped for three long days until the British were out of sight. And then they escaped from there.

The bullet wound made Rajamani limp for life. But she did not regret. Rather she felt proud that her limping was a result of her struggle for the cause of the freedom of India. For her brave act, the Emperor of Japan honored her in front of Netaji. She was promoted to the rank of Lieutenant in the Rani of Jhansi regiment.

After the the 2nd World War, the INA was disbanded. On Netaji's instructions, Saraswathi Rajamani returned to India along with her family. Her family had donated all their wealth for the cause of India's freedom. Back to India they had to live a life of poverty. Nothing was known about her family since then until in 2005 a newspaper reported how she struggled to make both ends meet with her freedom fighter pension, living in a cramped one-room flat in a poor environment.

Despite her struggles, she was still serving the society, collecting old clothes, stitching them, and donating them to the poor and needy. She even donated to 2006 Tsunami victims from her pension! The then chief minister of Tamil Nadu, Jayalalitha extended help by offering her a rent-free flat and Rs. 5 lakh.

Salute to the brave Saraswathi Rajamani. Jai Hind!

4

Jhalkaribai

Rani Laxmibai's Lookalike Who Defended Jhansi against British in 1857-58

Jhalkaribai! While she remains in oblivion in the pages of History, she is revered as one of the bravest daughters of Bharat Mata from the Bahujan community. She was one of the commanders of Durga Dal, the women contingent of the Jhansi army of Rani Laxmibai. She was also an advisor to the queen. Laxmibai consulted her on administrative and military affairs. Born and brought up in a humble background, she rose to power by sheer dint of her bravery and her love for the motherland.

Do you know it was because of the defence laid by Jhalkaribai against the British army that Rani Laxmibai could escape from Jhansi Fort? The British felt confused, as they thought she was the Rani of Jhansi. Such was the resemblance of Jhalkaribai with Laxmibai! Jhalkaribai purposefully misled the British army, leading from the front, giving a safe passage to the Rani of Jhansi.

Jhalkaribai was born to Jamuna Devi and Sadoba Singh, a Koli family in Bhojla village near Jhansi on 22 November 1830. The Kolis are a community with many subgroups; they inhabit the central and western mountain regions of India. She was the only child of her parents. She lost her mother when she was very young. Coincidently her lookalike Laxmibai also lost her mother when she was 4. Her father raised her as a single parent.

She was different from other girls of her community. Besides taking care of household chores, doing her duties of a lady of the household, Jhalkaribai was regularly involved in tending cattle and collecting firewood from the jungle. She was daring right from her childhood. She often went all alone with her axe to the jungle to collect firewood though she knew she might be attacked by wild animals.

Once she had an encounter with a leopard while herding her cattle. She killed the leopard with her herding stick! This feat of hers brought her fame in her neighborhood and beyond. On another occasion, she saved a village businessman from being looted by dacoits. She challenged a gang of dacoits who raided the house of the businessman and forced them to retreat. The villagers started revering her. The young and the old drew inspiration from her.

When Jhalkaribai grew of marriageable age, the villagers started looking for a groom for her. They wanted her to get married to someone as courageous as her. And they found a suitable groom in Pooran Kori, who was known to be brave and trained in the art of warfare. Soon after, Pooran Kori was inducted into the Jhansi army as a soldier. He became a well known personality in the Jhansi army for his skills and exploits.

On one occasion, Rani Laxmibai invited the women of the villages of Jhansi to attend Gauri (Goddess Shakti) *puja* at the Jhansi Fort. Jhalkaribai accompanied the other ladies to the fort. Laxmibai's eyes fell on her; she was struck by Jhalkaribai's uncanny resemblance with her. She learnt that she was the wife of Pooran Kori, one of the bravest soldiers of her army. She also learnt about her childhood exploits, how she killed the leopard and her encounter with the dacoits. Laxmibai immediately inducted her into the women contingent of the Jhansi Army called Durga Dal. More women joined Durga Dal.

The Rani herself trained the women army. Jhalkaribai's learning was fast. She soon became an expert in the art of warfare – horse riding, shooting, using of all weapons used in war, etc. By dint of her courage and her skills, she rose to the power of the Commander of Durga Dal.

Jhalkaribai was also a beauty with brains. Rani Laxmibai additionally appointed her as her advisor. The Rani started seeking her advice in administrative and military affairs and of creating strategies of defending Jhansi from possible attacks by the British and other enemy forces.

The British under Lord Dalhousie had rejected Damodar Rao's claim to the throne of Jhansi, as he was adopted. They applied the Doctrine of Lapse and annexed Jhansi to their empire. Meanwhile, in the early months of 1857, rumor about cartridges containing pork or beef fat being supplied by British sparked unrest amongst soldiers and the common men alike. And the first rebellion started in Meerut on May 10, 1857. Indian sepoys with the help of local civilians killed 50 Britishers. This news spread like wild fire and many a son and daughter of Bharat Mata rose in revolt against the British across the country. The news reached Jhansi. Laxmibai revolted against the British and declared independence.

Meanwhile, a group of mutineers, who were supporters of a rival prince claiming the throne of Jhansi, attacked the fort. Rani Laxmibai foiled their attempt, defeating them. The rulers of Orchha and Datiya, both allies of the British, attacked Jhansi in August 1857. They wished to divide Jhansi amongst themselves. The Rani assembled her forces. She set up a foundry to cast cannons within the premises of the fort. Yes! She successfully defeated the invaders. Jhalkaribai and Durga Dal played an instrumental role in defeating the enemy forces.

Laxmibai ruled Jhansi peacefully from August 1857 to January 1858. Towards the third week of March 1858, the British forces, under Commander Hugh Rose, marched towards Jhansi. They ordered the Rani to surrender and threatened destruction of the fort and the town if she refused. The battle between Rani Laxmibai and the British forces began on 24th March 1858 and continued for 10 days until April 2nd. Jhalkaribai played an active role in this battle. There were heavy casualties from both sides. At last British forces were able to penetrate the walls of the fort and into the fort and the palace. All because one of the Rani's commanders betrayed her, opening a well protected gate of the fort to the British forces.

It was Jhalkaribai who advised Laxmibai to run away from the fort so that she accumulated a force outside. The witty Jhalkaribai herself offered to defend the fort unto death by disguising herself as the Rani. Disguised as the queen, she galloped in her horse towards the enemy, taking command of the Jhansi army.

Meanwhile, her husband Pooran Kori died while fighting the British. Jhalkaribai fought like a wounded tigress when she learnt about it, killing many British soldiers, until she was caught. With her adopted son Damodar Rao tied to her back, Laxmibai jumped down several feet from the fort and managed to escape.

The British Commander Hugh Rose and his men were overjoyed, as they felt they caught the Rani alive. Rose asked Jhalkaribai what should be done to her. She said, "Hang me!" Later, they learnt that she was Jhalkaribai, the lookalike of Laxmibai. She was hanged to death by the British. Though the actual date of the hanging is not in records, it was probably April 1858, as she was caught on April 2nd.

According to Bundelkhand folklore, the British commander was so stunned by Jhalkaribai's wit, courage, and sacrifice that he said if every Indian woman was like her, the British would be bound to leave India soon.

Jhalkaribai was a Bahujan. But didn't she rise to power owing to her skills? Jhalkaribai struck fear in the hearts of the British army. Through her role in the 1857 War of Independence and for the freedom of Jhansi, through her valor and sacrifice, she has left behind a rich legacy for millions to emulate.

5

Bajiprabhu Deshpande

Led 300 Soldiers against 12000 Adilshahi Army, Defending Shivaji

So you have heard about the 300 brave Spartans led by King Leonidas who fought bravely in battlefield against thousands of Persians. A film was produced based on this historic battle titled *300*. I have watched it. Many of you might have watched it too. But have you heard about the brave 300 Maratha army led by Bajiprabhu Deshpande who fought bravely in battlefield against a 12000 Adilshahi army led by Siddi Masood? The soldier ratio was 1:40! The rear guard battle which took place at a mountain pass in Pawankhind lasted for 15 hours until the last warrior of all of the 300 Marathas perished! Bajiprabhu Deshpande selflessly sacrificed his life to save the life of his king Chattrapati Shivaji and for the motherland. 4000 of the Muslim army were killed while the rest were heavily wounded. This deadly battle is not glorified in History text books!

Bajiprabhu Deshpande was born into a Marathi Chandrasainya Kayastha Prabhu family around 1615 AD. Though socially proximate to the Maharashtrian Brahmin community, Bajiprabhu, since his childhood was more attracted towards martial arts. The tyranny of the Mughals had been plaguing India culturally, socially, and economically and the young Kayastha Prabhu boy was more interested in serving the country. Shivaji had meanwhile risen to power. Bajiprabhu Deshpande grabbed the opportunity to work under Shivaji.

Bajiprabhu had mastered the art of using the *dandpatta*, a sword weapon. The *dandpatta*, called a gauntlet-sword in English, is the pride of Maratha warriors. The *patta* has a long straight blade ranging in length from 10 to 44 inches with the gauntlet integrated in the sword as a hand guard. Maratha infantrymen, who were experts in using the *dandpatta*, used it in warfare against heavily armoured cavalry. Shivaji and Bajiprabhu Deshpande were renowned to be masters in the use of *dandpatta*.

By sheer dint of his skills in the art of warfare and his steadfast love for the motherland, Bajiprabhu rose to position in the Maratha army. Shivaji Maharaj appointed him as the military commander of South Maharashtra around the Kolhapur region.

During this time, Ali Adil Shah II was the Sultan of Bijapur. The Adilshahi Sultanate dynasty was started by Yusuf Adil Shah in 1489 with capital at Bijapur. Their territory included the Western area of the Deccan region of Southern India. Afzhal Khan was the ablest of commanders of the Adilshahi army. In 1659, Afzal Khan led a huge army against Shivaji's forces. Shivaji and his army were experts in fighting battles in hill areas rather than the plains. Moreover, his army was no match to the huge Bijapuri forces. Hence, he restricted his base in the hill forts. He moved to Pratapgad Fort in Satara, which was surrounded by dense jungles. Meanwhile, Afzhal Khan, who knew about Shivaji's strengths and was weak in fighting battles in hilly terrains, started plundering villages and razing temples to the ground besides destroying idols of the Hindu deities. The Muslim commander felt such actions would provoke Shivaji to come out in the open in the plains.

Meanwhile, leaders of both parties felt a battle between the two might lead to heavy casualties. Hence, Afzhal Khan offered for negotiations and a peace pact to which Shivaji agreed. Actually, it was the Muslim commander's secret plan to kill Shivaji during the meeting and thereby subdue the Marathas without use of force. Afzhal Khan offered to meet Shivaji in person. The meeting place decided was Par, a village lying one mile south of Pratapgad Fort. A crest below Pratapgad Fort was chosen as the venue. The meeting was arranged with two personal bodyguards accompanying the leaders on each side.

There was a track record of Afzhal Khan deceiving negotiators during meetings. In 1639, he treacherously murdered Kasturi Ranga, the king of Sera, a small South Indian kingdom, during a meeting. Shivaji went to meet Afzhal Khan after equipping himself with weapons hidden from view — *bichu*, a stiletto-like thin dagger and the *wagh nakh* (tiger claws), consisting of an iron finger-grip with four razor claws, which he concealed within his clenched fist. He wore armour under his clothes and a steel helmet under his turban.

In the meeting, Afzhal Khan applied his treacherous tactics and secretly attacked Shivaji during an embrace. Shivaji immediately reciprocated, disemboweling him with the *wagh nakh* and stabbing him with the *bichu*. A combat followed. Sambhaji Kavji, Shivaji's bodyguard killed the heavily injured Afzhal Khan.

After the death of Afzhal Khan, the Bijapuri army fled. Shivaji with his army pursued them and pushed into the Bijapuri territory. The Marathas captured Panhala Fort located near the city of Kolhapur. This fort was under the Bijapuri Sultanate from the beginning of the 16th century. Another Maratha force under the commandment of Netaji Palkar attacked Bijapur. The Adilshahi army foiled their attempts. Shivaji with few of his commanders and soldiers retreated to Panhala fort. This was the fort where Shivaji spent the next 500 plus days till Bajiprabhu Deshpande facilitated his safe passage to another location.

The Adilshahi force led by Siddhi Johar, an Abyssinian general, laid siege of Panhala Fort from all sides after they came to know about Shivaji's whereabouts. Johar had come with a huge army and Shivaji's puny force was no match to them. Hence Shivaji remained in the fort, strategizing to give a brave defense. Netaji Palkar made repeat attempts to break the Muslim army siege from outside, but in vain.

Meanwhile, at the Panhala fort, Bajiprabhu Deshpande chanced to come face to face with Shiva Nhavi, a barber of the Maratha forces. He had an uncanny resemblance with Shivaji. An idea clicked Deshpande's mind. He discussed the plan with Shivaji to which the latter agreed. The planning was made. Bajiprabhu Deshpande called

Shiva Nhavi and asked him if he would disguise as Shivaji and facilitate the king escape from the fort. The general also told him that as he was Shivaji's lookalike and his changed attire might further stamp his identity as the Maratha ruler, he might get caught by the Bijapuri forces. It might even lead to his execution by the Muslim forces. Shiva Nhavi readily agreed, offering himself to be martyred for the king and the motherland.

A plan was hatched at the Panhala Fort. It was decided that Bajiprabhu Deshpande and Shivaji along with a select band of the Maratha army would attempt to break through the Adilshahi siege at night and make for Vishalgadh, a hill *jagir* of the Maratha Empire in Kolhapur. The Adilshahi forces might give a chase only when they could find out that Shivaji had fled, breaking the siege. To stop them from pursuing Shivaji, Shiva Nhavi would then let himself be captured. This would make the Adilshahi forces feel that they had captured the Maratha king!

July 13, 1660. It was *Guru Poornima* — a full moon night. The weather was stormy. A band of 600 select men, led by Bajiprabhu Deshpande and Shivaji broke through the siege. The Bijapuri forces were about to pursue the Maratha forces when Shiva Nhavi allowed himself to be captured. He was taken to the Adilshahi camp. Shiva Nhavi knew he might be put to death but he was bravely ready to meet the consequences. This gave safe passage for the Maratha army to escape.

The Muslim army soon realized their blunder. Immediately they set to action — 12000 well armed soldiers advanced fast towards the 600 Maratha army. The chase was led by Siddhi Masood, the son-in-law of Siddhi Johar. The march of fast approaching hoofs near the Ghodkhind Pass (Horse's Pass) led Bajiprabhu Deshpande devise a plan immediately. Ghodkhind Pass was located seven to nine km ahead of Vishalgadh.

Bajiprabhu Deshpande let Shivaji and half of the troops escape to Vishalgadh fast and himself offered to stay back with the remaining soldiers at the Ghodkhind Pass to give resistance to the Adilshahi army. His brother Phulaji also offered to stay back to defend. Shivaji agreed.

The 300 brave Maratha army blocked the pass. A fierce battled between the Maratha and Adilshahi army followed. This place was also called Pawankhind, hence the christening, 'The Battle of Pawankhind'. The valour displayed by the Marathas during this rear-guard action is unmatched in military history. One by one the Maratha soldiers were martyred. But the puny force of 300 soldiers badly injured the enemy forces.

At the end of 15 hours, all of the 300 Maratha soldiers perished. 4000 of the Muslim army were killed while the rest were heavily wounded. Though grievously injured, Bajiprabhu Deshpande fought with two swords, using his two hands until he breathed his last. But this 15 hours of blocking the pass facilitated Shivaji's safe passage to Vishalgadh. The fort had been laid siege by Bijapuri Sardars. Shivaji and his 300 men defeated the Sardars and recaptured the fort.

Salute to the brave Bajiprabhu Deshpande and the valorous 299 Maratha soldiers. Salute to Shiva Nhavi. Jai Shivaji! Jai Hind!!

6

Karnavati

Garhwal Queen who Defeated Mughal Army in 1640; Cut Noses of Surviving Invaders

Rani Karnavati or the *Naak Kati Rani* of Garhwal as she is called! Not many of us are familiar with this brave queen of our motherland. She was more popular as the *Naak Katne Wali Rani* and invaders dreaded waging war against her. She became the ruler of the Garhwal region as the Queen Regent from 1631 till her minor son, who was then aged 7 years, became an adult. She not only ruled wisely but also effectively protected the Garhwal borders and repulsed all attacks. A major attack was carried out by the Mughals in 1640. Under her leadership, the Mughals were not only badly defeated, but also humiliated. She cut the noses of the surviving Muslim soldiers and created terror amongst them as well as in the Mughal court.

Garhwal! The very utterance of this term will transport you to the Himalayas and to the abode of Mahadev. The worship of Mahadev is predominant in this region. The historicity of this region dates back to antiquity, much beyond the *Mahabharata* and the *Ramayana* periods. This region is believed to be the place where the *Vedas* were compiled and the *Mahabharata* written. Amongst the earliest known kings in BCE was Kanak Pal, who ruled Garhwal from 823 BCE.

Karnavati was the queen of Mahipat Shah, the ruler of Garhwal, who reigned from 1622 to 1631 AD. He died while fighting against the Raja of Kumaon. As per the book *Garhwal Himalayas: A Study in Historical Perspective* by Ajay S. Rawat, Jesuit missionaries were active in the Himalayan region during this period. Their objective was to spread Christianity. Few wrote about the historicity of the places they stayed and visited. According to Azevedo, a Jesuit missionary appointed by the 'Society of Jesus' in Agra in June 1628 for the Mogor Mission to the Himalayas, Mahipat Shah died in 1631. Azevedo went to Tsaprang via the route of Srinagar in Garhwal. He wrote that he was witness to the funeral of the king of Garhwal, Mahipat Shah in 1631.

When Raja Mahipat Shah died, his son, Prithvi Pat Shah, the heir to the throne, was only seven years old. Rani Karnavati took over the reins of the Garhwali kingdom on behalf of Prithvi Pat Shah. Though contemporary inscriptions mention her name as Maharani Mata Karnavati, she was more popular as *Naak Kati Rani* after she successfully repulsed a Mughal attack and chopped off the noses of the surviving invaders. Folk songs in Garhwal since that period to this day glorify the queen on her bravery exhibited against Muslim invaders.

Many secular historians say that Rani Karnavati didn't rule Garhwal. But there are inscriptional evidences confirming her rule. A copper plate inscription of Samvat 1697 corresponding to 1640 AD of the Gregorian calendar is related to Rani Karnavati of Garhwal. She released it on behalf of her son Maharaja Prithvi Pat Shah. The copper plate confirms grant of land to the Hatwal Brahmins in Haat village of Chamoli district of Garhwal. One of the witnesses to this grant was Madho Singh Bhandari, one of the three brave generals in the Garhwal army.

The Mughal rule in India had no impact on Garhwal. Mahipat Shah was an independent ruler. He had three brave generals in his army — Madho Singh Bhandari, Rikhola Lodi, and Banwari Dass. Lodi had led successful war expeditions against the Tibetans and other kingdoms. There was a saying regarding the valor of Madho Singh Bhandari in the Garhwals — "There are only three 'Singhs' on this earth, one is the lion, the second is the cow's horn and the third Madho Singh". Such brave generals continued to command the Garhwali army, first under Mahipat Shah and then under Rani Karnavati. Madho Singh died in the battle of Chotta Chini against

Tibetans in 1640 AD. After his death, Rani Karnavati banked upon another brave Garhwali soldier. He was Dost Baig, an artillery officer in service since the time of Mahipat Shah. The queen appointed him as the commander. At the time of Mughal invasion, Dost Baig was the commander of the Garhwali army.

In 1640, Mughal Emperor Shah Jahan sent a huge army to invade Garhwal. 30,000 horsemen under the command of General Najabat Khan started their march towards this Himalayan region. Shah Jahan was aware that a minor ruler under a queen Regent ruled Garhwal. As most Mughal expeditions in subjugating kingdoms and bringing them under Mughal rule were a success, bringing Garhwal under Mughal supremacy was his objective. His aim was to further establish his supremacy in the Himalayan region.

Rani Karnavati had spies in the borders of her territory. She was alerted of the advancing Mughal army towards Srinagar. Garhwali forces checked the Mughal army ahead of their reaching the capital. A fierce battle ensued between the two parties. Garhwalis were proficient in fighting in hilly terrains, which the Mughals lacked though they were well equipped with weaponry. Garhwali forces soon started decimating the Muslim army. Witnessing that defeat was imminent, few of the Mughal soldiers fled the battlefield. In no time Mughals witnessed a crushing defeat. Many of them were butchered in battlefield.

Rani Karnavati humiliated the surviving Mughal soldiers in the battlefield. She wanted to teach the Mughals a lesson so that they never invaded her territory in the future. She chopped off the noses of the Mughal soldiers including Najabat Khan, the Mughal general. She sent a message to the Mughal court that if she could chop off their noses, she could also chop off their heads.

The surviving soldiers were let free after their noses were cut. They tried to force their way back to the Mughal kingdom, but many of them were encircled and massacred on the way by the Garhwali soldiers. Very few soldiers including Najabat Khan survived on the leaves and roots of trees in the mountainous jungles to reach the Mughal court. They narrated their saga of horror and torture to Shah Jahan. The Mughal emperor demoted Najabat Khan for bringing shame to the Mughal emperorship.

Since then Rani Karnavati came to be known as *Naak Katne Wali Rani* and later *Naak Kati Rani*. The Mughals including contemporary rulers of neighboring kingdoms and people started knowing her by her nickname and not her original name.

Many Indian kings followed the rules of Dharma and pardoned not only the prisoners of war but also the invading Muslim rulers. Prithviraj Chauhan pardoned Mohammed Ghori every time he was defeated in battle and begged for mercy. Ultimately in the 16th battle, Ghori defeated Chauhan and the outcome is known to all. Muslim rule in India began after the success of Ghori in this last battle. King Prithu of Assam pardoned the Muslim prisoners of war and allowed them to settle which led to the first Muslim settlements in the northeast. Rani Karnavati was one of the counted few rulers who had no mercy on foreign invaders. Due to her mercilessness, Mughals never dared to attack her kingdom again!

Mughal Darbaar ya Maasirul Umra, a translated book of Rani Karnavati's contemporary times, describes about the brave feat of Rani Karnavati. This book mentions how the Rani gave a crushing defeat to the Mughal army. It says that the queen was responsible for humiliating the Muslim army. The name of the Mughal general as Najabat Khan, who led the Garhwal expedition, also finds mention in this book. It also describes how Rani Karnavati chopped off the noses of the surviving Muslim invaders.

The Garhwal region witnessed big developments during the reign of Rani Karnavati. She was instrumental in facilitating a number of hydraulic constructions, especially irrigation systems to the benefit of farmers. It prevented water from sinking underground as it exited the hill into the gravels leading to the valleys. Under her patronage, several temples were built. Another of her development activities worth mentioning was the construction of the Rajpur Canal, the earliest of all the Dun canals. This canal started from the Rispana River, a tributary of the Song River, and brought along waters to Dehradun city.

Few years later, the Garhwali queen's grown up son Prithvi Pat Shah ascended the throne of Garhwal. Rani Karnavati continued assisting her son in the administrative, military, and judicial affairs.

Garhwal, the land of celestial beauty, is the kingdom that the Mughals could never win, all because of the mercilessness shown by Rani Karnavati. Had all the kings of Bharat fought and were merciless like her, the History of the country would have been different! Hail the Garhwali queen Karnavati!

7

Rana Sanga

Fiercely Defeated Delhi Sultan in Khatoli Battle

Rana Sanga! Indian history is full of acts of valor and daring glories. As we delve into the aspects of Indian history that has been kept out of reach of text books, we find many such unsung heroes whose bravery, magnanimity and courage made them look almost like super humans. It is a pity that our text books either make just a passing remark on such characters and acts, or just ignore them completely.

One such character was Maharana Sangram Singh aka Rana Sanga. Here, an effort has been made to look at a very important battle where Rana Sanga destroyed the Lodhi army of Delhi Sultanate and even captured a Lodhi prince. This particular battle was fought at Khatoli in the year 1518. Khatoli is a village near Harauti in Rajasthan.

Rana Sanga was the ruler of Mewar from year 1508 to 1528. He was born in the Sisodiya clan of Rajputs to Rana Rai Mal on 14 April 1484 at Malwa. He was a daring and courageous warrior who quickly started to expand his territories. This expansion brought him in direct conflict with the Lodhi dynasty of Delhi.

Sikander Lodhi had died in A.D. 1517 and his son Ibrahim Lodhi succeeded him. News of Rana Sanga extending his territories was a bad omen for the Delhi Sultanate, as Sanga's extended territory almost touched the boundaries of Delhi. To wipe this threat of a resurging Hindu power, Ibrahim Lodhi decided to stop Rana in his tracks. He collected and organised a large army and started to move towards Mewar to intercept Rana Sanga.

Maharana Sanga decided to meet the foe head on and moved with his army. Both armies met face to face at Khatoli or Ghatoli village near the borders of Harauti. Ibrahim's army was larger and better prepared in terms of numerical superiority and weapons. Rana Sanga and his army lacked it but they were motivated to the extent that they were ready to embrace death, fighting for the motherland. This holy death is the ultimate outcome of following Kshatriya Dharma, where a warrior gets either victory or death with no other option.

Ibrahim was himself commanding the army seated on his favorite war elephant. He had heavy cavalry as well as a well trained and equipped infantry. He placed his infantry in the front and his heavy cavalry on the flanks. He himself along with a reserve force was at the back of his lines.

Rana Sanga had an army mostly comprising of cavalry units from Mewar and Shekhawti. He also had a formidable infantry. Maharana decided to lead the army himself. His mere presence on the field was a great morale booster for his troops and tales of his daring and valor had already struck fear in his adversaries.

The battle started as a series of skirmishes between Lodhi horse and the Rajput horse. Rajputs had the upper hand in these skirmishes and they were repeatedly taunting the main lines of Sultan's army. Ibrahim decided to put an end to this and ordered his lines to advance and engage the Rajputs in a full frontal attack.

Maharana Sanga quickly assessed the situation and ordered his heavy cavalry to form a spear head. He himself decided to lead the charge. His army was motivated to thrash the Sultanate's army. Rajputs descended on the advancing Lodhi lines in a furious charge with Rana Sanga leading from the front. The impact and momentum of the charge was such that Lodhi army lines started to crumble and were scattered here and there. Lodhi cavalry quickly tried to counter the onslaught but the momentum of the charge was so intense that they were unable to withstand.

Ibrahim decided to throw in his reserve in order to salvage the day. His reserve moved forward but their forward movement was hampered by routing Lodhi horsemen and infantry. The reserve of

Lodhi army could not form a solid base against which they expected to turn the tables on Rajputs. A general and disorganised rout followed during which the Rajputs played havoc with the Lodhis. Ibrahim managed to run away but a royal prince of his family was caught. He was later released on payment of a hefty ransom.

In the words of a Lodhi era historian 'Sultan's armies scattered like dead leaves caught in a gale in front of Rajput cavalry charge'.

This battle lasted for just around 5 hours. These 5 hours were a nightmare for the Lodhis which they could never forget. This battle crippled the Lodhi army to such an extent that they could not challenge Sanga again for a while. This battle also gave Mewar control over north eastern Rajasthan.

Rana Sanga was wounded in this battle but that did not deter his courage from taking part in further battles. He lost an arm by a sword cut and an arrow made him lame for life. He was already blind by one eye before his coronation.

There is an interesting incident which shows the greatness of Sanga. After this battle, Rana Sanga returned to Mewar. On the day he was to assume his duties by sitting on the throne, he surprised everyone by sitting instead on the ground among lesser nobles. The whole court was bewildered. They asked Rana the reason for such behavior to which he replied that 'when an idol of deity is broken in any form, it is not worshiped but instead kept outside the house and a new idol is put in its place'. He said similar was his case as he had lost an arm and a leg so he should not continue as the Maharana. The whole court was stunned. Medini Rai, a Rajput chief took Rana Sanga by his hand and made him sit on the throne.

There are many such stories from Indian history which are worth sharing and applauding. It is a pity that most of our young generation is totally unaware of their own roots. Or have they been kept unaware by design?

8

Battle of Haldighati
Who Won? Rana Pratap or Akbar? The Real Story!

There was a big controversy regarding the outcome of the Battle of Haldighati as to who was the winner and the consequences thereof. This controversy was triggered by the decision of the Rajasthan Education board to revisit the theory that Akbar won the battle easily. Actually various facts point contrary to this theory which has been spoon fed by history text books. Before trying to look into the details of the aforesaid great battle, let's explore some facts which led to this bloody encounter or I should say series of bloody encounters.

As most of us know, Akbar was the Mughal emperor during that time. He had subjugated most of the kingdoms in Rajputana and had active military support of some of the biggest and powerful kingdoms of that time. Primary among these was the Kachchwaha state of Amber, currently known as Jaipur. Amber armies were usually at the forefront of Mughal armies and often acted as vanguard. It should also be mentioned here that whatever this bonhomie suggests, truth was that Mughals never fully trusted the Rajputs.

Man Singh, the crown prince of Kachchwaha clan considered himself as the primary leader of the Rajputs. He was also a distinguished commander of the Mughal army. The Sisodias of Mewar made mockery of this. Sisodia clan was led by Maharana Pratap Singh of Mewar, who was the grandson of famous warrior Maharana Sangram Singh or Rana Sanga as he was called. Sisodias had a long history of conflicts with Mughals and had already fought many wars with them. Akbar considered Maharana Pratap and kingdom of Mewar a thorn in his side. He wanted complete subjugation of Rajputs but this was not possible till the Sun flag of Mewar fluttered high. Akbar made diplomatic advances first by sending emissaries to Mewar, but without much success.

Akbar decided to use Rajputs against Rajputs and sent Man Singh as his emissary to Mewar. He wanted Rana Pratap to acknowledge him as the emperor and wanted Pratap to be his vassal, just like Man Singh. Maharana Pratap did not pay heed to any of the logics and schemes put forward by Man Singh and declared his independence. The mission failed; then something happened which brought war to the gates of Mewar even earlier than predicted.

During his stay in Mewar, Man Singh was invited to a royal dinner. Maharana Pratap refused to join him on the pretext that kings dine only with kings and Man Singh was just a crown prince and that too, of a vassal state of the Mughals. Pratap sent his son Amar Singh for the dinner. Man Singh considered this to be an insult and left. He started advising Akbar to attack and depose Maharana and capture Mewar. Akbar was already looking for a moment like this. He quickly ordered an attack on Maharana.

Akbar himself did not lead the army. He entrusted the task to Syed Hashim of Barrha along with his brothers and Man Singh. There is widespread difference in the opinion of historians as to the strength of the competing armies. Some sources place the army sizes to a ridiculously low strength as of Mewar to just 3000 and Mughals around 10000.

This estimation is highly doubtful going by the stature of commanders of the Mughal army. Man Singh himself was a commander ranking 5000 horse and other ancillaries. Syed Hashim was another commander matching him in stature. Mughal army was also supplemented by the Kachchwaha forces. Rao Lunkaran of Sambhar brought his Rajputs to the Mughal fold too. And the kinsmen of famous Salim Chishti of Fatehpur Sikri were also there present with their followers. This takes the the army strength of Mughals beyond 10000 and it is also highly doubtful that Akbar sent only 10000 men to overcome the kingdom which consisted of rough terrain and was his last big obstacle. Mewari records put the number of invading Mughal army to around 80000, which might look exaggerated.

Same sources put Mewari strength to around 20000 comprising of cavalry and Bhils who were the inhabitants of the rough terrain around. Almost all historians agree to the fact that whatever be the number of soldiers, Mewari forces were heavily outnumbered and Mughals were confident of an easy victory owing to this huge difference.

The Mughal army was commandeered by Syed Hashim of Barrha, Man Singh Kachchwaha, Jagannath Kachchwaha, Madho Singh Kachchwaha of Amber, Rao Lunkaran of Sambhar, Gazi Khan of central Asian provinces who was a military adventurer and worked for Akbar, to name a few.

On the other hand, Mewar army was commandeered by Maharana Pratap Singh himself along with his trusted lieutenant Ram Das Rathore, son of famous Jaimal Rathore who laid down his life defending Chittor during the seige. Jaimal was killed by Akbar, not during the actual fighting, but while overseeing the repair work of walls of Chittor by a long range musket shot.

Apart from these, other commanders of Mewar army were Ram Shah Tanwar of Gwalior who had sought refuge with Mewar after his state was taken over by Mughals. He was aided by his sons, Shaliwahan and two others. Another commander was an Afghan who was a direct descendant of Sher Shah Suri named Hakim Khan Sur. Famous Bhama Shah and his brother Tara Chand were also notable commanders of Mewar Army. Bhim Singh of Dodia had brought his kinsmen to fight alongside Pratap. Worth mentioning here is the name of Rao Punja, the Bhil commander and Jhala Maan who rendered excellent and supreme service to the history of Mewar.

The battle of Haldighati was fought on 18th or 21st (historians are divided on the actual date) June, 1576. It was not a long drawn battle but a rather short and intensely bloody affair.

Mughal army's vanguard was led by Jagannath Kachchwaha, Bakshi Ali Asaf Khan and Behlol Khan Pathan. Ahead of this van was a screen of skirmishers belonging to Syed Hashim. Behind the vanguard there was an advance reserve led by Madho Singh Kachchwaha. In the centre was Man Singh. Left flank was led by Gazi Khan and Rao Lunkaran and the Chistis of Sikri. The right wing was personally led by Sayyid Hashim of Barrha along with his brothers and kinsmen. Rearguard was brought up by Mehtar Khan.

Rana Pratap organised his army with himself commanding the centre. The Mewar vanguard was led by Ramdas Rathore along with Bhim Singh of Dodia and Hakim Khan Sur along with his Afghans. The right flank was under Ramshah Tanwar along with his three sons and the famous Bhama Shah and his brother Tara Chand. The left flank was under Jhala Maan or Bida Maan as he is sometimes called.

Rana Pratap was well aware of the numerical superiority of the Mughal army; so he decided on a full and ferocious attack with speed and hoped to pierce the Mughal lines and thus quickly end the battle.

As soon as the battle of Haldighati started, the screen of Mughal skirmishers was blown away by a ferocious cavalry charge. Without wasting time Mewar right flank of Ramshah Tanwar attacked the left of Mughal army, Gazi Khan and Rao Lunkaran. The Chistis could not face the fury of cavalry charge and ran away from battlefield towards their right. Mughal left flank was decimated to the extent that advance reserves had to be called upon. Jhala Maan on left flank fell upon the Syeds on Mughal right and was pressuring the Mughal lines to break up. Syeds were holding with difficulty.

Advance reserve and vanguard of Mughals had been already pressed into service. Vanguard of Mewar under Ram Das Rathore, Hakim Khan Sur and Bhim Singh clashed head on into the rushing Mughals. After decimating the Mughal left flank, Ramshah Tanwar wheeled to his left to join Pratap in the centre. The Mughal van managed to attack Rana Pratap with Behlol Khan leading the charge.

Pratap himself came forward to counter him; what happened next froze the blood in the veins of onlookers. Before Behlol Khan could even complete his blow, Pratap seated on his favorite horse Chetak delivered a sword blow on the helmet of Behlol Khan. The blow was struck with such ferocity and precision that Behlol Khan was vertically cut into two pieces along with his helmet, armour and even his horse.

This scene is depicted in many old art works and has been made immortal by bards and poets. Mughal army was petrified and their charge withered. Pratap found the right opportunity to move to the Mughal centre. Bhim Singh of Dodia was ahead of him already cleaving his way into the centre of Mughals. Bhim Singh reached there first and charged Man Singh who was seated on an elephant. In the ensuing tussle, Bhim Singh was killed.

Sensing trouble, the rearguard led by Mehtar Khan came to the fore to aid Man Singh. Meanwhile, Pratap had reached the scene, seeing Man Singh. Pratap attacked him. Chetak was a fearless steed and planted its front legs on the trunk of the elephant. He threw his spear at Man Singh. The mahawat of Man Singh came in between and was pierced. The force of the blow broke even the howda of the elephant. Man Singh was saved due to the sacrifice by his mahawat. This incident rattled him but his dwindling forces were bolstered by the arrival of Mehtar Khan whose soldiers now surrounded Pratap.

Chetak was already wounded by a sword cut on hind leg which was caused by the sword tied to the trunk of Man Singh's elephant. Rana Pratap was also wounded by now by a musket shot as well as a spear and a sword cut. Ram Shah Tanwar tried to come to aid of Maharana. While trying to reach there, he was killed by Jagannath Kachchwaha in the melee.

Meanwhile, sensing his Maharana in danger, Jhala Maan raced to his help and reaching there, he quickly snatched the royal banner from Pratap which confused the Mughals. They thought of Jhala to be Pratap and fell upon him. Jhala attained his martyrdom fighting meanwhile Pratap retreated from the battlefield.

Pretty quickly Mughals realised their fault and pursued Rana Pratap. Chetak was wounded badly but still took his master to safety. Pratap reached a rivulet which was quite wide for a horse to jump; still Chetak jumped and crossed it but died soon after. There is a cenotaph erected in the memory of this most famous horse of Indian history at the spot.

The Mughals had lost his track. Pratap had a half brother by name of Shakta or Shakti Singh. He had gone over to Akbar upon coronation of Rana Pratap. Upon seeing the valour and supreme sacrifice of Jhala, he changed his plans and once again joined Rana. He gave his horse to Rana thus helping him escape to safety. Some accounts say that Shakti Singh fought with the pursuers and killed two of them.

Meanwhile, the battle of Haldighati was raging on. Ram Das Rathore was among the last ones to be killed. The heroics of Rajputs of Mewar and the Bhils had stopped Mughal advance but the numbers were dwindling fast for Mewar. The remaining commanders knowing fully well that Pratap had reached to safety organised a well planned and executed retreat.

The Mughals dared not chase them due to the fear of an ambush. The retreat was so successful that Mewar army took even the baggage and camps with them. Mughals however had captured a prized elephant of Mewar named Ram Prasad. He was later gifted to Akbar, who changed his name to Pir Prasad. The beast was so loyal to Rana Pratap that he eventually starved himself to death few days later.

This battle might have been the bloodiest of battles in world history. It lasted just 4 hours or thereabout. The carnage was such that the place came to be known as Rakt Talai or the lake of blood. Local sources place the number of dead at around 18000, 4000 from Mewar army and 14000 from Mughal army. It might have been exaggerated but still gives a glimpse into the blood that flowed that eventful day.

The place Rakt Talai is still called by the same name and has a *mazaar* constructed in honor of Hakim Khan Sur who laid his life in this battle fighting against the Mughals. The cenotaphs of Ram Shah Tanwar and his sons Shaliwahan and two others are also there in Haldighati.

The Mughal army moved next day in pursuit of Maharana who had by now vanished into the hills and reorganised his army. He once again came face to face with Mughal army at Dewair a few days after the battle of Haldighati. This time, instead of a full frontal attack, he followed the strategy of thrust and parry with speedy charges and then retreating. Mughal army was decimated at Dewair and this led to overrunning of Mughal outposts in Mewar by Rana. Within a short span of time, he had taken back whole of Mewar from Mughals except the fortress of Chittor.

Meanwhile, on the Mughal side, Akbar was furious with Man Singh for failing to annihilate Rana. He refused to meet Man Singh for months following the battle of Haldighati.

All these facts point that the battle was in fact a stalemate with both sides not being able to attain their objectives. Superior numerical strength of Mughals could not achieve them their glory as the valour of Mewar army denied them an outright victory.

This battle of Haldighati has been made immortal by many writers, poets and bards in folklore. Haldighati is actually considered something close to a pilgrimage site.

9

Tonkham Borpatra Gohain

Ahom General Who Defeated and Killed Afghan Turbak Khan in 1533 AD

Indian History text books hardly glorify the exploits of Indian warriors who won in battles against Islamic invaders. Many freedom fighters, who played an instrumental role in freeing India from the clutches of the British, have not found a place in History. Instead, it is the invaders who are glorified. From the north to the south, east to the west, there are hundreds of winning exploits of warriors, both men and women. It is time History text books are rewritten!

It was the year 1533 AD. Turbak Khan, the experienced Afghan general of Nasiruddin Nasrat Shah, the Sultan of Bengal, attacked Assam with a huge army. Nasiruddin Nasrat Shah was the son of Ala-ud-din Husain Shah, founder of the Hussain Shahi dynasty in Bengal. He usurped the throne of Bengal after assassinating Shams-ud-Din Muzaffar Shah, an Abyssinian Sultan. After his death in 1519, he was succeeded by his son Nasrat Shah. The Sultan's army commandeered by Turbak Khan were armed with guns and cannons besides other weapons used in battle during that time.

According to the book *War Drums of Eagle King* written by P.W. Ingty, "Turbak was given command over a large army comprising of both land and naval forces, and with this impressive and powerful army he invaded the territories under Ahom influence. The forces led by Turbak Khan were well equipped with sufficient rations and armaments; their soldiers were well trained and seemed unbeatable as they moved steadily on the north bank of the Brahmaputra towards the core of the Ahom-held territories."

Ahom king Suhungmung was then the ruler of Assam. The 14th Ahom ruler, he ascended the throne of the Ahom kingdom under the title of Swarganarayan and Dihingia Raja in 1497. Under his rule, the Ahom kingdom expanded beyond the previous borders.

Suhungmung's army was commandeered by his general, Tonkham Borpatra Gohain (Barpatra Gohain is a title given by the king to the 3rd in rank in the Ahom court of ministers). The battle took place at Duimunisila along the banks of the mighty Bharali River. In the words of Leslie Shakespear from his book *History of Upper Assam, Upper Burmah and North-Eastern Frontier*, the Ahom Raja "sent large reinforcements by land and river. Turbak's forces were defeated, he himself killed, and his head, as was customary, was sent for burial on Charaideo hill. The beaten and disorganized forces were pursued by the victorious Ahoms through Koch territory to the Karatoya River."

The battle of Duimunisila in 1533 is the last of a series of battles fought between Turbak Khan and the Ahom forces that started in 1532. The first battle was fought between Turbak and Ahoms at Singri. This battle was commandeered by Suklen, the son of Suhungmung. Suklen was defeated and wounded in this battle. The Ahom forces retreated over to the south bank of the Brahmaputra. The Mohammedan forces followed. Several more battles followed at different places with neither party at the winning end. The Ahoms made a change of their war tactics this time. They positioned themselves in such a way so as to cut off all supply and communication lines of the army of Turbak Khan with their homeland and headquarters at Gauda, Bengal.

In the words of P.W. Ingty, "The indomitable Turbak Khan, however, decided to press on with his expedition in spite of this setback and also to depend upon locally available resources. Turbak Khan's forces soon reached the Dikrai River, where they found that the Ahoms had positioned themselves on the other bank of the river under Ahom general Tonkham, an experienced fighter.... Suhungmung had entrusted Ahom general Tonkham with the task of driving back the Muslim invaders. At this point of time, Turbak Khan's army was already running low of rations and there were no fresh supplies or reinforcements coming from Gauda. As a consequence of which the troops under Turbak Khan were in no position to take on the strongly entrenched Ahoms".

The Mohammedan forces waited and watched. The Ahom forces laid on them a series of guerilla attacks, which not only reduced the numbers of the enemy forces but also dampened their morale and spirits. In a few days' time Turbak's army weakened further. And the final battle took place at Duimunisila. The defeat of Turbak's naval forces weakened Turbak's battle strength and he was ultimately killed by the Ahom general. Historical references find mention of the first use of firearms by the Ahoms in these battles.

Leslie Shakespear further writes, "At the fight the recorded Mahomedan losses were over 2500 men, twenty-two ships and many big guns; so that with the losses in the pursuit the Moghul casualty list must have been a long one; while the booty that fell to the pursuers is stated to have been twenty eight elephants, a great number of guns and matchlocks, with a quantity of gold and silver ornaments and utensils. It is now that we find the Ahoms taking to firearms and utilizing the numbers captured from the Moghuls in preference to bows and spears."

After Turbak was killed, the Ahom forces of Suhungmung pursued the Mohammedan army till the Karatoya River in present day North Bengal. Later, the captured prisoners of war were allowed to settle in Assam.

10

Veer Savarkar

Active Role in Assassination of British Officials;
Coined 'Hindutva'

Orator, lawyer, politician, poet, writer, scholar, historian, playwright — these are only few labels that well describe the versatility of one of the greatest freedom fighters of India. He is Vinayak Damodar Savarkar, popularly known as Veer Savarkar. His role as a pro-independence activist, wherein he was involved in underground revolutionary activities, believing in armed revolution against the ruling British, was noteworthy. He opposed the peaceful freedom struggle spearheaded by Mahatma Gandhi.

Early Life and Education

Veer Savarkar was born to Damodar Savarkar and Yashoda Savarkar on 28 May 1883 at Bhagur, Nasik. He lost his parents at a very young age. His eldest sibling Ganesh, known as Babarao, who took responsibility of the family, supported him in all his endeavors. He did his schooling in the local village.

At the age of 18, i.e, in 1901, Savarkar married Yamunabai, whose father supported his university education. In 1902, he enrolled in Fergusson College, Pune where he completed his graduation. Shyamji Krishna Varma, a freedom fighter, lawyer and journalist helped Savarkar attain a scholarship and study Law in London. He enrolled in Gray's Inn Law College in London.

Why He was Called 'Veer'

Veer means 'braveheart'. An incident that Veer Savarkar encountered at the age of 12 earned him the title of 'Veer'. A horde of Muslims, in a rampaging mood, attacked his village. Savarkar led a group of his friends, all fellow students, and immediately reciprocated. Though outnumbered, he inspired his group to fight back until the last attacker was driven off. This brave victorious encounter at such a young age earned him the nickname 'Veer'. Henceforth, he was called Veer Savarkar.

Veer Savarkar's Role in Assassination of British Officials

Veer Savarkar and his brother Ganesh Savarkar formed a secret group called the 'Mitra Mela' in 1899. Veer was only 16 years old then. The aim of the group was achieving absolute Independence from British through use of arms. The group was renamed Abhinav Bharat Society in 1903 when Veer was still a student of Fergusson College. Soon, hundreds of freedom fighters from across the state joined the group. It spread its wings across the country and various branches were set up with thousands of patriots joining the common cause — freedom of Bharat. After Savarkar was enrolled to study Law, the group's activities extended to London too!

The group carried out a few assassinations of British officials. When in London, Veer Savarkar formed the Free India Society, comprising of Indians overseas. Following the assassinations, the Savarkar brothers were convicted and imprisoned.

One of the few British officials assassinated was Sir William Curzon Wyllie, political aide-de-camp at the India Office, London. Madanlal Dhingra, a keen follower and friend of Savarkar, shot dead the British official in 1909 in a public meeting. Dhingra was arrested, tried and hanged. Though the Savarkars were arrested following this incident, Veer's active role in this assassination was proven months later after his death in 1966 by Dhananjay Keer, who wrote a biography of Veer Savarkar. It was first published in 1950, titled, *Savarkar and His Times*. In its 1966 edition, Keer wrote that Savarkar gave Madanlal Dhingra a nickel-plated revolver on the morning of Wyllie's assassination and told him, "Don't show me your face if you fail this time." Dhingra's first attempt of killing the official had failed once.

On December 29, 1909, Anant Laxman Kanhere, a freedom fighter and member of Abhinav Bharat Society shot dead AMT Jackson, the Collector (district magistrate) of Nasik. The district magistrate was then watching a Marathi play called *Sharada*, in a theatre. Following this assassination, Ganesh Savarkar was arrested and banished to the Andamans.

The British continued interrogating more freedom fighters from the area. From Kanhere's accomplices, few of Veer Savarkar's letters were discovered. The Browning pistol that Kanhere used to assassinate the Collector was linked to Savarkar. Likewise, Veer Savarkar had sent 20 such weapons to India from England. The British sent a telegraphic warrant of arrest to London from where Savarkar was arrested. It was March 13, 1910. He was brought to India, tried, and sentenced to transportation to the Andamans for two terms of 50 years each.

Abhinav Bharat Society was disbanded in 1952.

The Hindutva Philosophy

Veer Savarkar coined the term 'Hindutva' and led the Hindutva movement, influencing the masses from across the length and breadth of the country. Later many an Indian, including Hindus who were secular, communists, and atheists described this movement and coinage of the term 'Hindutva' as fascist. They even approached the Supreme Court of India.

India's highest court of justice defined Hindutva as a 'way of life, not a religion' in its 1995 verdict against a number of appeals which arose from decisions of the Bombay High Court on this matter. Social activist Teesta Setalvad re-appealed the Supreme Court to check the 'devastating consequences' of its 1995 judgment on Hindutva. A seven judge constitution bench of the Court in 2016 declined to change the definition, as according to them, Hindutva had nothing to do with "narrow fundamentalist Hindu religious bigotry".

Coining the term 'Hindutva', Veer Savarkar fashioned the spirit of Hindu nationalism to create a collective 'Hindu' identity as an essence of Bharat. In his book *Hindutva: Who Is a Hindu?*, he defined a Hindu as one 'who was born of Hindu parents and regarded India as his motherland as well as holy land. The three essentials of Hindutva were the common nation (*rashtra*), common race (*jati*) and common culture (*sanskriti*).' Opposing the British view that India was just a geographical entity, Savarkar wrote in his book that Hindus of Akhand Bharat had existed since antiquity.

In his book, *Essentials of Hindutva*, Veer Savarkar wrote that 'Hindutva is an inclusive term of everything Indic'. He defined the term thus, 'Hindutva is not a word but a history. Not only the spiritual or religious history of our people as at times it is mistaken to be by being confounded with the other cognate term Hinduism, but a history in full. Hinduism is only a derivative, a fraction, a part of Hindutva. … Hindutva embraces all the departments of thought and activity of the whole Being of our Hindu race.'

Imprisonment and Release Terms

On March 13, 1910, Veer Savarkar was brought to India and tried for his involvement in the assassination of British officials. In July 1911, he was sentenced to transportation to the Andamans (Andaman cellular jail), also called 'Kalapani' for two terms of 50 years each.

Prisoners at Kalapani were subjected to repeated mistreatment and torture. They weren't allowed to meet friends and relatives. They were allowed to write only one letter a year to their friends or family. The Savarkars performed their duties in prison diligently. Obtaining permission from the jail authorities, Veer Savarkar taught fellow illiterate convicts to read and write.

After his associates filed mercy petitions, Veer Savarkar was shifted to Yerwada Jail in 1923. And in 1924, he was released under strict conditions and allowed to live in Ratnagiri. He was strictly forbidden to participate in politics for 5 years and barred to leave Ratnagiri district. Police restrictions on his activities were not dropped until he was granted provincial autonomy in 1937.

Few More Activities of Veer Savarkar at a Glance

1. Inspired by Lokamanya Tilak's announcement to boycott British clothes, in October 1905, he set up a bonfire during Dusshera and burnt all his foreign clothes and goods.

2. Based on the Great Uprising of 1857, Veer Savarkar wrote the book, *The History of the War of Indian Independence* with an aim to instill the spirit of patriotism and nationalism in the minds of the Indians and trigger them to fight against the British. The book was banned by the British. Likewise, many books and articles by Savarkar were banned.

3. He plotted an armed revolt against the Morle-Minto reform of the British in 1909. It was an Act passed by the British that brought about a limited increase in the involvement of Indians in British rule in India.

4. He worked on the abolishment of untouchability during his stay in Ratnagiri. He was successful in it for which he was compared to Lord Buddha by Baba Saheb Ambedkar.

5. Veer Savarkar was elected president of the Hindu Mahasabha in 1937. He served until 1943.

The list of his activities goes on and on....

Fasting until Death

Savarkar's wife, Yamunabai, died on 8 November 1963. On 1 February 1966, he renounced food, water, and medicines, observing fast until death, termed *atmaarpan*.

In an article titled *Atmahatya Nahi Atmaarpan* which he wrote before his death, he opined that 'when one's life mission is over and ability to serve the society is left no more, it is better to end the life at will rather than waiting for death'. Veer Savarkar died on 26 February 1966 at the age of 83.

11

Chennamma

Rani of Keladi Who Fought Bravely against Mughals and Gave Shelter to Shivaji's Son

S he was a Lingayat, a devotee of Mahadev. She belonged to a merchant family from Kundapur, Karnataka. She was beautiful, pious, and virtuous. With a pearl-like complexion, broad forehead, curly hair, and bright eyes, an aura of divinity emanated from her. She was Chennamma.

She was married to Somashekara Nayaka, king of Keladi, Karnataka in 1667 CE. After the king's death in 1677, Chennamma took the reins of the kingdom in her hands. She ruled efficiently for 26 years. During her rule, she fought several battles to victory. She fought bravely against Mughal Emperor Aurangzeb's forces. It was the enemy Mughal forces who withdrew, sensing defeat and begged for a treaty. It was for the first time that the Mughals proposed peace accord with an Indian ruler! She also defeated the Sultan of Bijapur and the ruler of Mysore.

Chennamma's Marriage

Somashekhara Nayaka became the king of Keladi in 1664. The Keladi kingdom during his reign stretched along the entire seacoast from Goa to Malabar. He was known far and wide for his handsome features, his efficient ruling, virtue, religious mindedness, power and wealth. Many a king from near and far kingdoms wished to make him a son-in-law. Somashekhara Nayaka turned down every marriage proposal that he received.

The king once went to the Rameshwara fair. His eyes fell on Chennamma, the daughter of Siddappa Shetty, who happened to visit the Rameshwara temple along with her friends. It was love at first sight for the king. He decided that if at all he married, he would marry her.

Somashekhara Nayaka sent his Chief Minister to the abode of Siddappa Shetty with a marriage proposal. The latter advised him that she wasn't from the royal blood, that the kings of Keladi married only royal princesses. But the king did not pay heed to his advice. Siddappa Shetty was bound to accept the king's marriage proposal. The wedding took place in the king's palace located in the capital city of Bidanur. It was the year 1667.

Chennamma's Role in the Affairs of Keladi

Chennamma started learning the art of warfare after she became the queen of Keladi. In no time she became an expert in the use of weapons. Raja Somashekhara Nayaka gave her complete support. Soon she became well versed in politics and statecraft. She also started learning music and literature and mastered both the subjects. She established a colony and facilitated settlement of scholars from near and far off states to spread knowledge of ancient wisdom in her kingdom.

The king sought the wise and witty Chennamma's advice in administrative affairs and the judiciary. Her advice never went wrong. The people of Keladi started banking upon the queen. She helped the king punish the wicked and protect the virtuous and aided in efficient ruling of the kingdom.

Chennamma as Ruler of Keladi

Chennamma became a widow after 10 years of her marriage, i.e. in 1677. The ailing king was murdered by Bharame Mavuta, the foster father of the royal court dancer named Kalavathi. An expert in black magic, Bharame Mavuta and Kalavathi had made the king their puppet. The king thereby failed in his duty of kingship.

Due to the king's deteriorating health and childlessness, many nobles had by then already begun to hatch conspiracies to usurp the throne. But Chennamma managed the affairs of Keladi with an iron hand. She appointed only trusted people as ministers. She adopted Basappa Nayaka as her son and geared up to train him in the art of warfare and the affairs of the kingdom.

Battle against Sultan of Bijapur

Bharame Mavuta conspired with the Sultan of Bijapur. News of a huge army of the Sultan approaching towards Bidanur reached the queen's ears. Two robust forts, one in Bidanur and another in the thick jungles of Bhuvanagiri were Keladi's strengths. As the queen wasn't prepared for a fight against a huge force at that moment, she followed her ministers' advice of transporting the throne of the kingdom, wealth of the royal treasury and all other valuables to Bhuvanagiri fort. When the enemy forces entered the Bidanur fort, they found it empty with no treasury or people.

At Bhuvanagiri, Rani Chennamma assembled her forces. Meanwhile, few of Keladi's commanders and ministers who did not support her at the beginning and had left her earlier arrived in Bhuvanagiri to take part in the battle against the enemy forces. Meanwhile, the Sultan's forces marched towards Bhuvanagiri. A battle ensued between the two forces in the midst of a thick forest and a narrow pass. The Sultan's army was badly defeated.

Battle against the Ruler of Mysore

When Chennamma became the ruler of Keladi, Chikkadevaraya Wodeyar was the ruler of Mysore. He declared war against Keladi, as he was driven by the notion that he could easily defeat a woman ruler. The chieftains of Sode, Sirsi and Banavasi also declared war on Keladi. But the Queen managed to defeat them all.

Three wars in total took place between Keladi and Mysore. Chennamma emerged victorious in the first and last. She treated the prisoners of war with honor and respect and set them free. Due to this act of the queen, Chikkadevaraya Wodeyar started respecting her. This was followed by a treaty of friendship between the two kingdoms.

Shelter to Son of Shivaji

Rajaram Raje Bhonsle, the younger son of Maratha ruler Chhatrapati Shivaji, was crowned at Raigad as the Maratha chief after the death of his half brother Sambhaji. It was 12 March 1689. On 25 March 1689, the Mughals started laying siege to the region around Raigad. The Marathas fought with the Mughals and managed to let Rajaram escape through Kavlya ghat to Tamil Nadu. He was to seek refuge in the fort of Jinji.

Jinji Fort, located in Villupuram, Tamil Nadu, was built by the Cholas in the 12th century and was later enhanced by the Vijaynagara kings. It was built at a strategic place to fend off any invading armies. The fort came under the control of the Bijapur Sultanate from 1649. Chhatrapati Shivaji Maharaj defeated the Bijapuri forces in 1677 and captured the fort. The Maratha king ranked Jinji Fort as the most impregnable fortress in India. Such was its fortification! The Marathas chose this fort as a hideout for their chief Rajaram till the Mughals calmed down.

Rajaram reached the fort of Keladi in disguise. He sought refuge from Rani Chennamma and asked her help for his safe passage and escape to Jinji Fort. The queen knew that if she gave shelter to Rajaram, the robust Mughals would certainly attack her kingdom. Yet she wasn't bothered. She agreed. She welcomed Rajaram with the warmest of hospitality.

Battle against Aurangzeb's Forces

Aurangzeb sent a messenger with a letter along with diamonds and precious stones to the Keladi court asking Rani Chennamma to hand over Rajaram to him. By the time the messenger reached her court, the queen had already facilitated Rajaram's safe escape to Jinji Fort. The queen replied that handing over Rajaram was impossible. Aurangzeb had already sent his son Azamath Ara with a huge army to invade Keladi, as he expected that the queen would not give in to his request.

Queen Chennamma was fully prepared for the war. The brave Keladi soldiers led by the queen waylaid the huge Mughal army in

Keladi through a thick jungle amid downpour. They started butchering the Mughal soldiers following Guerrilla warfare techniques. Azamath Ara had defeated many kings, but now the very thought of getting defeated in the hands of a woman troubled him, as defeat was for sure.

Keladi forces captured a large number of horses and considerable war material of the Mughals. More than half of the Mughal forces were killed. It continued for a few days with the queen at the winning end. The Mughal army had been dwindling fast.

Meanwhile, Azamath Ara received a letter from Aurangzeb to leave Keladi and proceed towards Jinji Fort to attack Rajaram. An elated Azamath Ara begged for a peace treaty. The generous Rani Chennamma instead of crushing the rest of the forces or taking Azamath Ara prisoner, agreed for peace. Indian rulers had always followed the rules of Dharma in warfare. This was the reason why foreigners could stamp their identity and rule in the Indian soil. Had Aurangzeb's letter not reached Azamath Ara and had the Mughal prince not begged for peace, defeat of the Mughals was for certain!

Rani Chennamma built the Mirjan fort. She ruled Keladi until her death in 1696.

Salute to Rani Chennamma! India will remember her valor and courage for eternity.

12

Kuyili

First Human Bomb of India against British

The very utterance of the term 'human bomb' will transport you to a terrain of horror, of some violent attack wherein the attacker dies during action. You will only visualize about the harm, damage and destruction that it may cause to life and property. But this is no story about any hostile individual. We are delving about a brave lady warrior who became a human bomb for the sake of the motherland. She did not carry any bomb but set herself ablaze at the guns and ammunition storehouse of the British. As a result the warehouse exploded and all guns and ammunition of British stored in the warehouse were destroyed. This helped Rani Velu Nacchiyar easily defeat the British. She is long forgotten and wiped away from the pages of History. Many of us aren't aware of or familiar with her. She was Kuyili of Tamil Nadu.

Kuyili was the commander of the Udayal Padai contingent of women army of Velu Nacchiyar, the queen of Sivagangai, Tamil Nadu. A warrior to the core, she was known for her valor and unconditional love for her motherland, always ready to sacrifice her life. She was a faithful follower of the queen. Velu Nacchiyar trusted her the most.

Not much information about Kuyili's birth and childhood is available in records. She was born at Kudanchavadi near Sivagangai. She belonged to the Sambavar community from Tamil Nadu. 'Sambavar' draws its origin as followers of Mahadev. They are believed to be ancient priests of Mahadev. Sambavars find mention in History and other records as warriors, priests, agriculturalists, poets, writers, dancers, and musicians.

Velu Nacchiyar was married to Muthuvaduganathaperiya Udaiyathevar, the king of Sivagangai. The couple was blessed with a daughter. Muthuvaduganathaperiya Udaiyathevar was killed in a battle against the combined forces of the British and Nawab of Arcot at Kalaiyar Koil on 25 June 1772. The invading British army plundered Kalaiyar Koil and collected jewels worth 50,000 pagodas.

Rani Velu Nacchiyar fled with her daughter Vellacchi to Virupachi, a neighboring kingdom ruled by Palayakaarar Kopaala Naayakkar. She was all determined to take vengeance against the British. She remained in hiding at Virupachi near Dindigul for eight years. Dindigul was located at a distance of around 100 km from Sivagangai. During the eight long years in hiding, she managed to arrange a huge army. Her army also included a big contingent of women warriors under the banner of Udayal Padai in memory of Udayal, who sacrificed her life for the queen. This wing was commandeered by Kuyili. Velu Nacchiyar herself trained them to perfection. Kuyili was a beauty with brains and was one of the ablest of the queen's commanders.

In 1780, Velu Nacchiyar formed an alliance with two neighboring rulers and was all geared up for a war against the British. She marched with her allies and army towards Sivagangai. On the way, they encountered enemy troops at intervals, first at Madurai Kochadai, then at Thirubuvanam, and at Kalaiyar Koil. The queen's army defeated the enemy forces at all the three places.

The queen and her army were now on their way to Sivangangai to recapture the fort and drive away the British from the city. At this juncture, her spy from Sivangangai alerted the troops and advised them not to march towards Sivangangai at the moment as British troops were all ready with heavy guns and ammunition including cannon barrels at several places at a distance of a kilometer each in and around Sivangangai.

The enemy British forces were superior in terms of guns and ammunition using which they could kill their opponents from a long distance. Rani Velu Nacchiyar wished that the enemy's ammunition and guns were destroyed so that she could successfully achieve victory. Marching ahead at this time would only mean casualties for her army and a possible defeat. The spies also told that the British stored the guns and ammunition at a warehouse inside the Raja Rajeswari temple at Sivagangai palace.

The queen and her army set up camps to wait till the situation in Sivagangai calmed down. She held a meeting with the commanders including Kuyili and discussed on the future course of action.

Kuyili happened to see a group of women at a distance walking barefoot towards the route to Sivagangai. They looked like devotees. She rushed towards them. During ancient and medieval times, and to this day, devotees on particular festive occasions walk several miles to visit their favorite places of worship. Kuyili asked them where they were heading to. They replied that the next day was *Vijayadashami*. And that they were heading towards Raja Rajeswari temple dedicated to Maa Shakti and Mahadev located within the Sivagangai palace premises. It was only on *Vijayadashami* day that the British allowed entry of women to the Raja Rajeswari temple for worship.

Kuyili walked back towards the camp. An idea struck her mind. She immediately devised a plan and discussed it with the queen. She undertook complete responsibility by volunteering for the task. She chose the next day — *Vijayadashami* for executing her plan. Velu Nacchiyar readily gave her consent to the commander's plan.

The brave Kuyili divided the Udayal Padai wing into groups. She instructed all the women soldiers what they would be doing step by step. They all disguised as worshippers and hid weapons tucked under their sarees. Velu Nacchiyar, also disguised, mingled in the group. And the groups, one after another, headed towards Raja Rajeswari temple. Three rounds of worship were to be carried out at the temple, which the queen and the women army were well familiar of. They strategized to strike after the third round after the general devotees would leave.

As decided, after the third round of worship after maximum devotees left, Kuyili, Velu Nacchiyar and the women army attacked the British. Captain Benjour and the entire British troop were taken unawares. In a short while many British soldiers were slain. British sepoys rushed towards the warehouse in the temple to bring ammunition.

Allowing the British bring ammunition from the warehouse would mean heavy casualties of the Udayal Padai soldiers. The warehouse had to be destroyed. Kuyili immediately rushed towards the deity where a large *ghee* oil lamp was burning. Two British sepoys shot at her. The wounded Kuyili rushed forward. There was a pot of *ghee* oil nearby. The valorous woman captain poured the *ghee* from the pot and emptied it over herself. Holding the *ghee* oil lamp, she rushed towards the warehouse. British sepoys rushing towards the warehouse suddenly stopped as they realized what was going to happen. In no time, the warehouse exploded. Kuyili had lit herself in the warehouse turning into a human bomb. She perished and turned into ashes in no time. But her sacrifice led to the destruction of the warehouse of guns and ammunition of the British forces.

A face-to-face fierce battle ensued between the British and Rani Velu Nacchiyar's forces. More of the Rani's forces joined the battle. The British stood no chance before the queen's mighty warriors. They were defeated. Captain Benjour surrendered. He pleaded begging for his life at the same time promising that the British would never interfere into the affairs of Sivagangai kingdom in the future. Velu Nacchiyar spared the captain's life and let him free.

Rani Velu Nacchiyar regained her kingdom, all because of the supreme sacrifice by Kuyili.

13

Unknown Hindu Yogi

How He Shot Dead a British Captain in Front of British Army in 1857!

The War of Independence of 1857! Part of the many divisions of the British army marched towards Kanpur, then called Cawnpore, from Calcutta on 21st of September. They were to reach Lucknow via Benares, Allahabad, Futtehpore, and Kanpur. Around 2200 Indian sepoys had laid siege of the British Residency in Lucknow including Sikandar Bagh. Sikandar Bagh was a villa and garden spread over an area of 4.5 acres located in Lucknow. It was built as a summer residence during the first half of the 19th century by Wajid Ali Shah, the last Nawab of Oudh. This villa had a fortified wall along the boundary on all four sides.

The Ninety-Third Sutherland Highlanders, also a part of the British army, used rail, bullock carts to reach this destination. They also marched on foot, especially in areas where rail facility was not available. Elephants were used to carry tents and other necessities including ammunition. En route to Kanpur, the Highlanders reached Benares on the 17th of October 1857.

The British Army dreaded the freedom fighters of the region from Benares to Allahabad. In the words of William Forbes-Mitchell, a Sergeant with the Ninety-Third Sutherland Highlanders, who wrote about the 1857 War of Independence in his book *Reminiscences of the Great Mutiny*, "From Benares we proceeded by detachments of two or three companies to Allahabad; the country between Benares and Allahabad, being overrun by different bands of mutineers, was too dangerous for small detachments of one company."

According to this book by William Forbes-Mitchell, railway tracks have been built up to Lohunga, about forty-eight miles from Allahabad. This line was to connect Kanpur. No stations were built. A considerable force of the British army assembled in Allahabad.

Missionary workers involved in converting the Hindus to Christianity were active in this region during that time. Mitchell mentions about meeting a group of missionary workers at Futtehpore, located seventy-two miles from Allahabad. He wrote, "I met some native Christians whom I had first seen in Allahabad, and who were, or had been, connected with mission work, and could speak English. They had returned from Allahabad to look after property which they had been obliged to abandon when they fled from Futtehpore on the outbreak of the Mutiny." This proves that the War of Independence of 1857 affected missionary workers too. Had the war been a success, India would have been a different nation today! Maybe there was lack of communication amongst the freedom fighters across the length and breadth of the country, which led to their failure.

Freedom fighters from Banda and Dinapore and adjoining areas, "numbering over ten thousand men, with three batteries of regular artillery, mustering eighteen guns" crossed the Yamuna River to check the advances of the British army. Mitchell mentions about this in his book, but there is no mention whether any skirmish between the two forces occurred.

The British Army reached Kanpur. Indian sepoys and civilians of Kanpur had laid siege of the city in June 1857. The sepoy forces captured 120 British women and children, killed them, and threw their dead bodies in wells. This came to be known as the Bibighar Massacre. The incident drew hateful criticism amid the British in India and their home country. The angry British recaptured Kanpur and started widespread retaliation, killing and hanging captured sepoys and civilians. Brigadier Wilson of the Sixty-Fourth Regiment was in command of Kanpur when more forces of the British directed for Lucknow reached this city.

Mitchell happened to meet a man, a local guide, a Mohammedan from Peshawar, who could speak broken English and who knew many secrets. He took him to the "slaughter-house in which the unfortunate women and children had been barbarously murdered, and the well into which their mangled bodies were afterwards flung."

The Peshawari guide narrated a secret related to Nana Sahib, who led the uprising in Kanpur. Nana Sahib was the adopted son of the exiled Maratha Peshwa Baji Rao II and adopted brother of Rani Lakshmi Bai of Jhansi. According to the guide's account, Nana Sahib, through a spy, tried to bribe the commissariat bakers who had remained with the English. He asked them to put arsenic into the bread they baked for the British. The bakers were Mohammedans. They refused to add poison to the bread. After the Bibighar Massacre, Nana Sahib had these bakers "taken and put alive into their own ovens, and there cooked and thrown to the pigs."

The British army marched from Kanpur towards Lucknow. They reached the outskirts of a village on the east side of Secunderabagh (Sikandar Bagh) in November (1857). They made a short halt at the centre of the village. They came across a Yogi in meditation, which Mitchell described as 'naked wretch'. The British never termed the Indians with respect then. The Yogi looked like a bodybuilder. His head was cleanly shaven except a *shikha* (a tuft of hair at the back of head) adorning it. It was a ritual followed by not only Brahmins but also many other Hindus. Out of the seven *chakras* or energy centres in the human body, the *shikha* is believed to cover that part of the skull wherein lies the *Shasrara Chakra*. The tuft of hair is retained to protect it. Mitchell's book finds no mention of the name of this Yogi. His body was smeared with ashes and his face painted in white and red. He was seated on a leopard's skin. He was counting a rosary of beads when the British army saw him.

In the words of Mitchell, the Yogi "was of a strong muscular build, with his head closely shaven except for the tuft on his crown, and his face all streaked in a hideous manner with white and red paint, his body smeared with ashes. He was sitting on a leopard's skin counting a rosary of beads".

James Wilson, a British soldier aimed his bayonet at the Yogi, addressing him a 'painted scoundrel' and 'murderer'. Another officer, Captain A. O. Mayne, Deputy Assistant Quartermaster-General of that troop, stopped him. Mayne said that Hindu Yogis were harmless. He had just scarcely uttered the words and his sentence not yet completed when the Yogi stopped counting the beads, took out a pistol, and fired at the chest of Captain Mayne in seconds. It all happened at the lightning's pace! Mayne lay dead. The British army could not stop his action then.

Here is what Mitchell described about the encounter, "The words had scarcely been uttered when the painted scoundrel stopped counting the beads, slipped his hand under the leopard skin, and as quick as lightning brought out a short, brass, bell-mouthed blunderbuss and fired the contents of it into Captain Mayne's chest at a distance of only a few feet. His action was as quick as it was unexpected, and Captain Mayne was unable to avoid the shot, or the men to prevent it."

Immediately, the army was set to action. The Yogi was already surrounded by thousands of the British army at the time of the assassination. They quickly bayoneted and shot him dead.

Was he really a Yogi? Or was he only waiting, disguised, to kill a high ranking British officer without fearing for his life? No records of History mention this! Thanks to the account by Mitchell. Salute to the valor of the unknown Yogi. Jai Hind!

14

Gurjars in Freedom Movement in 1824

100s of Gurjars Martyred and 100s Hung in Single Tree

History textbooks hardly find mention of many significant events. Before the Freedom Struggle of 1857, there were numerous small uprisings across the length and breadth of the country. One big uprising needs special mention here. It was the Uprising of 1824 where hundreds of freedom fighters, principally Gurjars bravely resisted and sacrificed their lives. It is an irony that this War of Independence of 1824 is not described in History text books. Rather it finds mention in a historical account by James Grant. *Cassell's Illustrated History of India* by James Grant (1822-1887. Vol. 2. Pg 13.) finds a detailed description about the First War of Independence of 1824.

It was the year 1824. The British had by then annexed a major part of India. Koonja Bahadurpur (earlier under Dehradun and presently under Roorkee Tehsil, Haridwar District, Uttarakhand), a well developed village with a small fort was under the *riyasat* of Raja Vijay Singh. His *riyasat* extended as far as Saharanpur and Meerut. The Raja declared his independence and held siege of the fort. He made Kalyan Singh (Kalua) his general. He started collecting taxes.

On one instance, when the British were transporting their treasury from Jawalapur to Saharanpur, escorted by 200 British soldiers, Kalyan Singh, led by his men, attacked them. The Gurjars looted the treasury and killed a number of the British forces. Soon after, British forces tried to curb the uprising, but in vain. Freedom fighters turned more active, looting and butchering the Britishers.

British forces employed Gurkhas for this task and marched towards Koonja Bahadurpur. In the words of the author of the book *Cassell's Illustrated History of India*, "…On the 2nd of October 1824, an express reached Deyrah from Mr. Grindall, the local magistrate of Saharanpore, stating that part of the district has risen in rebellion that upwards of 800 men principally Goojurs, headed by a notorious freebooter named Kower, had taken possession of the ghurry of Koonja, in that neighborhood and was committing every species of atrocity. He announced his advent as Kali, the last of the Hindoo avatars, for the purpose of putting an end to the reign of foreigners. Mr. Grindal solicited the aid of 200 rank and file of the Sirmoor Battalion, which had been formed of disbanded Nepaulese in 1815; and this detachment instantly marched, under Captain Young (commanding the corps) accompanied by the Hon Frederick Shore, of the Bengal Civil Service, who with his accustomed zeal and love of enterprise, marched with the little band. Mr. Grindall joined the detachment at Secunderpore with 150 men of the Sirmoor Battalion, attended by Lieutenant Debude, of the Engineers and Dr. Royle, as volunteers."

"After a forced march of 36 miles, these forces reached the scene of action in the Deyrah Doon, a valley through which the Ganges flows in the form of a stream, full of green islets, and fordable with difficulty, and where the forests abound with elephants, tigers, leopards, black bears, and striped hyenas."

"The rebels were found drawn up outside the fort and along the skirts of the village of Koonja in fighting order, and they instantly opened fire upon the advancing column, which was quickly led to the attack by Captain Young….."

A fierce fight ensued between the Gurjars and the British army outside the fort. A number of Gurjars attained martyrdom. The walls of the fort were high and Captain Young's target was to enter the fort. Escalade was impossible, as there was neither detachment nor ladders. And they had no gun to blow open the gate.

On Mr. Shore's suggestion, a large tree was cut and its branches were lopped off by the Gurkhas using their sharp kookeries. They obtained ropes. Using the ropes and the tree, they rammed against the gate. They made several attempts. At every attempt the Gurjars attacked, thrusting long spears through the opening of the iron gate of the fort. The British opened fire. In the fifth attempt, the British succeeded in making an aperture in the gate, but only large enough to admit of entrance in a stooping posture.

Captain Young dashed through the opening attended by two soldiers and followed closely by Shore and others. In the words of the author, "As he rushed on, without having time to look about him, a man sprang from a corner of the rear, and aimed a desperate blow at the back of his neck, and would assuredly have killed him, but the quick eye of Shore, who had just reared his tall form after bursting through the aperture, saw his friend's danger, and with the full swing of his sword, sent the lifeless trunk of the Goojur bounding past Young." Due to the effect of the blow by the Gurjar mutineer, Young's neck turned blue.

A fierce fight ensued thereafter. 150 Gurjars were slain by the British forces inside the fort. Meanwhile, a 'gallant, athletic and gigantic *pehelwan*', as described by the author, who by then had killed seven soldiers of the British forces using his sword and shield, came to the notice of Shore. He was involved in combat at the flat roof of a house adjoining the ramparts.

Frederick Shore approached him for a combat on the rooftop. A fight ensued between the two. In the words of the author, "The Indian was perfectly naked, with the exception of a middle cloth, and he was gaily and fantastically painted, 'for this, his last battle'. He was armed with a sword and a shield and scornfully addressed Shore as they advanced towards each other. 'What you too have turned sipahee to fight the Goojurs?' The next moment their swords were seen flashing in the setting sun; but, in the combat, Shore fought at a great disadvantage, his shield having been rendered nearly useless by the loss of its corded handle, and he could only grasp the two rings to which the latter had been attached."

During the fight Shore was heavily wounded. Kalyan Singh, the Gurjar *'pehelwan'* was able to hit several blows with his sword on Shore's chest. He was about to kill him when Captain Young turned up. He opened fire at Kalyan Singh. In the author's own words, "At this time Captain Young reached the place where the two were fighting and levelled his 'Joe Manton' at the Goojur's breast; the first barrel flashed in the pan, but a ball from the second pierced his chest just as he was making a desperate cut. The sharp blade swept under Shore's unsteady shield and gashed his side at the moment his antagonist fell back dead." Shore never recovered from his wounds. In the words of the author, "His originally robust constitution never recovered the wounds received at Koonja, though he survived till 1837, when he died at Calcutta, in his thirty-eighth year."

In the fight in the fort with the Gurjars, 37 British forces lost their lives and several were wounded. They captured Raja Vijay Singh; he was later hanged at Saharanpur. Hundreds of Gurjars lost their lives. Raja Vijay Singh's head and Kalyan Singh's waist (*dhad*) were hung on the main gate of Dehradun Jail. Later the head was transferred to Thomson College (University of Roorkee).

The British captured the local Gurjars, especially men, of Koonja Bahadurpur. In a single day, 100s of them were hung by neck until death on a huge tree. This tree still contains the iron rings (*kunde*) where they were hung.

Salute to the sons of the soil, who sacrificed their lives for the freedom of the motherland.

15

Naiki Devi

Gujarat Chalukyan Queen Who Defeated Mohammad Ghori in 1178 Battle

It has been rightly said that a woman becomes a hundred times more powerful when she becomes a mother. Here is a historical saga of a brave mother, a young Chalukyan queen, who led a huge army with her young son tied to her lap against Mohammad Ghori in battlefield. Hundreds of enemy soldiers were slain by her flashing sword. She won! We are delving about Naiki Devi, the Chalukyan queen of Gujarat, from the late 12th century. Lakshmi Bai of Jhansi fought in battle with her young son tied to her back. That was how brave mothers of India fought in battlefield in the bygone days! But do we get to read in detail about their heroic and inspiring feats in our history books? No!

Naiki Devi was the daughter of Paramardin, the Kadamba chief of Goa. According to one account, Paramardin has been identified with Mahamandalesvara Permadi, also called Sivachitta, a Goan chief. Naiki Devi was married to king Ajayapala of Gujarat. Ajayapala, who belonged to the Chaulukya (Solanki) dynasty, ascended the throne of Gujarat in 1171. The Chalukyan kingdom included parts of Gujarat and Rajasthan with capital at Anahilavada, modern Patan. This dynasty was founded by Mularaja in 940 CE after supplanting Samantsimha, the last ruler of the Chapotkata dynasty. The Chalukyas were also known as Solankis and Agnivanshi Rajputs.

Ajayapala's rule was short lived. He died in 1175. After his death, his elder son Mularaja II became his successor. But as he was a minor, his mother Naiki Devi acted as the Queen Regent. She looked after the complete administration and military affairs of the kingdom. Besides, she trained herself in the art of warfare to lead possible future battles.

During this time, Mu'izz ad-Din Muhammad of Ghor, also called Mohammad Ghori, was the Sultan of the Ghurid Empire in Afghanistan. The Ghurids were originally Buddhists but converted to Islam after Mahmud of Ghazni conquered Ghor in 1011. Mohammad Ghori ruled Ghor along with his brother Ghiyath ad-Din Muhammad.

It was Mohammad Ghori who laid the foundation of Muslim rule in India. Do you know his first expedition of attacking, looting, and plundering India was foiled by Naiki Devi? After capturing Multan in 1175, Mohammad Ghori made plans to attack India. He heard a lot about the wealth and riches of India.

With base at Multan, Mohammad Ghori marched with a huge army to Uch, the southern part of Pakistan's Punjab province. From there the Muslim army crossed the desert and started marching towards Anhilwara, the Chalukyan capital in 1178. 13th century Persian historian Minhaj-i-Siraj wrote about Muhammad of Ghor advancing towards Anahilavada, the Chaulukya capital through the routes Uchchha and Multan. Ghori did learn about Gujarat being ruled by a boy. Little did he know that the Chalukyan army would offer stiff resistance under the leadership of the boy's mother Naiki Devi!

Meanwhile, Naiki Devi heard from her spies about the advancing Muslim army towards her capital. She heard their forces were huge. Immediately, she sought help from neighboring feudatory rulers, namely Jalor Chahamana ruler Kirtipala, Arbuda Paramara ruler Dharavarsha, Naddula Chahamana ruler Kelhanadeva, and more. They agreed to help.

Mohammad Ghori camped at Kayadara near Mount Abu and sent a messenger to the court of the Chalukyan queen with a condition that he would not attack, loot, and plunder Gujarat if the queen herself surrendered to Ghori along with her sons and handed over to him all of the gold and women of the Chalukyan kingdom. The queen pretended to agree.

Mohammad Ghori waited in his camp for the arrival of the queen, her sons, gold, and women. Naiki Devi approached towards the camp on a horse with the minor king of Gujarat Mularaja II tied to her lap. Approaching hoofs alerted the Ghurid Sultan. He was overjoyed that the Chalukyan Rajputs easily accepted defeat and accepted his conditions. Soon, sound of more hoofs followed and then it was unending.

The combined forces of the Chalukyan army led by Naiki Devi surrounded the camp of Mohammad Ghori. A fierce battle ensued between the two forces. Soon the Battle of Kayadara witnessed major casualties from Ghori's army. Swords and spears clashed amid war cries. Naiki Devi tore into the enemy forces killing the enemy soldiers on either side with her sword. As she fought, her son watched the fast dwindling enemy forces from her lap! Firishta, a Persian historian from the 16th century mentions how the ruler of Gujarat defeated the Muslim army "with great slaughter". Ghori's army was badly defeated. The Sultan and the remaining Muslim army fled from the battlefield. Chalukyan army chased them out of the territories of Gujarat.

Minhaj-i-Siraj wrote how the huge Chaulukya army with elephants defeated Ghor. In his words, "the army of Islam was defeated and put to rout". 16th century Muslim historian Badauni also mentions Ghori's defeat. He also mentions how the 'remnant of the defeated army' returned to Ghazni out of great difficulty.

Mohammad Ghori was so badly defeated in this expedition that he did not think about attacking India until 1191! Never again did he attack Gujarat in his life!

Salute to the brave Naiki Devi! Jai Hind!

16

Tarabai Bhosale

Maratha Queen Who Successfully Led War against Aurangzeb's Forces

Tarabai Bhosale! She was the daughter-in-law of Chhatrapati Shivaji Maharaj and the queen of Chhatrapati Rajaram Bhosale. She ruled the Maratha Empire from 1700 until 1708 as the Queen Regent as the heir to the throne Shivaji II was a minor when the king died. After the death of Rajaram Bhosale, Mughal attacks on Maratha supremacy continued. But Tarabai Bhosale dealt it with an iron hand. She herself led her army into the battlefield and successfully fought against the Mughal forces. According to Jadunath Sarkar, a prominent Bengali historian, it was because of the administrative genius and strength of Tarabai that the Maratha Empire survived the awful crisis from 1700 to 1707 — when Mughals tried their best to occupy Maratha territories, but in vain. She valorously defended her territories. But have we ever read about the unflagging courage and indomitable spirit of this brave daughter of Bharat Mata? Ironically never, except few from Maharashtra!

The Marathas comprise of 96 clans — 60 Somvanshi and 36 Suryavanshi. Mohites belong to the Maratha Royal Deshmukh clan. Tarabai Bhosale was a Mohite. She was the daughter of Maratha general Hambirao Mohite. Since her childhood, she was fiercely independent. Rather than taking part in activities pertaining to girls of her age, she was more interested in getting trained in the art of warfare. She was inspired by the heroic exploits of her commander father. She was well-trained in the art of sword fighting, archery, cavalry, and war tactics. She learnt military strategy from her father.

Tarabai Bhosale was married to Shivaji's younger son Rajaram Bhosale when she was just eight years old. Rajaram Bhosale was older to her by 5 years. She was Rajaram's second wife. Rajaram was then already married at the age of ten to Jankibai, the daughter of Prataprao Gurjar, the chief of Shivaji's Maratha army. Hambirao Mohite later succeeded Prataprao Gurjar as the Maratha army chief. Rajaram was also married to Rajasbai Ghatge from Kagal.

Before we delve about Tarabai Bhosale, let us dig into the history of the Marathas to know better about the situation when she became Queen Regent and what led to war with Mughals. The occasional war between the Mughals and Marathas, also termed 27 Year War or Maratha War of Independence started in the year 1680 in the Deccan after the death of Shivaji. It started with Aurangzeb's invasion of the Maratha enclave in Bijapur. Even before this, after the establishment of the Maratha kingdom by Shivaji in 1674, there were constant conflicts with the Muslim rulers, but Shivaji resisted the attacks. Do you know during Shivaji's reign the Maratha Empire had about 300 forts with 50,000 foot soldiers, 40,000 cavalry, and a strong naval base along the west coast? The 27 year war that started in 1680 ended in 1707 with the death of Aurangzeb. Initially Shivaji's successor Sambhaji gave stiff resistance to the Mughal forces. After his death in 1989, Marathas under Rajaram Bhosale continued with the resistance efforts until the king died of an illness in 1700. And then Tarabai Bhosale took the reins of the Maratha kingdom in her hands and offered stiff resistance to the Mughal forces.

Rajaram Bhosale was born to Shivaji and his younger wife, Soyarabai. After the death of Shivaji, Sambhaji, who was the elder son and 13 years older to Rajaram, was the strong contender to the Maratha throne. Soyarabai conspired with few of the Maratha nobility and installed Rajaram as the king. However, Sambhaji claimed the throne after winning over the Maratha generals to his side. He imprisoned Soyarabai and Rajaram and got rid of the nobility who supported them. Meanwhile, the Mughal Maratha war continued. Soyarabai and Rajaram remained in prison until Sambhaji was captured and executed by the Mughals in 1689. The Maratha nobility freed the duo and Rajaram Bhosale became the king of the Maratha Empire.

Rajaram was crowned at Raigad on 12 March 1689 at the age of 19. On 25 March 1689, the Mughals started laying siege to the region around Raigad. The Marathas fought with the Mughals and managed to let Rajaram escape through Kavlya ghat to Tamil Nadu. He was to seek refuge in the fort of Jinji. Rajaram reached the fort of Keladi in disguise and sought refuge from queen Chennamma and asked her help for his safe passage and escape to Jinji Fort. The queen knew that if she gave shelter to Rajaram, the robust Mughals would certainly attack her kingdom. Yet she wasn't bothered.

Aurangzeb sent a messenger with a letter along with diamonds and precious stones to the Keladi court asking Rani Chennamma to hand over Rajaram to him. By the time the messenger reached her court, the queen had already facilitated Rajaram's safe escape to Jinji fort. The queen replied that handing over Rajaram was impossible. Aurangzeb had already sent his son Azamath Ara with a huge army to invade Keladi.

Do you know Rani Chennamma almost defeated the Mughal forces when the latter proposed for a peace treaty? The Rani agreed for peace. Rajaram Bhosale remained in Jinji for few years and then continued the Maratha Mughal war until his death in 1700.

After the death of Rajaram Bhosale, there were two legal heirs (both minors) to the throne — Shivaji II, Tarabai Bhosale's son and Sambhaji II, Rajasbai's son. Shivaji II was elder, then aged only four years. Tarabai Bhosale proclaimed her son Shivaji II as the heir to the throne and successor to Rajaram and declared herself as Queen Regent, taking charge of the administrative, judiciary, and military powers of the Maratha Empire.

Ramchandra Nilkanth, the veteran administrator of the Maratha Empire during Rajaram's presence in Jinji, wanted Sambhaji's son Shahuji to claim the throne. But Shahuji was then under the custody of Aurangzeb. Tarabai Bhosale carried out the royal thread ceremony of her son in the hill fort of Vishalgarh with the help of her supporters.

Tarabai Bhosale was 25 years old when she became the Queen Regent of the Marathas. Mughal chronicler Khafi Khan wrote about Tarabai, "The chiefs then made Tarabai, the chief wife and the mother of one son (of Rajaram) Regent. She was a clever intelligent woman, and had obtained a reputation during her husband's lifetime for her knowledge of civil and military matters."

When Rajaram was in Jinji Fort, the teenage Tarabai stayed at Panhala. Under the tutelage of Ramchandra Nilkanth, she studied statecraft and administrative knowledge. She further trained herself in military affairs. Later she joined her husband at Jinji. In the words of Richard M. Eaton, author of *A Social History of the Deccan, 1300-1761: Eight Indian Lives, Volume 1,* "The experience and skills gained at this time evidently infused her with considerable self confidence. For in February 1999, after she and Rajaram had returned to Maharashtra from Jinji, it was Tarabai, not her husband who resolved a dispute between the kingdoms' commander-in-chief Dhanaji Jadhav and another prominent chieftain." Tarabai Bhosale decided the dispute against the powerful Dhanaji Jadhav.

After Tarabai Bhosale assumed power, she became the supreme force of the Marathas. She regulated things so well that not a single Maratha leader acted without her order. And the power of the Marathas increased by the day, a proof of which was chronicled by Muslim historian Khafi Khan. He wrote about her, "She won the hearts of her officers, and or all the struggles and schemes, the campaigns and seizes of Aurangzeb up to the end of his reign, the power of the Marathas increased day by day." The Portugese in Goa termed her the 'Queen of the Marathas.'

Tarabai Bhosale singlehandedly directed Maratha defense against Mughal forces sent by Aurangzeb from 1700 to 1707. Aurangzeb was then deemed one of the mightiest rulers, but his might failed in front of Tarabai. She moved tirelessly from fort to fort and motivated the Maratha forces. She mobilized resources and mastered Aurangzeb's own game of offering bribes and counter bribes to commanders on both sides of the conflict.

Indian kings often strategized about launching offensive against enemy forces and create terror in their minds. This involved setting out to invade enemy territories even before the enemy thought about planning an attack. This strategy often helped check the enemy's future plans of attack. Narasimhadeva of Orissa followed this strategy and defeated Turkic Afghan Tughan Khan in 1244 AD. For several years the Delhi Sultanate and the Nawabs of Bengal did not even think of attacking Narasimhadeva's territory after this strategy worked. Tarabai Bhosale followed a similar strategy. She sent large forces beyond the Maratha speaking Deccan deep into Mughal territories to the north. This she did despite Maratha forts in the Deccan falling into Aurangzeb's hands.

Here is a list of successful raids by Marathas under Tarabai Bhosale as part of the above strategy:

- 1700 AD: She sent a troop of 50,000 soldiers as far north as the region west of Chanderi in modern Guna of northwestern Madhya Pradesh
- 1702: Invaded Khandesh, Berar, and Telangana, Maharashtra's northern and eastern borderlands
- 1703: Attacked urban centres in Khandesh and Malwa (Ujjain, Burhanpur, Munda, Sironj)
- 1705: Attacked cities in Gujarat and Khandesh.

Khafi Khan wrote about these raids of Tarabai Bhosale, "They penetrated into the old territories of the Imperial throne, plundering and destroying wherever they went…. The commanders of Tarabai cast the anchor of permanence wherever they penetrated, and having appointed *kamaish dars* (revenue collectors), they passed the years and months to their satisfaction, with their wives and children, tents and elephants. Their daring went beyond all bounds. They divided all the districts (*parganas*) amongst themselves, and following the practice of the Imperial rule, they appointed their *Subadars* (provincial governors), *kamaish dars* (revenue collectors), and *rahdars* (toll collectors)."

After the death of Aurangzeb in 1707, the 27 year war between the Marathas and Mughals ended. Shahuji was released by the Mughals. He claimed the Maratha throne. As he was Sambhaji's son and Shivaji II was still a minor, most of the Maratha nobility supported Shahuji. Tarabai Bhosale was sidelined. The Maratha queen then established a rival court in Kolhapur in 1709. But she was deposed by Rajasbai who put her own son Sambhaji II to the throne. Tarabai and Shivaji II were imprisoned by Rajasbai. Shivaji II died in 1726. Tarabai was released from prison after she reconciled with Shahuji. But she was left with no political power.

Tarabai assumed some power during her later years. She breathed her last at the age of 86 in December 1761 after the 3rd Battle of Panipat that saw the Maratha army decimated by Ahmad Shah Abdali. Had the brave Tarabai Bhosale not taken charge of Maratha power in 1700, the Marathas might have faced a similar defeat long beforehand. Had she continued ruling as the queen after 1707, the History of the Marathas would have been different. Maybe they would have established Hindu supremacy by subjugating the Mughals and ending their rule! The 7 years of her successful raids and attacks into Mughal territory corroborate this.

Salute to Tarabai Bhosale! Jai Hind!

17

Baji Rout

Youngest Freedom Fighter Martyred at 12 Years

He was a boat boy from Odisha. A patriot to the core. He was witness to oppression by the British and hated them. When British police asked him to ferry them to the other side of the Brahmani River, he flatly refused. British police asked him again to obey their orders. He refused again. They manhandled him and threatened him with death. Yet he remained adamant. Better die for the motherland than give in to the commands and demands of the British! And the British hit him hard on his head and fractured his skull. He attained martyrdom on the Brahmani River bank. He was only 12 years old then. We are delving about Baji Rout, India's youngest freedom fighter. It is unfortunate that we haven't read about him in our History text books. Except in Odisha, the name of Baji Rout hardly finds a place in books and media.

Baji Rout was born on 5th October 1926 at Nilakanthapur village in Dhenkanal, Odisha. His father was a boatman, who died when he was an infant. After his father's death, the financial condition of his family turned worse. His weak and sick mother started earning in meager amounts by grinding and husking paddy in well-to-do homes in her village. Baji Rout received no formal education. From a young age, he started ferrying people in the Brahmani River, following his father's occupation.

During the 1920s, the British entrusted local feudatory rulers, especially *zamindars* and landlords in many a princely state to collect taxes and perform other duties on their behalf in Odisha. Civil rights of the people deteriorated with chances of their growth and development being crippled completely. They were deprived from the freedom of association and expression. They could neither meet in groups nor voice their opinion freely. The poor became poorer and the feudatory rulers and people under them grew richer. Lands of many civilians were grabbed by these feudatory rulers. Anyone raising their voice was punished and British troops handled the situation using military force. Oppression by the British reached new heights.

Bihar, Jharkhand, and parts of Odisha were all parts of the Bengal Presidency of the British Raj. Bengal Presidency was then the biggest province of British India. The British created the province of Odisha in 1936 based on language spoken by the inhabitants. They further reinforced the powers of the feudatory rulers, which in turn further worsened the condition of the people, especially the peasants. The system of forced labor and compulsory extraction of money became rampant. Few areas remained under direct control of the British.

The natives, comprising of the oppressed, set up Praja Mandals (People's Front) at various places in Odisha in 1938 to raise voice against the feudatory rulers and the British and fight against oppression and plunder. The Nilgiri chapter of Praja Mandal saw peasants demanding fairer laws. This was dealt with an iron hand with the natives subjected to even harsher and brutal measures in response.

Baji Rout and many natives joined the Dhenkanal Praja Mandal group. This group submitted a petition demanding freedom of speech and association among other things. But their petition was rejected. Stern measures were taken against the natives. Many were put behind bars. A series of repressive measures were forced upon the people. Public meetings were banned. But Dhenkanal Praja Mandal group did not pay hid to the ban. They continued meeting and discussing at public places. British police opened fire at the defenseless natives, killing many. Besides, many were wounded. Womenfolk were raped by the British police. They burnt down the houses of the villagers, who supported or were part of the Praja Mandal group. The teenage Baji Rout was witness to all of this. His blood boiled the more against the feudatory chiefs and the British.

Baji Rout earned a living by ferrying people in the Brahmani River. During the period of tension when the British police started atrocities against the natives, Baji Rout and other boatmen of the region became alert. Praja Mandal members advised the boatmen and boat boys to keep guard at the banks of the river to keep check of the people who sided with the feudatory rulers and the British police and prevent them from crossing the river. Their crossing the river would only mean further plunder of the villages on the other side of the river by these enemies. For the last three nights, Baji Rout kept guard on the river bank, resting on his boat, despite incessant rains.

On the 10th of October 1938, Baji Rout was asleep on his small ferry boat fastened to a tree. His boat had a thatched shed. At the darkness of the night, in the wee hours of 11th October, British police arrived at the place where Baji's boat was parked. They had opened fire on a group of villagers in Bhuvan, two kilometers away from there. Just a night ago, they had killed two villagers. They woke up Baji Rout and ordered him to ferry them across the river to the other side.

British police pointed their guns at Baji and ordered him to ferry them fast. Baji Raot said,

"This boat of mine belongs to the Praja Mandal. It cannot be hired out to you — the enemy of the people."

The British police were taken aback listening to what the boy said. They never expected such a reply. A British policeman caught hold of him and shook his body violently while another hit him hard on his head with the heavy butt of his gun. And they continued ordering him to ferry them to the other side.

Baji Raot collapsed on the ground. The impact of the blow of the butt of the gun on his head was so fierce that his skull had a fracture and blood started oozing out profusely. But soon after Baji Rout got up, jumped to the river bank and called out loud repeatedly, asking his friends to come. His voice echoed across his village and the sleeping villagers awoke to his call. Soon Praja Mandal members reached the spot.

By this time, the British police have unfastened the boat and were ready to ferry themselves on their own to the other side. Few of the Praja Mandal members who came with ropes fastened themselves to the boat by their waists and stood firm on the river bank like trees deeply rooted in the soil. British police cut the ropes and rowed away.

From a little distance, the British police fired shots at the Praja Mandal members standing on the river bank. Few attained martyrdom on the spot while few were fatally wounded. Baji Rout breathed his last at the river bank. Among the other martyrs were Hurushi Pradhan, Lakshman Mullick, Raghu Nayak, Guri Nayak, Nata Mullick, and Fagu Sahu.

Sachidananda Routray has well paid a tribute to Baji Rout with these opening lines of his poem:

> It is not a pyre, O Friends!
> When the country is in dark despair,
> It is the light of our liberty.
> It is our freedom-fire."

Salute to Baji Rout and all the martyrs! Jai Hind!

18

Tirot Sing

Meghalaya King, Who was Guerrilla Terror to British from 1829 to 1833

U Tirot Sing! The very utterance of his name instilled terror in the minds of the British for 4 long years from 1829 to 1833 in the Khasi Hills in Meghalaya. This Khasi king of a principality in Meghalaya did not bow to the supremacy of the British. He did not surrender to their oppression and injustice or let his people suffer at the colonial enemy's hands. He kept the flame of freedom struggle alive and inspired the neighboring kingdoms of the Northeast to rise in revolt against the British.

But do we get to read in detail about this brave son of India from Meghalaya? No! Like many other unsung warriors of India, the name of Tirot Sing is in oblivion in the pages of History! How do we then get inspired from the brave feats of our ancestors from the east to west, north to south? History books must be rewritten! Glories of the brave sons and daughters of Bharat Mata should be featured. And let us bask in their glory, their patriotism, their sacrifice and feel proud and get inspired from their saga.

U Tirot Sing was the king of Nongkhlaw, a principality located in the Khasi Hills of Meghalaya. He was also the constitutional head of leading clans within his territory. He drew his lineage from the Syiemlieh clan of the Khasi tribe that migrated from Central Mongolia through Kashmir to Assam and the Khasi hills.

The British established their supremacy in parts of the northeastern states after the Treaty of Yandaboo signed in 1826 with

Burma. It was a peace treaty that led to the end of the First Anglo-Burmese War. This war that continued for two years led to the death of fifteen thousand European and Indian soldiers. As per the treaty, the British would occupy Assam, Manipur, Rakhine (Arakan), and the Taninthayi (Tenasserim) coast south of the Salween River besides supremacy in Cachar and the Jaintia Hills district. After the treaty was signed, the British planted tea gardens in most of these places and stationed British planters and forces.

The road leading from the Brahmaputra valley to Cachar and other regions of the Barak valley was hilly, treacherous, and daunting. There were no direct roads that connected the two valleys. Before the treaty of Yandaboo was signed, the British had already established their supremacy in the Barak valley. After the treaty was signed, the British found it difficult and time consuming to maintain a communication link between the two valleys.

The British wanted to establish a strategic road to link the two valleys, from Guwahati to Sylhet. That would mean it should be constructed via the Khasi hills for the road to be short and less time consuming. Passage through the Khasi hills would save the British several weeks of time.

David Scott, the political agent of the British for the northern territory, approached U Tirot Sing for seeking permission for the construction of a road through his kingdom. David Scott promised free trade for the Khasis with other regions through this road once the road project was completed. Scott also promised to give Tirot Sing complete control over Bordwar (territory that leads to passage to Assam) in the Meghalaya Assam border.

U Tirot Sing summoned all the chiefs of the leading clans and convened a session in his *durbar*. He presented to the chiefs the proposal presented by the British. The discussion went on for two days with few opposing and few agreeing. And then it was decided that Tirot Sing would give his consent to the British proposal. One key reason was that good roads in the Khasi Hills would also benefit the local tribes. Moreover, the proposals forwarded by the British were advantageous for the Khasis. Little did the Khasis know the clever policy of the British!

Following the acceptance of the proposal, a British garrison with labourers to construct the road was posted at Nongkhlaw. The construction process started in full swing.

Meanwhile, the British reinforced their forces stationed in Guwahati and Sylhet. Why increase forces and add more weapons to the artillery when there were no wars to be fought in the near future? Moreover the British temporarily set up bases only for the purpose of road construction. Tirot Sing came to know about this development. He sensed the ulterior motive of the British to ultimately grab the entire hill territory cleverly and treacherously.

Tirot Sing immediately served a notice to the British to quit Nongkhlaw. But the British did not pay any heed to the notice. Neither did they think it important to discuss with the Khasi chief related to the notice. They continued with their construction activities. Meanwhile, the British stationed more British officers and laborers in other posts across the Khasi hills in the name of road construction.

During this time, Balaram Singh, Raja of Ranee, another principality of Meghalaya, disputed U Tirot Sing's claims to the Bordwar. To establish his claim U Tirot Sing marched towards Bordwar in December 1828. The British forces blocked his way to proceed further. This angered Tirot Sing and the ulterior motive of the British trying to establish their supremacy in the Khasi hills was further demonstrated.

Tirot Sing declared war against the British. On 4th April 1829, the Khasi army under Tirot Sing attacked the British garrison at Nongkhlaw. Several British officers were killed. The British immediately responded. They send fresh troops with artillery to the Khasi hills to control the situation.

The open battle led to the martyrdom of many Khasi warriors. The Khasi army, equipped with swords, shields, bows and arrows were no match to the British forces who were equipped with firearms and killed the opposite forces from a distance.

If this open war were to continue, the British would certainly win. Tirot Sing devised a plan. He held a meeting with the other chiefs and together they decided to employ guerrilla warfare techniques. The guerrilla warfare involved involvement of a small group of combatants in ambushes, hit-and-run tactics, sabotage, raids, etc. using arms.

Tirot Sing perfectly gave shape to his strategy, attacking the British in small groups in different places. He organized the Khasi chiefs from other principalities and together they created terror amongst the British. His advantage was his familiarity with the hilly terrain of the region.

Tirot Sing mastered the art of guerrilla warfare. He himself trained his men. The emergency situation led to the requirement of more arms. Sing entrusted a select band of Khasi warriors and deployed them in caves to manufacture tribal weapons. He also entrusted spies all over the region to stay updated about any movement from the British. Accordingly, he planned every attack. The Khasi king and his men conducted night raids on the British outposts. A number of the British units were destroyed and many Britishers were massacred. This worried the British. The remaining Britishers stationed in the Khasi hills stayed in panic.

Additional forces were sent by the British in the Khasi hills. Tirot Sing and his men hid in secret caves. They continued with their guerrilla warfare tactics. The British carried out search operations in each and every corner of Khasi hills to capture Tirot Sing but in vain. This continued for four long years!

Kanaiyalal Maneklal Munshi, freedom fighter, politician, founder of Bharatiya Vidya Bhavan, and author wrote about Tirot Sing, "Tirot Sing, and his 10,000-man army, evaded the British and occasionally swooped down upon the plains, causing alarm all over Assam. Once the panic was so great that even in Guwahati, the headquarters of the British, large numbers of people including high officials kept boats ready to evacuate at a moment's notice."

It is but a fact that during Mughal and British rule, many Indians themselves were traitors. Had these traitors not existed there would have been no Mughal or British rule. It is because of these traitors that Mughals and British ruled India for a long time.

The British were successful in luring a Khasi chief with gold coins to pass on information about the whereabouts of Tirot Sing. Based on the information provided by the traitor chief, the British were able to capture the Khasi king on January 13, 1833. Had the traitor not informed the British about Sing's whereabouts, the history of Meghalaya would have been different!

The British imprisoned Tirot Sing at Dhaka Jail till he breathed his last on 17 July 1835.

Salute to Tirot Sing! Jai Hind!

19

The Bishnois

15th Century Legacy of Vaishnava Theology and Ecology Conservation

Filmstar Salman Khan made headlines after he was sentenced to five years in prison by a Jodhpur court for his role in the blackbuck killing case of 1998. He was lodged in Jodhpur jail for two days after which he was granted bail. It was the Bishnois' compassion for wildlife that led to Salman Khan's conviction. Who are the Bishnois? How did they emerge as protectors of blackbucks? How are they related to ecology conservation?

The Bishnoi community has an enduring legacy of protecting the environment. They are well known for the sacrifices they have made to protect wildlife and nature. The pledge to protect nature and wildlife is imbibed into their religious beliefs. There are many Hindu communities in India that follow Nature conservation practices as part of their religious actions and beliefs.

In the present scenario where natural resources are under heavy pressure with deforestation, mining, industrial pollution, etc. taking a toll on the ecological balance, the earth ceases to be a safe place to live in. Though numerous organizations, NGOs and groups have emerged across the length and breadth of the world in the name of environmentalism, yet they are not able to make any difference to the ecological imbalance. Hindu communities have been playing an instrumental role in environmentalism, for years, conserving Nature and wildlife as part of their religious practices.

Dr. Pankaj Jain, Associate Professor at University of North Texas, in his book *Dharma and Ecology of Hindu Communities: Sustenance and Sustainability* delves on a number of rituals that exist in Indic religious traditions wherein the environment is revered. The book highlights nature worship and how it inspires Hindus to act in an environmentally conscious way. Dr. Pankaj Jain draws example of three Hindu communities, viz. the Swadhyaya movement, the Bishnoi, and the Bhil communities in this context. He presents the texts of Bishnois, their environmental history, and their contemporary activism.

Bishnois hail from the Jodhpur and Bikaner area of Rajasthan. The word Bishnoi is derived from the Rajasthani term for *bish* meaning twenty and *noi* meaning nine, which refers to the 29 principles of the adherents of the Bishnoi sect. It also refers to 'Vishnu', meaning followers of Vishnu.

Guru Jambheshwar, also known as Jambhaji, founded the Bishnoi sect in the 15th century. The only child born to Hansa Devi and Lohat Panwar in 1451 at Pipasar (Nagaur, Rajasthan), Jambhaji spent his youth herding cows. At the age of 34, he founded the Bishnoi sect. He advocated the worship of Vishnu and recorded his preaching in poetic form. He announced a set of 29 tenets or principles to be followed by the Bishnois. These are contained in a document called *Shabadwani*, containing 120 shabads written in the Nagri script. According to him, God is a divine power that is everywhere. He advocated the protection of plants and animals, citing their importance and their peaceful coexistence with nature. For the next 51 years, until his death in 1536, he traveled across the country, preaching the 29 principles.

The 29 principles of the Bishnois revolve around preserving biodiversity and encouraging good animal husbandry (8 principles are dedicated to these). These tenets encourage ban on killing animals and felling green trees and advocate providing of protection to all life forms. They consider blackbucks and many other animals as sacred. The Bishnois ensure the firewood they use is devoid of small insects. They avoid wearing blue clothes because the dye for colouring them is obtained by cutting a large quantity of shrubs.

Seven principles are dedicated to directions for maintaining healthy social behavior. Ten tenets focus on maintaining personal hygiene and basic good health and the rest of the principles provide guidelines for worshipping God daily.

Not many are familiar with the Khejarli massacre that saw the sacrifice of 363 Bishnois in an effort to save trees from being cut. In September 1730, Abhay Singh, the Maharajah of Jodhpur sent soldiers to cut Khejri trees in the village of Khejarli, located 26 kilometres south-east of the city. The trees were to be burned to produce lime for the construction of a new palace. The Khejri trees were sacred to the Bishnois.

Amrita Devi, a local Bishnoi woman, protested and prevented the soldiers from cutting down the trees. She considered it an insult to her faith. She declared that she would lay down her life to save the trees. She and her three daughters Asu, Ratni and Bhagu hugged the trees so that the axes hit them first before hitting the trees. More Bishnois joined them. The soldiers warned them to move away. But they remained adamant and remained as they were, hugging the trees. The soldiers struck them and they fell dead. 363 Bishnois sacrificed their lives to save the Khejri trees until the news spread and the Maharajah intervened and stopped the massacre.

Brian H. Collins, who reviewed *Dharma and Ecology of Hindu Communities: Sustenance and Sustainability* writes, 'Chapter 4 examines Rajasthan's Bishnoi community, founded in the fifteenth century by Guru Jambhesvara following a severe drought that drove farmers to cut down trees and hunt local game to survive. Out of this ecological catastrophe, the result partly of the drought and partly of the human response, Jambhesvara had a spiritual awakening and began to spread a teaching of conservation and living in harmony with nature. Jambhesvara's Vaisnava theology, which contained elements of both nirguna ("God without Qualities") and saguna ("God with Qualities") teachings, resulted in a list of twenty-nine rules for the community, eight of which concern protecting animals and trees, including an injunction against wearing blue clothes because "the dye for coloring them is obtained by cutting several shrubs". One striking story Jain recounts about the Bishnoi is the legendary "Khedajali sacrifice," believed to have taken place in 1730 and commemorated with a festival since 1979, in which 363 Bishnois were killed protecting their sacred khejari trees from the ministers of the local ruler Abbay Singh. In 1983, the Bishnoi actively lobbied to ban hunting in their state, threatening to follow the example of a non-Bishnoi who burned himself alive to protest the poaching of a blue bull. Like the Swadhyayis, the Bishnoi do not see themselves as environmentalists, despite their willingness to put the wellbeing of plants and animals before their own lives.... only in the Bishnoi does he find "the evolution from a religious ethos into ecological ethos." '

This saga of valor and sacrifice of the Bishnois for preservation of the ecology continues to this day. This Vaishnavite sect has been conserving the flora and fauna of the region for centuries, even to the extent of sacrificing their lives. Protecting the environment is part of their religious tradition. Yes, religious actions and beliefs of certain communities can contribute to environmental protection!

20

Kanaklata Barua

Freedom Fighter Martyred at 17 for Holding High the
National Flag

"You can kill our human bodies but not our souls made of
iron. O Britishers! Whatever measures you adopt to stop us will
fail. We shall continue to proceed. None can stop us from hoisting
our national flag at the police post." — Kanaklata Barua.

Her high pitched voice echoed all around with these words.
It boosted the morale of her fellow freedom fighters in
procession — all members of the 'Mrityu Bahini' group or
as the name suggests 'Death Squad'. 'Do or die' was their slogan
firm. She was Kanaklata Barua, a 17 year-old teenager, who nurtured
dreams of freeing Mother India from the clutches of the British. The
British officers pointed their guns at Kanaklata Barua who held high
the national flag.

The aura of the Tricolor filled the milieu all around. No fear of
death! And they marched forward with the Tricolor fluttering high
in the Gohpur sky. They reached the police station. She was about
to hoist the flag when the British shot at her. She died on the spot.

What happened next? The brave freedom fighters in the group
did not let the national flag fall. Mukunda Kakoti held the flag, but
he was shot dead too. One after another more valorous sons of the
soil joined. Gunshots injured them. Yet the fear of death or injury
did not stop them. They proceeded. Ultimately Rampati Rajkhowa
succeeded in hoisting the tricolor at the Gohpur police post! It was
20 September 1942.

This is only one example of a small incident in the Gohpur police station area of Darrang in Assam. Likewise, many such valorous stories of the sons and daughters of Bharat Mata from across her length and breadth are unheard of, and unsung in History text books. It is their collective efforts, their sacrifice, their martyrdom year after year, which ultimately forced the British to leave India.

How do we know about the sacrifices of our brothers and sisters by our motherland? How do we draw inspiration from their brave, valorous, and patriotic endeavors? Here is a saga of the brave Kanaklata Barua, one of the youngest freedom fighters, who opposed British rule. She attained martyrdom at age 17!

She was born on 22 December 1924 to Krishna Kanta and Karneshwari Barua at Borangabari, Gohpur, Darrang district (now in Sonitpur District), Assam. She was also called Birbala, Kanka. She was nicknamed Kali because of her dark complexion. Her ancestors were ministers in the court of the Ahom kings.

Kanaklata Barua lost her mother when she was only five. Her father, a farmer and social worker, remarried but he died when she was thirteen. She studied at the local school till Class III but then dropped out to take care of her younger siblings Rajani Kanta Barua and Dibyalata Barua and to do household chores.

Since her childhood, Kanaklata Barua was different from the other girls of her age. She was more patriotic in approach and nurtured hatred against the British. Freedom movements during her time attracted her attention. Some political events like 'Chaiduar Ryot Sabha' under the leadership of Jyoti Prasad Agarwala in 1931 and persecution of eminent leaders like Cheniram Das, Mahim Chandra, Lakhidhar Sarma and Mahadev Sarma further deepened her hatred against the British. She wished to follow their path and take an active role in India's freedom movement.

Kanaklata Barua lived in a joint family where her grandfather and five paternal uncles with their family also stayed together. Her efforts to take part in secret meetings of freedom fighters were foiled by her grandfather. He did not allow her to attend such meetings. However, she succeeded in convincing her step mother Jonaki Barua, who managed to let her go secretly.

Meanwhile, Jyoti Prasad Agarwala, the Assamese cultural icon, poet, and freedom fighter established a group called the Mrityu Vahini (Death Squad) in Tezpur to give shape to the 'Quit India' movement in the region. Kanaklata Barua joined the Mrityu Bahini wing of the Gohpur sub division.

On 20 September 1942, the Mrityu Bahini decided to hoist the national flag at the Gohpur police station. A procession of unarmed villagers led by Kanaklata Barua started their march towards the police station. Kanaklata held the flag high, shouting slogans of 'Do or Die'. The police warned the procession of dire consequences if they proceeded further. Undeterred, the procession continued marching ahead.

It was then that the teenage Kanaklata said aloud these inspiring words, "You can kill our human bodies but not our souls made of iron. O Britishers! Whatever measures you adopt to stop us will fail. We shall continue to proceed. None can stop us from hoisting our national flag at the police post."

Kanaklata was only 17 years of age at the time of her martyrdom.

Note: The words uttered by Kanaklata Barua in this post may not be exactly the same but denote the exact meaning.

21

Uda Devi

The Unsung Heroine Who Killed 32 British Soldiers in Sikandar Bagh in 1857

Like many unsung warriors of the Indian freedom movement, she finds no place in History text books. She played an instrumental role in the Indian War of Independence in 1857. She led a troop of women sepoys against the British soldiers. A brave and witty warrior, she acted as a hidden sniper climbing onto a peepal tree unnoticed by the enemy soldiers. Positioning herself comfortably onto a branch, she started shooting at the advancing British soldiers in the battle of Sikandar Bagh. She shot dead 32 Britishers and wounded many until a British soldier shot her and she fell down dead from the tree. She is Uda Devi. She is deemed the first sniper of India.

Not much information is available about the birth and childhood of Uda Devi. She hailed from the rural region of Awadh, Uttar Pradesh. Since her childhood, she hated the British and wished to get trained to wage a war against the enemy and free the country. She approached Begum Hazrat Mahal, the second wife of Nawab Wajid Ali Shah of Awadh for training. Hazrat Mahal had taken charge of the affairs of Awadh and seized control of Lucknow after her husband was exiled to Calcutta. The Begum facilitated Uda Devi's training and she emerged a sharp shooter in no time. Devi was also entrusted to form a women battalion and train them in the use of arms.

Uda Devi inspired many women from her village to join her troop and she herself trained them. Meanwhile, she got married to Makka Pasi, a soldier in the Begum's army.

The War of Independence in 1857 started in Meerut cantonment on May 10 where Indian sepoys with the help of local civilians killed 50 Britishers. This news spread like wild fire and many a son and daughter of Bharat Mata rose in revolt against the British across the country. Indian sepoys and civilians of Kanpur laid siege of the city within a month, i.e. in June 1857. The sepoy forces captured 120 British women and children, killed them, and threw their dead bodies in wells. This came to be known as the Bibighar Massacre. The incident drew hateful criticism amid the British in India and their home country. The angry British recaptured Kanpur and started widespread retaliation, killing and hanging captured sepoys and civilians.

In Lucknow, some 90 kilometers away from Kanpur, sepoys started their agitation against the British. They started with the siege of the British Residency in Lucknow including Sikandar Bagh. It was November 1857. Sikandar Bagh was a villa and garden spread over an area of 4.5 acres located in Lucknow. It was built as a summer residence during the first half of the 19th century by Wajid Ali Shah, the last Nawab of Oudh. This villa had a fortified wall along the boundary on all four sides.

The British forces attacked Sikandar Bagh. There were around 2200 sepoys including Uda Devi with her women troop within the villa. The British were larger in numbers and were superior in ammunition strength. After several attempts, they were able to manage to make a hole in the fortified wall and enter the boundary walls. A fierce battle ensued. Colin Campbell led the British troops assisted by officers like Captain Dawson, Quaker Wallace, to name a few.

The British started storming the villa. Though the Indian sepoys retaliated, thousands of them were murdered under the orders of Colin Campbell. The British, remembering the Bibighar Massacre, were merciless in their killings. Makka Pasi including many others attained martyrdom in front of Uda Devi's eyes. Uda Devi vowed to avenge his death. She devised a plan.

Advising her surviving troop to attack from different sides, Uda Devi herself climbed a peepal tree after she saw a group of British soldiers approaching towards them. She was armed with a pair of heavy old-pattern cavalry pistols, one loaded in her arm and another, also loaded, perched in her belt. She carried a pouch full of ammunition that hung from her waist. She perched herself in a branch, hiding herself amid the dense leaves in such a height that she could easily take aim at the British soldiers passing beneath. She was dressed as a male soldier.

Uda Devi fired at the British soldiers one after another and their dead bodies piled up under the peepal tree. Captain Dawson, surprised at the sudden turn of events, as there were no freedom fighters nearby, asked Quaker Wallace to look up at the tree. He suspected of a hidden sniper positioned in it. Wallace was able to locate Uda Devi, whom he mistook for a man. He aimed at her and shot her dead. Uda Devi fell down with a thud. Colin Campbell and Captain Dawson were amazed to find a woman disguised as a man causing such a large number of fatalities among his men. He bowed his head over her dead body in respect in recognition of her brave feat.

William Forbes-Mitchell, a Sergeant with the Ninety-Third Sutherland Highlanders in British India, wrote about Uda Devi in his book *Reminiscences of the Great Mutiny*, which was first published in 1893: "In the centre of the inner court of the Secundrabâgh there was a large peepul tree with a very bushy top, round the foot of which were set a number of jars full of cool water. When the slaughter was almost over, many of our men went under the tree for the sake of its shade, and to quench their burning thirst with a draught of the cool water from the jars. A number however lay dead under this tree, both of the Fifty-Third and Ninety-Third, and the many bodies lying in that particular spot attracted the notice of Captain Dawson. After having carefully examined the wounds, he noticed that in every case the men had evidently been shot from above. He thereupon stepped out from beneath the tree, and called to Quaker Wallace to look up if he could see any one in the top of the tree, because all the dead under it had apparently been shot from above. Wallace had his rifle loaded, and stepping back he carefully scanned the top of the tree. He almost immediately called out, 'I see him, sir!' and cocking his rifle he ... fired, and down fell a body dressed in a tight-fitting red jacket and tight-fitting rose-coloured silk trousers; and the breast of the jacket bursting open with the fall, showed that the wearer was a woman, She was armed with a pair of heavy old-pattern cavalry pistols, one of which was in her belt still loaded, and her pouch was still about half full of ammunition, while from her perch in the tree, which had been carefully prepared before the attack...."

By this time all opposition from the Indian sepoys and civilians ceased. All of the two thousand two hundred freedom fighters were martyred within the four walls of Sikandar Bagh, especially within the building and the centre court. In this battle, one hundred and eight British soldiers were killed and wounded.

22

Roipulliani

84 Year Old Mizoram Village Chief Who Defended her People from British Aggression

Roipulliani! None, except few in Mizoram, must have heard her name. History books find no mention of this brave warrior of Mizoram who ruled her dominion like a tigress.

Until the 1870s, Mizoram was divided into principalities with each ruled by a chief. The British had not yet established their supremacy in Mizoram. But they occupied neighboring level lands and highlands where they planted tea gardens. They entrusted British officials to look after the tea plantations. Besides, they established bazaars or trade marts where they sold products to the tribals and locals and minted money.

The British interfered into the affairs of the chiefs of Mizoram in 1871 following a raid by few Mizo chiefs in tea plantations. They killed British officers, looted guns and held many as captives. Two major British forces attacked Mizoram from two directions, burning villages and razing homes to the ground until a peace treaty was signed.

The Mizos defied the treaty 14 years later, which led to war between the British forces and Mizo chiefs at various places in Mizoram. Hundreds of Mizos were martyred. The British were superior in terms of military strength and ammunition. In March 1890, the expedition came to an end with the British on the winning side. And in April 1890, Captain Browne was appointed the Political Officer and administrator of Mizoram. British rule in Mizoram thus started in April 1890. But not all chiefs of the different principalities of Mizoram accepted the supremacy of British.

Vandula was a small principality located in the south of Mizoram. After the king of this principality died, his widow Roipulliani, became his successor. She started ruling Vandula from the village of Ralvawng. She neither recognized nor bowed to the supremacy of the British. She refused to pay any tax or deliver anything to the British.

Ever since the British started their rule in Mizoram, they collected taxes, farm produce, animals like chicken, pigs, etc. from the Mizo chiefs. They also employed Mizos as coolies (forced manual labour). According to the treaty signed with different chiefs, the latter were allowed to rule their respective jurisdictions provided they paid what was decided. Revolt of any kind would only lead to direct rule by British.

Before the British started their rule in Mizoram, the chief of Vandula had raided British tea plantations and had held British and Indian workers employed by British as captives, who were later freed. The Indian captives, though freed from the Mizos, were employed by the British to collect taxes and assist them in other errands.

The British sent one of the errand boys to the court of Roipulliani, demanding delivery of coolies. They also demanded farm produce, chickens, and other things. Roipulliani refused flatly. She said,

"This freed slave should not say anything to us. His face is loathsome and revolting in my sight. I do wish someone would kill him."

On his 2nd visit to Ralvawng for the same demands, he was killed.

Roipulliani never paid any tax to the British nor gave in to any of their demands. The following was her declaration, which she followed till the end of her rule:

"My subjects and I have never paid any tax to anyone, neither have we done any forced labor. We are the owners of this land. We must evict and chase out any and everyone who is an alien."

Would the British remain silent at this? Certainly not! To subdue Roipulliani, Captain Shakespeare and his troops camped at the banks of the Mat River on the outskirts of Ralvawng village. It was August 1893. He sent a messenger with a demand of 100 maunds of rice, 20 chickens, 10 pigs, 10 goats, 1 gayal (domesticated ox), and 30 guns. The queen herself along with her son Lalthuama was to take all of these to the camp where Captain Shakespeare would be waiting.

Roipulliani and her son Lalthuama refused to comply with the demand put forth by the British. Rather than giving in to the enemy's demand, they preferred war. The chief, then aged 84, declared war against the British. They started making preparations for war. Roipulliani sent messengers to the chief of the north principality for help for the war to which the latter agreed.

The British would not let Roipulliani prepare for war. This might lead other principalities to rise in revolt. Before the two forces would meet in the battlefield, Captain Shakespeare and his forces treacherously laid an unexpected surprise attack on the villages of Vandula. He held Roipulliani and his son captives. Both were sent to Chittagong jail and imprisoned.

Roipulliani died on 3rd January 1895 at the age of 86 in Chittagong jail. Her body was transported to Mizoram for the last rites.

Salute to Roipulliani! Jai Hind!

23

Kartar Singh Sarabha

Sikh Freedom Fighter Martyred at 19; Bhagat Singh Regarded Him as Guru

"Today there begins 'Ghadar' in foreign lands, but in our country's tongue, a war against the British Raj. What is our name? Ghadar. What is our work? Ghadar. Where will be the Revolution? In India. The time will soon come when rifles and blood will take the place of pens and ink."

— Kartar Singh Sarabha.

He was a Sikh freedom fighter. At the young age of 17, he joined the Indian freedom struggle overseas as a member of the Ghadar Party. He returned to India to give shape to the freedom movement the big way. He led rebellions in Punjab until he was caught by the British. He attained martyrdom at the young age of 19. It is unfortunate that History books do not glorify the brave exploits of Kartar Singh Sarabha and many freedom fighters from the east to the west, north to the south.

Kartar Singh Sarabha was born on 24 May 1896 into a Sikh Jat family to Sahib Kaur and Mangal Singh in Ludhiana. He lost his father at a very young age and grew up under the care of his grandfather Badan Singh Grewal. Till Standard VIII, he studied in Ludhiana and then enrolled at a school in Orissa at his uncle's place where he cleared his 10th. For his higher studies his grandfather sent him to get enrolled in the University of California, Berkeley in 1912. Though he confirmed his family that he had enrolled in the university, few say that he didn't study and instead worked as a mill worker.

On 12 April 1913, Indian workers in the Pacific Coast including Canada, USA that majorly comprised of Sikhs formed a group called the Ghadar Party. Sohan Singh Bhakna was the key founder. Another founding member was Har Dyal. The objective behind its establishment was securing India's independence from British rule. Its headquarters was at San Francisco.

Meanwhile, Kartar Singh Sarabha met Indian students at Nalanda Club at Berkeley. Conversations with fellow Indians aroused his patriotic sentiments. During this time he also met Sohan Singh Bhakna who was double his age, who inspired him to join the Ghadar Party. Bhakna was a Sikh peasant from Bhakna village in Amritsar district. Kartar Singh Sarabha immediately agreed.

And then started his robust training as a Ghadar member! He was all the more determined to free India from British rule. He learnt the art of using weapons including the use of gun and pistol from local Americans. He also learned how to make a bomb. Do you know Kartar Singh Sarabha also learnt how to fly an airplane?

Ghadar Party started publishing a weekly paper called *The Ghadar* published under the auspices of the Yugantar Ashram in San Francisco. This paper carried the caption on the masthead: *Angrezi Raj Ka Dushman*. Kartar Singh Sarabha wrote in the first issue:

"Today there begins 'Ghadar' in foreign lands, but in our country's tongue, a war against the British Raj. What is our name? Ghadar. What is our work? Ghadar. Where will be the Revolution? In India. The time will soon come when rifles and blood will take the place of pens and ink."

The Ghadar also declared:

"Wanted brave soldiers to stir up rebellion in India

Pay-death

Price-martyrdom

Pension-liberty

Field of battle-India".

Kartar Singh Sarabha stopped his studies and joined Har Dyal to assist him in running the revolutionary newspaper *The Ghadar*.

The Gurmukhi edition of the paper was printed under his aegis. Sarabha wrote articles for the paper and composed patriotic poetry.

Ghadar Party soon gained support from Indian expatriates from foreign lands worldwide. After World War I, Ghadar Party came to India to start the rebellion against the British in the Indian soil. They started organizing uprisings in Punjab in 1915, challenging the supremacy of the British. More freedom fighters from across the country joined the Ghadar Party to give shape to the movement the big way.

More key members of the group were Rashbehari Bose, Har Dayal, Gulab Kaur and Bhai Parmanand. In this context, Sohan Singh Bhakna later said regarding the members of the Ghadar Party, "We were not Sikhs or Punjabis. Our religion was patriotism".

Kartar Singh Sarabha and the other leaders of the Ghadar Party decided to wage war against the British in India. In the issue of *The Ghadar* dated 5 August 1914, "Decision of Declaration of War" against the British was published. Sarabha and hundreds of Ghadar members from foreign lands landed up in India after this in 1914. Thousands of copies of the paper were distributed among army cantonments, villages and cities. Sarabha met Rash Behari Bose in Benares and informed him that 20,000 more Ghadar members from abroad would be arriving to join the war against the British.

Meanwhile, Sarabha and other Ghadar members led small rebellions in Punjab. They started visiting the villages and motivated the people to join the fight against the British. On 25 January 1915 in a meeting by Ghadar members which also included Kartar Singh Sarabha and Rash Behari Bose, Amritsar 21 February was the date decided for the uprising.

It is but a fact that during Muslim and British rule, many Indians themselves were traitors. Had these traitors not existed there would have been no Muslim or British rule. It is because of these traitors that Muslims and British ruled India for a long time. It was because of a traitor within the Ghadar Party that the British came to know beforehand about the rebellion plans of the Ghadar Party. Accordingly, the British arrested many freedom fighters including Kartar Singh Sarabha in 1915. Hundreds of Ghadar members were arrested at the ports by the British.

The failed Ghadar conspiracy was also termed the First Lahore Conspiracy Case as the trials were held in Lahore. While many members left India to evade arrest, many were arrested. 291 freedom fighters, all members of the Ghadar Party, were convicted as conspirators. 42 of them were executed and 114 got life sentences. While 93 freedom fighters got varying terms of imprisonment, 42 defendants in the trial were acquitted. Kartar Singh Sarabha was sentenced to death by hanging on 13 September 1915 in the same trial. He was hanged in the Central Jail of Lahore on 16 November 1915. He was then aged only 19 years old.

It is said Kartar Singh Sarabha, who was also a patriotic poet, sang the following lines at the time of his hanging:

Sewa desh di jindariye badi aukhi
Gallan karniya dher sokhaliyan ne
jihne desh di sewa 'ch per paeya
Ohna lakh musibtaan jhalliyan ne

Serving ones country is very difficult
It is so easy to talk
Anyone who walked on that path
Must endure millions of calamities.

Kartar Singh Sarabha could have fled abroad to evade arrest. But he did not. He embraced death bravely. He soon became the symbol of martyrdom across Punjab and other states of India. Do you know Bhagat Singh was inspired by Sarabha's freedom struggle and regarded him as his Guru? Salute to Kartar Singh Sarabha and the other brave Ghadar warriors who sacrificed their lives for the freedom of the motherland. Jai Hind!

24

Bhagat Singh, Rajguru, and Sukhdev

What You Must Know

March 23, 1931. Time: 7.30 pm. Place: Lahore Jail. It was a Monday. On this day, Bhagat Singh aged 24, Sukhdev 23 and Rajguru 23 were hanged to death by the British. This cruelty and heartlessness of the British Raj was directed towards instilling fear in the hearts of other freedom fighters, but in vain. A thousand Bhagat Singh, Rajguru and Sukhdev sprang up from across the country. In the long run, the British had to leave India! A true Indian indeed experiences goose bumps at the very utterance of the names of martyrs who sacrificed their lives for Maa Bharti.

Every *Shaheed* fought for the freedom we enjoy today. At an age, when we pursue our studies and career, they dedicated their entire time and energy to gain freedom of Bharat. We breathe free and live free because of the collective sacrifices of our freedom fighters. We owe them every breath, every moment.

Do you know Sukhdev's father died when he was a toddler? He was brought up by his uncle Lala Achintram. Since a very young age, Sukhdev was actively involved in several Indian freedom movements. Besides, being an active senior member of Hindustan Socialist Republican Association (HSRA), he organized revolutionary cells not only in Punjab but also other areas of North India.

The HSRA was established in Kanpur in 1924 by Sachindra Nath Sanyal to carry out armed resistance against the British. Sanyal was a senior leader and a close associate of Rash Behari Bose, who was one of the key organizers of the Ghadar mutinee that saw thousands of Indians settled abroad rise in armed rebellion against British. He mentored Bhagat Singh and Chandrasekhar Azad.

Since his childhood, Rajguru could not tolerate the atrocities meted out to the Indians by the British. There is an interesting story behind Rajguru leaving his home. He failed in English in school. His brother punished him in front of his new bride by making him read aloud a chapter in English. Annoyed, Rajguru left his home with only 11 paise in his pocket.

Rajguru was a scholar in the scriptures. He joined the Hindustan Socialist Republican Association as an active member. He was also called Raghunath. He soon became an ace shooter, earning the title of 'Gunman of HSRA'. Such was Rajguru's love for Bharat that he even tested himself touching a hot iron rod. When Chandrasekhar Azad asked him about his insane act, he replied that if he was caught by the police, they would certainly torture him. Hence he was testing if he could bear a torture!

Bhagat Singh was only 12 years old when the Jallianwala Bagh massacre took place where thousands of unarmed people were killed by the British. He was witness to the dead bodies lying amid pools of blood at the site. The sight deeply disturbed him. Thenceforth, he pledged to offer himself for the cause of the freedom of Bharat. He joined the Young Revolutionary Movement at the age of 15; the youth in the group vowed to overthrow the British using violence. And his journey of revolutionary activities against the British started subsequently.

When Bhagat Singh was 20, his parents fixed his marriage. He ran away to Kanpur to avoid the wedding, leaving behind a letter that read: "My life has been dedicated to the noblest cause, that of the freedom of the country. Therefore, there is no rest or worldly desire that can lure me now".

Bhagat Singh, Sukhdev, and Rajguru were against Gandhiji's concept of non-violence and the non-cooperation movement. The trio, along with other freedom fighters, was actively involved in several revolutionary activities.

It was the Lahore conspiracy case that led to the execution of the trio. James A. Scott was then the Superintendent of Police in Lahore. During this time, Lala Lajpat Rai and his followers protested against the Simon Commission, as it had no Indian members. He led a protest march on 30 October 1928 in Lahore. Scott ordered *lathi* charge of the protesters. Lala Lajpat Rai and thousands of other protesters were injured. Rai died of injuries 17 days later.

To avenge Lala Lajpat Rai's death, Bhagat Singh along with Chandrashekhar Azad, Shivaram Rajguru, Sukhdev Thapar, and others planned to kill Scot. But they accidentally killed Saunders in Lahore. The group escaped safely.

The next big attempt that Bhagat Singh planned was exploding a bomb inside the Central Legislative Assembly to protest against the anti-Bharat Trade Dispute Act and the Public Safety Bill. It was 8 April 1929. Along with Batukeshwar Dutt, Singh succeeded in the attempt injuring few British officials and disrupting the assembly proceedings. Both shouted slogans of *Inqalab Zindabad*. They did not run away. They were subsequently arrested and jailed. They were sentenced for life following trial.

Meanwhile, the HSRA had set up bomb factories in Lahore and Saharanpur. On 15 April 1929, the police discovered the Lahore unit followed by discovery of the Saharanpur factory few days later. Several HSRA members including Sukhdev, Kishori Lal, and Jai Gopal were arrested. Few of the members like Hans Raj Vohra, P.N. Ghosh and Jai Gopal turned hostile, thus changing their role to informers for the police. Based on their information, 21 conspirators including Bhagat Singh, Jatin Das, Sukhdev, and Rajguru were arrested on account of three interconnected cases: Lahore murder (Saunders), Assembly bombing, and bomb manufacture.

During their stay in jail, Jatin Das and Bhagat Singh sat on a hunger strike, revolting against vast discrimination shown between Indian and European prisoners besides illegal detention of prisoners. After a 64-day hunger strike, Jatin Das became *Shaheed* on 13 September 1929.

On 14th February 1931, a mercy appeal was filed before Lord Irwin to save Bhagat Singh, Rajguru, and Sukhdev, who were given death sentence. The appeal was filed by Madan Mohan Malviya, then President of the Indian National Congress (who later left the party in 1934). But his efforts failed. That was followed by implementation of a plan to rescue Singh and fellow inmates from the jail. But that attempt failed too.

A final effort to rescue Bhagat Singh and fellow inmates was made by Bhagwati Charan, who attempted to manufacture bombs for the purpose. He was the husband of Durga Devi, an HSRA member. Unfortunately, before he could give shape to his plan, the bombs exploded accidentally, leading to his death. Such was the patriotism and love for fellow patriots and Maa Bharti!

Eventually, Bhagat Singh, Rajguru and Sukhdev were hanged. Their bodies were secretly cremated early at dawn outside Ganda Singh Wala village; the ashes were thrown into the Sutlej River. Three of the patriots were acquitted and the rest given lesser sentences.

The death sentence was given based mainly on the evidence provided by Hans Raj Vohra, P.N. Ghosh and Jai Gopal. Had they not turned hostile, history would have been different!

Salute to the sacrifices of every *Shaheed* and every freedom fighter, who fought for the cause of Bharat! Jai Hind!

25

Chandrashekhar Azad

The Journey for 'Swatantrata'

Magistrate: What is your name?

Chandrashekhar Tiwari: *Azad* (Free).

Magistrate: Your father's name?

Chandrashekhar Tiwari: *Swatantrata* (Independence).

Magistrate: Where is your residence?

Chandrashekhar Tiwari: Jail.

This was the conversation between the court magistrate and Chandrashekhar Tiwari after the latter was arrested for his participation in the non-cooperation movement in December 1921. He was then only 15 years old! The transition from Chandrashekhar Tiwari to Chandrashekhar Azad happened at the age of 15 after this. 'Azad', who attained martyrdom at 24, continues to impact and influence the sons and daughters of Bharat Mata and will continue to influence till eternity.

Chandrashekhar Azad was born to Sitaram Tiwari and Jagrani Devi Tiwari on 23 July 1906 at Bhavra village in the present-day Alirajpur district of Madhya Pradesh. He was also called Bhim, as he looked like a bodybuilder and his physique resembled Bhim, the second Pandava prince of *Mahabharata*. During his childhood, Azad mingled with the Bhil children and became an expert in archery, wrestling, and swimming.

Chandrashekhar's mother wanted him to become a Sanskrit scholar. He thus enrolled at Kashi Vidhyapeeth, Benares to study after his early education at Alirajpur. Azad was average in his studies. Attaining a degree, he did not want to serve the British. Hence, he had a deep aversion for studies. Meanwhile, during his stay in Benares, he drew inspiration from the freedom fighters. He decided to actively participate in the freedom struggle and drive the British out of India.

At the age of 15, Chandrashekhar joined Gandhi's non-cooperation movement. And he earned the title of 'Azad' following his answers to the magistrate during trial after his arrest. Thereafter he became popular as Chandrashekhar Azad.

Chandrashekhar Azad became more aggressive after suspension of the non-cooperation movement in 1922 by Gandhi. He wanted to achieve India's complete independence by any means. During this time, he met Pranvesh Chatterji, a young freedom fighter who introduced him to Ram Prasad Bismil, the founder of Hindustan Republican Association (HRA). HRA's aim was to free India and advocated equality of all people. During his introduction with Bismil, Azad pledged to serve the cause of the HRA, i.e. the freedom of India by putting his hand over a lamp. He did not remove it till his skin burnt. This impressed Bismil. Azad became an active member of the HRA.

Soon Azad became a master propagandist. He secretly distributed leaflets instilling the spirit of nationalism in India's youth to fight unitedly against the British. He collected funds for the HRA. Many more freedom fighters joined him; worth mentioning were Shri Yogesh Chatterji, Shri Rabindranath Kar, Shri Sachin Sanyal, to name a few. He imparted training in the art of warfare; so did other members of the HRA.

To collect more money to buy arms, Chandrashekhar Azad took the lead in committing robberies of government property. In 1925, he was involved in the "Kakori Train Robbery" and attempted to blow up the Viceroy's train in 1926.

On 30 October 1928, Lala Lajpat Rai led a protest march in Lahore against the Simon Commission, as it had no Indian members. Scott, then the Superintendent of Police in Lahore, ordered *lathi* charge of the protesters. Lala Lajpat Rai and thousands of other protesters were injured. Rai died of injuries 17 days later. To avenge Lala Lajpat Rai's death, Chandrashekhar Azad along with Bhagat Singh, Shivaram Rajguru, Sukhdev Thapar, and others planned to kill Scot. But they accidentally killed Saunders in Lahore. The group escaped safely.

After the death of Bismil, Chandrashekhar Azad reorganised the HRA under a new name called Hindustan Socialist Republican Army (HSRA) in 1926. Bhagat Singh, Sukhdev, and Rajguru were actively involved in this group. Manmath Nath Gupt, a fellow member of HSRA, described the activities of the HSRA in his writings. For some time, Chandrashekhar Azad made Jhansi the hub of the group's activities. He used the forest of Orchha to practice shooting and train the youth in the art of warfare. He stayed in disguise in a hut under the name of Pandit Harishankar Brahmachari near a Hanuman temple on the banks of the Satar River.

On 27 February 1931, Chandrashekhar Azad waited in hiding with Sukhdev Raj for a secret meeting at Alfred Park in Allahabad. The British had been looking for Azad for a long time, but in vain. They could never capture him. After an informant notified the British about his whereabouts, the police surrounded him in the park. In the process of defending himself and Sukhdev, Azad killed three British policemen and wounded few others. He was able to help Sukhdev Raj escape. After a long shootout, when he realized that his capture was for certain, he shot himself dead with his Colt pistol, holding true to his pledge to never be captured alive. He was then only 24 years old!

"Dushman ki goliyon ka hum samna karenge,
Azad hee rahein hain, Azad hee rahenge"

("Will face the enemies' bullets, Will remain free, Will Remain Free")

This was his slogan, which he voiced often!

The British could never have trapped Azad had the informer not informed them. History of India would have been different! Azad was another Netaji Bose in the making!

Was Jawaharlal Nehru the informant who notified the British about Azad's whereabouts? According to an article by *Daily O*, Sujit

Azad, the nephew of Chandrashekhar Azad, claimed that Nehru had provided the British specific information about Azad's whereabouts. According to him, based on information provided by Nehru, the British accosted him leading to his martyrdom. Sujit Azad also claimed that Azad handed over HSRA funds to Nehru hoping to free Bhagat Singh in exchange. Nehru took the money, but did not keep his words. He played no role in freeing Bhagat Singh!

On the day of his death, Chandrashekhar Azad had visited Jawaharlal Nehru. A verbal fight ensued between them. After he left Nehru's house that day, he was trapped in Alfred Park by British forces. Isn't it a coincidence? Besides, Nehru had confirmed in his autobiography that he did meet Azad in early 1931.

So did Jawaharlal Nehru betray Azad by informing the British about his whereabouts?

26

Khudiram Bose

An Orphan at 7 to Hanging by British at Age 18

Ekbaar biday de ma ghure ashi
Hasi hasi porbo phnashi dekhbe bharatbasi…
Dosh mash dosh din pore
Jonmo nebo mashir ghore Ma go
Tokhon jodi na chinte paris
Dekhbi golay phnashi

Mother bid me farewell once, I will be back soon.
Whole of India will watch me while I wear the noose smiling….

10 months and 10 days from now
I shall be born to my maternal aunt O Mother
If you don't recognize me
Look for the noose around my neck.

This was the song I grew up with, the haunting lines that fetched lumps in my throat, gave me goose bumps, and brought tears to my eyes. My father narrated to us siblings, neighbors, and relatives the valorous historical saga of freedom fighter Khudiram Bose and his martyrdom for Maa Bharti. The echo of this song is ingrained in my brain like the graphic outline of my heart's movement! This was the song 18 year old Khudiram sang when he was about to be hanged to death by the British. He was asking his mother (Mother India) to bid him goodbye. This song was composed in first person narrative in honor of Khudiram Bose by poet Pitambar Das.

18 years, 8 months, 8 days! This was his age when he was hanged to death by the British. One of the youngest freedom fighters for Maa Bharti from Bengal! It is but unfortunate that stories of many of our brave freedom fighters have been wiped away from the pages of History, especially History text books.

About Khudiram Bose at a Glance

- Birthday: December 3, 1889
- Birthplace: Habibpur village under Keshpur Police Station in Midnapore district of Bengal
- Parents: Trailokyanath Bose and Lakshmipriya Devi
- Schooling: Tamluk Hamilton High School (established in 1852), the second oldest school in Midnapore (West Medinipur) and Midnapore Collegiate School.

Naamkaran (Naming)

Do you know Khudiram Bose was the only son of his parents? He had three sisters. Two elder brothers were born, but both of them died in toddlerhood. Soon after Khudiram was born, his parents followed a ritual that was believed to save a child from dying at an early age. They sold him symbolically to their eldest daughter Aparupa in exchange of three handfuls of *khud* (a form of crushed rice). And hence his name Khudiram!

An Orphan at 7

When Khudiram Bose was 6 years old, he lost his mother. A year later, i.e. at the age of 7, he lost his father. Symbolically, Aparupa Roy, his eldest sister, was his mother, as he was sold to her at birth. She was married to Amritalal Roy. The couple brought Khudiram Bose to their home at Hatgachha village in West Medinipur district. They brought him up as their own son.

Freedom Movement Activities from Age 13

At the age of 13, Khudiram Bose happened to attend the public lectures of Aurobindo Ghosh and Sister Nivedita in West Medinipur. It was the year 1902. Aurobindo Ghosh moved from place to place to instill the spirit of nationalism in the youth through lectures so that they rise to fight against the British and free Mother India. He helped establish a series of youth clubs in Bengal and other regions of India. One club worth mentioning was the Anushilan Samiti established in 1902. Khudiram Bose joined the Anushilan Samiti at the age of 13 and got involved in secret planning sessions directed towards attacking the British. Thereby, he came in touch with Barindra Kumar Ghosh, younger brother of Sri Aurobindo. He became a volunteer at the age of 15.

Do you know Khudiram Bose was first arrested by the British at the age of 15? He was arrested for distributing pamphlets against the British. In 1905, he planted bombs near police stations, targeting British government officials.

What Led to Khudiram Bose's Martyrdom?

Anushilan Samiti youth club had been actively involved in various patriotic activities. One was the club's attempt of killing Douglas Kingsford, the Chief Magistrate of the Presidency court of Alipore. Kingsford had sentenced many young freedom fighters of the region with harsh punishments besides inflicting on them corporal punishment. He was famed for notoriety amongst the Indians but was in the good books of the British administration. Anushilan Samiti's first attempt of assassinating Kingsford failed. Meanwhile, Kingsford was promoted to District Judge and transferred to Muzaffarpur, Bihar.

Khudiram Bose and Prafulla Chaki were entrusted for another attempt to assassinate Douglas Kingsford in Muzaffarpur. To execute this task, the two arrived in Muzaffarpur. Hem Chandra Kanungo Das, who learnt the art of bomb making from Nicholas Safranski, a Russian revolutionary in exile in Paris, provided them a bomb.

At Muzaffarpur, Khudiram Bose and Prafulla Chaki stayed in a *dharamshala* under the names of Haren Sarkar and Dinesh Chandra Roy respectively. For three weeks, they closely observed the routine activities of Douglas Kingsford. On the day of the execution, they surveyed the Muzaffarpur Park, disguised as school boys. This park was located opposite the British Club where Kingsford regularly visited. It was 29th April 1908. As they were noticed by a constable in suspicion, they chose the next day for the task.

A day later, i.e. on the dark night of 30th April, before the clock struck 9, Khudiram Bose threw the bomb at a carriage he believed to be carrying Kingsford. A loud explosion followed. The carriage, which looked similar to the one that carried Kingsford, was then right outside the British Club. Unfortunately, it was occupied by the wife and daughter of barrister Pringle Kennedy, a leading pleader of Muzaffarpur Bar. They later succumbed to their injuries.

In a little while, the entire city was in chaos and the news of the bombing spread like wild fire. Police forces were deployed everywhere and every passenger embarking or disembarking in railway stations in/near Muzaffarpur were thoroughly checked and interrogated.

Khudiram Bose parted ways with Prafulla Chaki and walked from one village to another non-stop barefooted the whole night. After walking for around 25 miles, he reached a station called Waini (later named Khudiram Bose Pusa Station) the next morning, i.e. on May 1, 1908. At the railway station, two constables saw an exhausted and perspiring Khudiram Bose asking for a glass of water at a tea stall. His extremely dusty feet further gave them reasons to suspect the more. They confronted him and arrested him.

Do you know the two armed constables who arrested Khudiram Bose were Indians working under the British? Had they and many others employed by British sided for the cause of Mother India, History would have been different. Perhaps India would have gained independence much earlier from colonial rule!

Meanwhile, Prafulla Chaki was intercepted by the police too. Knowing that his arrest was for certain, he shot himself dead before he could be further questioned, jailed or sentenced by the British.

The handcuffed Khudiram Bose was brought to Muzaffarpur. He was unaware that Prafulla Chaki had attained martyrdom. Hence, when interrogated by district magistrate Mr. Woodman, he took complete responsibility of his actions. He didn't give in to tortures when asked about the co-conspirators of the incident. Such was his love for the motherland at such a young age! After he gave his statement, the body of Prafulla Chaki was brought to the same spot. Khudiram's effort to save his friend turned vain.

Khudiram Bose was eventually hanged to death on 11 August 1908. He died smiling, as reported by the *Anandabazar Patrika*. Salute to Bose and all brave sons and daughters of the soil who sacrificed their lives for the freedom of Maa Bharti.

Paona Brajabashi

Fearless Manipur General Who Led Fierce Battle against British in 1891

Many of you have heard about the 300 brave Spartans, who under the leadership of King Leonidas fought bravely in battlefield against thousands of Persians. But have you heard about the brave 300 Manipur army led by Paona Brajabashi who fought bravely in battlefield against the British in 1891? Historians describe this Anglo-Manipur Battle of Khongjom as one of the fiercest battles in the annals of Indian history. This was the last War of Independence of Manipur against the British.

There is another valorous instance from Indian History - of 300 Maratha army led by Bajiprabhu Deshpande who fought bravely in battlefield against a 12000 Adilshahi army led by Siddi Masood in 1660. Indian History is full of such heroic exploits. The only pity is that we, as the citizens of the country, hardly know about our brave warriors who gave a stiff resistance to Muslim rule and British supremacy. These brave warriors from east to the west, north to the south, hardly find a place in History text books.

When all of the 299 Manipuri soldiers were martyred in the battle of Khongjom in 1891, Paona Brajabashi singularly fought until he was caught by the British. Tribal weaponry used by the Manipuri warriors were no match to the advanced artillery used by the British. Paona Brajabashi was so skilled in the art of warfare that the British commander admired him. Here is a conversation between the British commander and Paona Brajabashi in the battlefield after he was caught.

British commander: We shall reward you with a big post if you join the British Army. And if you refuse, you will be executed.

Paona Brajabashi: Death is more welcome than treason.

Saying this, the brave Manipuri warrior took off his protective cloth wrapped as headgear and offered his head. "I refuse your offer. Behead me," he said.

This is the saga of our brave freedom fighters, who fought until their last breath and embraced death rather than accept British supremacy. This is the historical chronicle that will inspire generations and will continue to inspire the sons and daughters of Bharat Mata till eternity.

Khongjom, the place where the last Anglo-Manipuri war took place is located on the Indo-Myanmar road in the district of Thoubal, 36 km from Imphal. At the foot of this hill, Paona Brajabashi and the brave Manipuri warriors fought against the British until their martyrdom. A War Memorial has been built on the top of Kheba hill in Khongjom. 23rd April is celebrated as Khongjom day in Manipur every year in memory of the martyrs.

Not much information is available about Paona Brajabashi, except his role in the 1891 Battle of Khongjom. He was the Major general of the Manipur army.

The Burmese had annexed Manipur in 1819 until the war between the British and Burmese took place in 1824. The British won and the Treaty of Yandaboo was signed in 1826. It was because the British supremacy in Bengal was threatened that the British declared war against Burma. Thousands of Manipuri soldiers participated in this war, siding with the British against a promise that if won, their sovereignty won't be questioned by the British.

Except a few Manipuri territories, the sovereignty of Manipur was restored as promised. Due to internal conflicts between the princes of Manipur, the British grabbed an opportunity of cleverly interfering into the internal affairs in the name of 'friendship relations' and gradually establishing their supremacy by recruiting political agents in every region. The Manipuris revolted which resulted in the Anglo Manipuri war in 1891. It started on 31 March and ended on 27 April.

Maharajah Chandrakirti, the king of Manipur died in 1886. He was succeeded by Maharaja Surchandra, though there were eight princes including step brothers as contenders to the throne. Surchandra's ineffectiveness in governance led to political instability in Manipur and the eight princes divided into two groups. Each prince wished to be the king. Crown prince Kulachandra and his younger brothers, backed by the support of Tikendrajit, the Senapati revolted against Maharajah Surchandra on September 21st 1890. Maharajah Surchandra lodged a complaint to Lord Landsdown, the then Viceroy of India, against his step brothers. He also complained against Senapati Tikendrajit.

Landsdown sent Mr. JW Quinton, the Chief Commissioner of Assam with 400 Gurkha soldiers under Colonel Skene to capture Tikendrajit. They reached Imphal on 22nd March 1891. They attacked Kangla, the palace of Manipur the next day. Many innocent civilians including women and children were killed in this attack by the British. The Manipuris retaliated, killing five British officers including Mr. JW Quinton, the Chief Commissioner of Assam and wounded many.

On 31st March 1891, the British declared war against Manipur. They sent three huge forces of their army from three different directions. British troops that entered from the North were commandeered by Major General H. Collet, the west by Colonel RHF Rennick and the south by Brigadier General T. Graham.

The west front took possession of Kangla on 27th April 1891 despite resistance from the Manipuri warriors, so did the North. It was the south front led by Brigadier General T. Graham that witnessed the stiffest of resistance. And the battle in this south part of Manipur was fought at Khongjom. One of the Manipur army units fighting against this front was led by Paona Brajabashi.

Before the declaration of war by the British, Paona Brajabashi was posted as a Subedar in the Manipur army. The Maharajah promoted him and Chongtha Mia Singh to the post of majors. Following the orders of the Maharajah, Paona Brajabashi and Chongtha Mia proceeded to Pallel through Burma road with 300 soldiers. They reached Thoubal and made their camp on the

Western Side of the Khongjom River. They took position in trenches on 22nd April.

The south British front had occupied Pallel, Kakching and Langathel then and they camped at Langathel hill. Early morning on 23rd April, the British under Brigadier General T Graham fired guns from the top of the hill camp towards the Manipuri camps.

This was followed by the marching of the British army towards the base of the hill of Khongjom where the Manipuri forces under Paona Brajabashi and Chongtha Mia waited to attack. A fierce fight ensued between the two parties. The Manipuri warriors gave a stiff resistance until all of the Manipuri soldiers except Paona Brajabashi were martyred. Though heavily wounded, Paona continued to fight unabatedly and with renewed zest. His enthusiasm in the battlefield drew admiration from the British forces. At last the British were able to capture him. It was then that the aforementioned conversation took place between Brigadier General T. Graham and Paona Brajabashi. As the brave Manipuri warrior refused the offer, he was beheaded in the battlefield.

Manipur fell into British hands on 27th April. The British pulled down the native royal flag and hoisted the British Union's Jack Flag. They appointed Churachand, a five year old as the King of Manipur and started direct rule. H.St Maxwll, the Political Agent, was appointed as the Superintendent of Manipur. On 13th August, the British hung Senapati Tikendrajit, the prince of Manipur and General Thangal to death in broad daylight.

Salute to Paona Brajabashi and the brave Manipuri warriors. Jai Hind!

28

Shivdevi Tomar

16 Year Old Jat Girl Who Killed 17 British Soldiers during Revolt of 1857

Vande Mataram!

We breathe free, we live free;
This freedom we owe truly
To adversity, martyrdom, strategy,
To love, patriotism, sacrifice
Of our brothers and sisters by our motherland.

We invoke you, O patriots!
O sons and daughters of Bharat!
To shower us with your prowess,
So that we keep up to your legacy;
Let your courage, let your nationalism
Prevail in this generation;
And subsequent generations for eternity.

Yes! We breathe free and live free because of the collective sacrifices of our freedom fighters. Who doesn't know about the brave sons and daughters of Mother India — Bhagat Singh, Chandra Sekhar Azad, Subhash Chandra Bose, Rani Lakhsmi Bai, Mangal Pandey, to name a few?

But there are many unsung heroes and heroines of Indian Independence Movement, who have not found a place in History books. Besides men, women too played an instrumental role in India's struggle for independence.

Not everyone is familiar with 16 year-old Shivdevi Tomar, who bravely fought against the British during India's War of Independence of 1857. She hailed from Baraut, Baghpat, around 54 kilometers from Meerut, the place from where the Revolt started. Except her role in India's freedom struggle in 1857, there are no available records about her childhood and upbringing.

It was a Sunday. Date: May 10, 1857. Place: Meerut cantonment. By this time, many Indians across the country were agitated against the British. Rebellions did occur at many places earlier, but in vain. The episode of greased cartridges had been hurting the sentiments of the Indian soldiers. Numerous British soldiers were off duty and the British officers stationed at Meerut Cantonment were preparing to attend church that day. Indian soldiers at the cantonment attacked the British soldiers including officers. The people of Meerut joined them. 50 Britishers were killed in the attack.

Soon, this news spread like wild fire and many a son and daughter of Bharat Mata rose in revolt against the British across the country. The freedom struggle in the villages adjoining Meerut was triggered by one Shahmal Singh Tomar from Baraut. He laid siege of Baraut and declared independence. The flag of independence flew high in the Baraut sky.

On 18 July 1857, British forces attacked Shahmal Singh Tomar and his men at Badka village near Baraut. Shahmal Singh Tomar and the villagers fought bravely. Tomar was martyred in the attack. 32 of the freedom fighters who sided with Tomar were captured. They were hanged to death from a *peepal* tree in the outskirts of Bijraul village near Baraut. The British then destroyed the houses of Baraut, leaving everyone homeless. Not only this, the British also plundered the village, looted wealth and precious belongings and left the villagers without food and shelter.

16 year-old Shivdevi Tomar was witness to the atrocities carried out by the British. She was never trained in warfare, yet she decided to fight or perish. She held a secret meeting with one of her brave friends Kishandevi and few of the youths of the village. And they

decided to attack the British. She motivated them to rise in rebellion. Fighting unto death was their slogan firm!

Holding a sword, Shivdevi Tomar, leading her group of few villagers attacked the British forces at Baraut. They knew they might not come back alive, as they carried only swords and sticks whereas the British were equipped with guns. Yet, this drawback did not deter their spirits.

Shivdevi Tomar fought like Goddess Kali. She tore the British soldiers into pieces with her sword, killing 17 of them and wounding many. So did her team of brave freedom fighters. It was Shivdevi Tomar, who gave shape to maximum number of casualties of British soldiers.

The British forces were taken unawares. They never expected a rebellion from Baraut. They surmised that the brutal hanging to death of the 25 freedom fighters in the outskirts of Bijraul village had frightened them. But they were wrong.

The rest of the surviving British soldiers fled to save their lives. Not a single British remained in Baraut.

Villagers gathered around the heavily wounded Shivdevi Tomar, appreciating her courage. Suddenly, while her wounds were being treated, the British forces arrived and pumped several bullets into her. She attained martyrdom.

Such is the saga of the brave daughter, who sacrificed her life for the motherland.

29

Veerapandiya Kattabomman

Tamil Nadu Chieftain Who Opposed British Rule, Defeated Them Twice and Hanged at 39

The Indian Independence Movement happened in bits and parts across the country many years before the 1857 Uprising. These movements every now and then indeed terrorized the British. They feared that if such movements gain momentum and the chieftains and people get united for the cause, their 'rule and loot a rich India' strategy would fail. They curbed these movements in every possible way — killing, destroying sites, hanging the freedom fighters so that Indians who thought about an uprising took a lesson.

But this barbaric policy of the British did not deter the spirits of the true sons and daughters of the soil. It is but an irony that many an Indian also sided with the British, helping them arrest the freedom fighters and were rewarded. Had they also fought for the freedom of our motherland, we would have attained freedom much before 1947. And the bigger irony at present is that such anti-India forces are still breeding, harming our motherland culturally, socially, politically, and economically.

Our History text books are filled with the glorius saga of our invaders. The contribution of many freedom fighters from across the country has not found a place in these books. How do we know about the sacrifices of our brothers and sisters by our soil? How do we draw inspiration from their brave, valorous, and patriotic endeavors?

Here is a saga of a brave Telugu chieftain Veerapandiya Kattabomman, one of the earliest freedom fighters from Tamil Nadu, who opposed British rule. He refused to pay taxes, fought against them, until he was hanged at the age of 39. He embraced death, but did not give in to the demands of the British. As aforementioned, his friends helped the British arrest him. Otherwise History of that region of India would have been different!

Veerapandiya Kattabomman was born on January 3, 1760 to Jagaveera Kattabomman and Aarumugathammal, a Nayakkar family at Panchalankurichi of present Thoothukudi district of Tamil Nadu.

Lineage and Legacy of Veerapandiya Kattabomman

The downfall of the Vijaynagara Empire in Tamil Nadu saw the rise of governors of the kingdom declaring independence and establishing independent kingdoms. The Nayakkars ruled the Pandya region. They divided their territories into 72 palayams or regions. They appointed a palaiyakkarar, the feudal title for a class of territorial administrative and military governors, for each palayam.

The palaiyakkarars were entrusted with the role to administer their respective territories, collect taxes, run the local judiciary, and maintain an army for the Nayakkar rulers. Veerapandiya Kattabomman's ancestor was a minister in the court of Jagaveera Pandyan, a Pandyan desendent. As the king was issueless, he declared Kattabomman as his successor. On February 2, 1790, Veerapandiya Kattabomman, aged 30, became the chieftain of Panchalankurichi palayam.

Events Leading to British Supremacy of Nayakkar Kingdom

After the death of Nayakkar king of Madurai, Vijaya Ranga Chokkanatha in 1731, his queen Meenakshi ascended the throne. Chanda Sahib, the Mughal Empire's Sepoy and Divan of the Carnatic, betrayed Queen Meenakshi and seized the throne for himself. He was also a vassal to the Nawab of Arcot. The Nayakkar kingdom with all the 72 palayams thus came under the control of the Nawab after Chanda Sahib was beheaded in a mutiny in Tanjore.

But the chieftains of the 72 palayams refused to recognise the Nawab as their ruler. They stopped paying taxes. Meanwhile, the Nawab faced bankruptcy and borrowed a huge sum from the British. Not able to return his dues, he ceded the right to collect taxes and levies from the 72 palayams to the British.

Veerapandiya Kattabomman Did Not Submit to British Supremacy

Eventually by the 1790s, the British mercilessly looted the wealth of Tamil Nadu in the name of tax and other levies. All chieftains of the 72 palayams except Veerapandiya Kattabomman gave in to the demand and savagery of the British. Veerapandiya Kattabomman did not submit to British supremacy.

Veerapandiya Kattabomman Killed British Deputy Commandant Clarke and other British Soldiers

Veerapandiya Kattabomman did not pay any tax to the British despite repeat orders. Months passed by. The British then entrusted the Collector of the region Jackson to solve the issue. Jackson ordered Kattabomman to meet him but the chieftain refused. Finally, under repeat requests, Veerapandiya Kattabomman agreed to meet him but at the same time determined not to give in to the enemy's demand. The venue of the meeting was Ramalinga Vilasam, the palace of Sethupathi of Ramanathapuram.

The British treacherously planned to capture the Panchalankurichi chieftain at Ramalinga Vilasam so that they could set an example for other possible defaulters. As Veerapandiya Kattabomman was resolute in his decision of not submitting to British supremacy, the meeting ended in a combat. Kattabomman killed Clarke, the Deputy Commandant of the British. In the process of getting himself and his men to safety, he killed several British soldiers.

Lousington's Attempt to Meet Veerapandiya Kattabomman

Following the failure of Jackson to solve the issue of Panchalankurichi palayam and his inability to capture Veerapandiya Kattabomman, the British sacked him. They appointed Lousington as the new Collector of Tirunelveli. It was the year 1799.

Lousington wrote a letter to Kattabomman, expressing his desire to meet him. The Panchalankurichi chieftain agreed on one condition — whatever was robbed from him at Ramalinga Vilasam in Ramanathapuram should be restored to him first. This was unacceptable to Lousington.

Veerapandiya Kattabomman Defeated Combined Forces of British

Ettayapuram is the neighboring palayam of Panchalankurichi, Veerapandiya's principality. Lousington bribed its palaiyakkarar to wage war against Veerapandiya. The palaiyakkarar, who was in a dispute with Veerapandiya, accepted the bribe. Lousington sent British troops to strengthen Ettayapuram's forces. The combined forces attacked Panchalankurichi. The valorous Veerapandiya Kattabomman and his army easily defeated them.

Thereafter, the British army under the commandment of Major Bannerman, stationed themselves at all the four entrances of Panchalankurichi fort with a motive to attack. Veerapandiya Kattabomman and his forces reciprocated with a daring attack on the southern entrance. They killed the British troops stationed there including their commander Lieutenant Collins. They also destroyed their weaponry. Unable to withstand the sudden heavy loss, the rest of the British troops withdrew to Palayamkottai.

The Treacherous Capture of Veerapandiya Kattabomman and Barbarism of British

The British forces were far more superior in weaponry, ammunition, and troops. Veerapandiya and his army did fight bravely and defeated them. But he knew that the British forces would come back with bigger reinforcements and heavy artillery and the small fort of Panchalankurichi would not be able to survive a barrage from their heavy cannons. With an objective to seek help from neighboring palaiyakkarars and arrange a huge army, Veerapandiya Kattabomman with his aides left the fort that night. Next day, the British attacked the fort with additional forces.

The British were able to capture 17 close aides of Veerapandiya including Thanapathi Pillai. They beheaded Thanapathi Pillai, perched his head on a bamboo pole, and displayed it at Panchalankurichi to create terror amongst the Indians. They executed the rest of the 16 prisoners openly to demoralize the sentiments of the freedom fighters. The British were able to capture Soundarapandian Nayakkar, also an associate of Veerapandiya. They exceeded all limits of barbarism in their treatment of Soundarapandian Nayakkar. They brutally killed him by smashing his head repeatedly against a village wall until the inner contents of his brains spattered all over it.

A big reward to the one who could help the British in arresting Veerapandiya Kattabomman was announced. The Tamil chieftain moved from place to place in hiding until he reached the Thirukalambur forests close to Pudukkottai. The palaiyakkarar of Pudukkottai instead of helping his fellow Indian sided with the British and helped them capture him. After trial, the British hanged Veerapandiya Kattabomman unceremoniously on a tamarind tree. It was 16 October 1799. He was then aged only 39. The fort of Panchalankurichi was razed to the ground and all of his wealth was looted by the British.

30

Kanhoji Angre

18th Century Maratha Navy Admiral Who Was Never
Defeated by European Forces

Kanhoji Angre! He is a familiar name in Maharashtra, but almost unknown to the rest of India. Do you know he was involved in naval battles with the British, Dutch and Portuguese in the Indian waters many times? For more than four decades, he guarded the western coast of India and became a terror to European powers at sea. He always led his sailors to victory. He never faced defeat. He emerged as a master of the Indian waters from Surat to south Konkan.

This brave Maratha Navy Admiral elevated the naval prestige of Maharashtra in particular and India in general in the Indian waters during a period when the Mughals, British, Portugese, and Dutch held power. He remained victorious until his death! Such was Kanhoji Angre's power, supremacy and control in the waters that enemy forces termed him a pirate. He captured many ships of the British, Dutch and Portuguese.

India has around 7,517 kilometers of vulnerable coastline. Historical records corroborate the stationing of naval forces by the Mauryas, Guptas, and Cholas in the Indian waters. The Chola Navy led naval expeditions between 900 to 1100 AD. Few successful naval expeditions include conquest of Indonesia (then known as Sri Vijaya) and Ceylon islands. It was under Rajaraja Chola I and his son Rajendra Chola I, that the Chola dynasty expanded their territories with a robust military and naval base. Chandragupta

Maurya's Prime Minister Kautilya (Chanakya) in his book *Arthashastra* had written about ocean waterways.

The history of Indian maritime dates back to thousands of years, as early as the pre-*Rigveda* period. The *Rigveda* finds mention of Varun, the God of water and the celestial ocean, as having knowledge of sea routes. Sanskrit terminologies like *Navadhyaksha, Nava Dvipantaragamanam, Samudrasamyanam, Matsya Yantra,* etc. that find mention in ancient manuscripts refer to the existence of sea routes, ships, exploration, sea warfare, navigation, and sea trade in ancient times. Excavations at Lothal in coastal Gujarat in present Mangrol harbour substantiate the historicity of the port area dating back to 2300 BC corresponding to the Indus Valley Civilization.

Besides land route, though trading happened between India and other foreign countries via sea route, it was during the emergent period of European colonialism that there was danger of occupancy of the Indian waters. From the 17th century, the strong Maratha Navy under the kingship of Chhatrapati Shivaji, defended the Indian waters in the west against numerous foreign forces. The Maharaja's naval force was well trained and their ships were mounted with cannons, always ready for action.

Shivaji Maharaj had almost 200 fighting ships of various sizes. He erected watch posts on the Andaman Islands, which helped him keep a watch on foreign ships. His naval forces attacked English, Dutch and Portuguese ships and captured British vessels. Such was the robustness of the Maratha naval forces and ships in the Indian waters that Shivaji, who started the robust bases, came to be known as the 'Father of Indian Navy'.

One of the bravest Maratha naval commanders was Kanhoji Angre. Under the leadership of Angre, enemy forces could not use the sea route freely in the west waters for four decades. Other Maratha commanders worth mentioning are SidhoJi Gurjar, Mainak Bhandari, and Mendhaji Bhatkar.

Kanhoji Angre was born to Ambabai and Tukoji in 1669 at Angarwadi, a village located six miles from Pune. Tukoji served under the army of Shivaji at Suvarnadurg, a fort and a naval post in a small island in the Arabian Sea between Mumbai and Goa. He was entrusted to command 200 posts. Kanhoji Angre spent his early life in Suvarnadurg and often accompanied his father in his heroic exploits at the sea. He grew up watching the Maratha ships making out for the open sea and the naval fleet falling upon the enemy's fleet victoriously. And thus began his practical training of seamanship from a young age!

After the death of Chatrapati Shivaji, the Maratha navy had shrunken. His son Sambhaji carried on his father's mission, with SidhoJi Gurjar as the Admiral. Sambhaji died in 1690. The chief of Satara appointed Kanhoji Angre as the Admiral (*Surkhel*) in 1698. He won this title after he attacked merchant ships of the British and looted their wealth. His plundering of British, Portugese, and Dutch ships continued. By 1700, he was deemed as the 'most daring pirate' in European records!

The Maratha empire turned weak over time. Shahu Bhonsle, the grandson of Shivaji, ascended the throne in 1707. Kanhoji Angre started gaining authority in most of the naval bases. The king signed a pact with Angre and made him the head of the Maratha Navy. When there were rumors about his authority, the king sent an army under Peshwa Bhyroo Pant to control him. The Peshwa was defeated and held prisoner. Another pact was signed. Kanhoji Angre was made Admiral of the entire Maratha Navy fleet. He was also appointed as the head of 26 forts and fortified places of Maharashtra.

Kanhoji Angre made Kolaba his headquarters and formed bases at Vijayadurg (485 km from Mumbai). Later, over time, he expanded his base to cover Alibag (southern tip of Mumbai), and Purnagad (port at Ratnagiri). He started attacking English, Dutch and Portuguese ships that were moving to and from East Indies.

For the next forty years, Angre was the undisputed leader of a heavily disputed stretch of coastline. He had a fleet of only 80 ships then with many of these used as mere fishing boats by the Kolis (local fishermen), who knew the complete paraphernalia of the sea routes in that region. It was by devising winning strategies that he maintained his hold! He gallantly defeated the English, Portuguese, Siddis who were aided by Mughals, the Dutch, and the Sawants of Wadi.

Kanhoji Angre led several victorious exploits at sea in between 1698 until his death in 1729. And all of these without fresh reinforcements, no resources or allies to help! On 4th November 1712, he captured Algerine, the armed yacht of William Aislabie, the British President of Bombay. He killed Thomas Chown, a British chief and took his wife prisoner. He let release of the captured yacht and the lady prisoner on 13 February 1713 against a ransom of 30,000 Rupees.

In 1712, Kanhoji Angre captured several British vessels, namely *EastIndiamen*, *Somers* and *Grantham*, near Goa. These British vessels were captured en route from England to Bombay. Ten forts were ceded to Angre by the British in 1713 as a result of the latter's defeat. The British made several attempts to capture Angre after Charles Boone was appointed the new Governor of Bombay on 26 December 1715, but in vain. During the naval battles, the British lost three ships to Angre. In 1718, Angre blockaded Mumbai port and collected ransom. Governor Boone himself led an army against Angre in 1720 and stormed the Vijaydurg fort. But he lost the battle and retreated.

On 29 November 1721, the British led by General Robert Cowan and Portugese led by Viceroy Francisco José de Sampaio e Castro jointly attacked Kanhoji Angre. But they were no match to Kanhoji's valor. They were badly defeated. Similarly, several attempts by Dutch and the Siddis failed too.

After Angre's death on 4th July 1729, his sons Sekhoji and Sambhaji continued with the Maratha naval campaigns.

31

Pasaltha Khuangchera

And Brave Warriors of Mizoram Who Fought against Britishers

Warriors of every state in India fought against British supremacy and oppression. A question may arise in the minds of many — Did our ancestors really fight back or did they just accept foreign rule without resistance? History books won't tell you about the brave feats of many of our ancestors who laid their lives resisting against foreign aggression!

At the national level, while only a selected few freedom fighters are glorified, many a name has remained in oblivion even in regional history text books. There are thousands of warriors, both men and women, who resisted British rule, fought bravely, and sacrificed their lives for the motherland.

Mizoram is a land of brave warriors. Bengkhuaia, Saithawma, Rani Roipulliani, Pasaltha Khuangchera, Ngurbawnga – they and more valorous sons and daughters of Bharat Mata from Mizoram fought bravely against the British. Many were martyred during their fight for freedom. They are immortal in folklores and some quiet pages of unread historical records.

Until the 1870s, Mizoram was divided into principalities with each principality ruled by a chief. The north was inhabited by descendants of Lallula, northeast by Manga, northwest by Lallianvunga (Lalphunga, Vanhnuailiana, and Vuta), southwest lowlands by Lai, southwest highlands by Thangluah, west by Lianlulla, and the hills by Rolura. And then, there were numerous sub-groups of these tribes.

Most of Mizos from these principalities raided the neighboring lowlands. The Mizos followed the policy of striking before being struck at and shooting before asking questions. One of their strategies was expanding their territories.

The British had not yet established their supremacy in Mizoram. But they occupied neighboring level lands and highlands of Assam, Tripura, and Manipur where they fiercely colonized. They planted tea gardens in the areas surrounding Mizoram in Assam, Tripura, and beyond. They entrusted British officials to look after the tea plantations. Besides, they established bazaars or trade marts where they sold products to the tribals and locals and minted money.

Bengkhuaia, Chief of Sailam

Amongst the Mizo chiefs and their followers raiding neighboring villages and dominions of British supremacy, the most furious was those conducted by Bengkhuaia, the chief of Sailam. Bengkhuaia and his men raided Alexendrapore and Katlichera, both tea estates in Cachar of Assam.

James Winchester was a Scottish planter employed by the British. Bengkhuaia and his men killed Winchester including other Britishers and their Indian employees and looted the guns. They carried away Winchester's 6 year old child Mary Winchester and more captives to Mizoram. It was January 1871.

It was said the Mizos did not harm the child. Instead they brought her up with care. The queen of Sailam, Bengkhuaia's wife, let the child Mary stay at their residence. As neither understood one another's language, the Mizos named her Zoluti. Bengkhuaia entrusted care and upbringing of Mary under Pi Tluangi, wife of the village elder Vansuakthanga. Pi Tluangi took care of her like a princess, sleeping with her, and making garments and toys for her. Soon Mary, christened as Zoluti, started her new life happily in this remote village in Mizoram.

Another Mizo chief raided Monierkhal and Nudigram and took away guns.

The British immediately set to action. They sent two forces under a common expedition termed 'The Lushai Expedition' divided into 'Right Column' and 'Left Column' on 8 October 1871. The British forces destroyed Mizo villages, burnt and razed houses to the ground, one by one as they entered Mizoram and forced their way into Sailam where, according to them, Mary Winchester was held captive. The Mizos retaliated bravely, but their tribal weaponry were no match to the advanced artillery of the British.

The right column of the The Lushai Expedition reached Sailam village on 21 January 1872. They laid a siege to the village in the morning at 0830 hours. Bengkhuaia and the Mizos retaliated, but in vain. Many a Mizo were martyred. The British forces destroyed the granaries and crops of Sailam. As the British continued their gunshots and shelling, Bengkhuaia tendered his submission to save his people and his village. The Mizos gathered around the British general. The British rescued Mary Winchester. It was said Mary refused to accompany the British; she was lured with sweets! In a year's time, Mary had become a family member of the Mizos!

Treaty, Defiance, and 2nd Expedition of British

Ultimately, the Mizo chiefs assembled and a treaty was signed. All the captives including Mary Winchester were set free. According to the pact, the Mizos would no longer raid villages and allow British entry into Mizoram but continue ruling their own jurisdictions. The guns were returned. Mizos also delivered jewelleries, animals, and rice to the British as decided in the pact.

This was the first interference of the British in Mizoram the big way. There were minor interferences in the mid 1800s following raids by the Mizos. The peace treaty was followed diligently by the Mizos for the next 14 years. In 1888, few Mizos started raiding the British occupied dominions in the neighboring highlands and lowlands once again, killing British officers during the raid. They carried away guns and held several people captives. The raids were conducted mainly because of two reasons. Mizos did not like British entry or settlement in their dominion. The British cleared many a forest area and turned them into plantations or grasslands. These jungles had earlier served as hunting grounds for the Mizos.

The British retaliated in a more aggressive manner this time compared to the first. They started the 'Lushai–Chin Expedition' sending three huge forces to Mizoram from the north, east, and south with an aim to put Mizoram under British rule. It was the year 1888. The British burnt down villages, destroyed crops, killed many Mizos during their expedition. The Mizos bravely hit back. It continued for days. The British were no wonder superior in terms of military strength and ammunition.

In March 1890, the expedition came to an end and in April 1890 Captain Browne was made the Political Officer and appointed the administrator of Mizoram. British rule in Mizoram thus started in April 1890.

Saithawma

The Mizos looked for opportunities to strike at the British and drive them out of Mizoram. Saithawma, a Mizo chief, had earlier revolted against the British. Hence, the British interfered, dethroned him, and put another chief as the ruler of that principality.

Saithawma had been looking for the right opportunity to strike. In September 1990, Captain Browne along with a group of Britishers were on their way to Shillong from Aizwal. The Manga and Kalkhama Mizo tribes led by Saithawma attacked them near Changsil, about 33 Km from Aizawl. They killed all of the followers of Captain Browne.

Saithawma shot at Browne, who was riding on a horse. Browne fell off his horse with a thud and slipped into the hilly jungle. The Mizos assumed him to be dead. Later, an wounded Browne somehow managed to crawl to the nearest Changsil fort where British forces were stationed. It was 9th September 1890.

Pasaltha Khuangchera and Ngurbawnga

On 10th September 1890, Pasaltha Khuangchera, a Mizo warrior along with his friend Ngurbawnga attacked Changsil fort. They regretted for not participating in the attack the previous day, as they were involved in some urgent family errands.

The highly outnumbered British soldiers armed with guns and ammunition were no match to the two brave Mizo warriors –

Pasaltha Khuangchera and Ngurbawnga, equipped with village weapons. During the firing, several bullets hit Ngurbawnga and he died. Pasaltha Khuangchera could have fled the spot and saved his life. But he didn't. He would not let the dead body of his friend remain at the enemy's site.

According to Mizo custom, the dead body of a warrior is never left behind nor forsaken in a battlefield. Pasaltha Khuangchera picked up the body of his friend on his shoulders and started rushing towards the path leading to his home at the same time retaliating with his tribal weapon at the enemy who were following behind. Many bullets hit him. Pasaltha Khuangchera fell dead, one of his hands still holding the body of his dead friend on his shoulders. Meanwhile, Captain Browne breathed his last at Changsil fort.

A series of skirmishes between the British and Mizos followed at Changsil and Aizwal. RB McCabe succeeded Captain Browne as the administrative-in-charge of Mizoram. The British followed their old tactic of burning down the Mizo villages and arresting the Mizos. At many a place, battle between the British and Mizos continued for days. Though inferior in military strength and ammunition, the Mizos did not surrender. More British forces joined the already outnumbered forces. By 1892, the British subdued the Mizos.

There are many more untold sagas of the brave warriors of Mizoram. Salute to Bengkhuaia, Saithawma, Rani Roipulliani, Pasaltha Khuangchera, Ngurbawnga, and all the warriors of Mizoram. Jai Hind!

32

Lakshmi Bai

Motherless at 4 to Battlefield Warrior Against British Forces and Martyrdom at 30

Motherless at 4, marriage at 14, mother at 23, widow at 25, rebel and defender of Jhansi at 29, battlefield warrior against British forces and martyrdom at 30! Lakshmi Bai was an inspiration for all freedom fighters, especially the women gentry from 1858 to 1947. The saga of the brave lady warrior is immortalized in golden letters in History.

She inspires us till today and shall continue to inspire future generations till eternity. None would have imagined that Manikarnika Tambe, as Lakshmi Bai was known before marriage, belonging to a simple Marathi Brahmin family from Varanasi, could weave a chronicle of valor, courage, queenship, and sacrifice.

Born on 19 November 1828, Manu (nickname) spent her early life in Varanasi. Her father Moropant Tambe worked in the court of Peshwa Baji Rao II of Bithoor in Kanpur. The last Peshwa of the Maratha Empire, Baji Rao II was banished to Bithoor by the British against an annual pension and an estate. Bithoor is located along the Ganga; it is the birthplace of Luv and Kush, the twin sons of Ram and Sita.

After Manu lost her mother Bhagirathi Bai at the age of four, the Peshwa of Bithoor brought her up as his own daughter. She started living at the Peshwa's palace. The Peshwa named her Chhabili, which means playful. He facilitated her education the royal way at the palace. Soon she became proficient in horsemanship, fencing, shooting, use of the sword, unlike other children of her age.

The childless Peshwa Baji Rao II had adopted Nana Sahib (who played an instrumental role in the Revolt of 1857) and his younger brother as his sons. Manu and Nana Sahib became close playmates; together they learnt the art of warfare.

Nana Sahib was four years older to Manu. Once, while riding his elephant, Nana Sahib refused to give in to Manu's request for a ride. An offended Manu declared that one day she would own and have ten elephants to ride. No wonder, her declaration did come true soon! Even she didn't think in her wildest of imaginations that she would be queen one day!!

The king of Jhansi, Gangadhar Rao Newalkar, of Maratha lineage, happened to see Manu, then aged 14, riding a horse and practicing the sword. He was on a visit to Bithoor. He was so impressed by her boldness and beauty that he instantaneously decided to marry her. His first wife had died childless. Manu's father and the Peshwa agreed to Gangadhar Rao's marriage proposal though the king was older to Manu by several years.

The marriage was solemnized at the Ganesh Temple located within the premises of Jhansi Fort. Gangadhar Rao christened Manu's name as Lakshmi Bai.

Gangadhar Rao had been a statesman. Though Jhansi prospered under his regime, he was feared by one and all in his kingdom. For even the pettiest to the gravest of crimes, lawbreakers were hanged to death. Rani Lakshmi Bai stopped this practice.

The king followed her advice on administrative, judicial, and all matters related to his kingdom. Gangadhar Rao was an art and culture aficionado. He had a library that contained a huge collection of Sanskrit manuscripts. He regularly hosted theaters and himself participated in roles.

Jhansi had an army of around 5,000 men. Lakshmi Bai added a regiment of women and named it Durga Dal. An excellent horse rider, she herself drilled and trained them. Her favorite horses were Sarangi, Pavan and Badal. She practiced regularly along with the women army. She allotted armed women guards at the women's quarters in Jhansi.

One of the commandants of her women army was Jhalkaribai, who was her look-alike. Jhalkaribai was married to Pooran Kori (also called Puran Singh), an artillery man from the Jhansi army unit. During her childhood, she herded cattle and had no formal education. Like the Rani, she was brave and underwent training in war weapons and horse riding. She killed a leopard with a herding stick in the forest when she was young. Knowing about her exploits, Rani Lakshmi Bai appointed her and further trained her.

At the age of 23, Rani Lakshmi Bai gave birth to a son. He was named Damodar Rao. Rivalry within family members for succession to the throne led to the poisoning of Damodar Rao at four months of age. Subsequently, the child died.

Raghunath Rao (elder brother of Gangadhar Rao) was the immediate predecessor of Gangadhar Rao. After Raghunath Rao's death, there emerged four contenders to the throne of Jhansi – Janki Bai, the widow of Raghunath; Kishan Rao and Gangadhar Rao, his brothers; and Ali Bahadur, the king's illegitimate son. After Gangadhar Rao's first wife died childless, hope prevailed amongst the remaining contenders. But Lakshmi Bai's marriage with the king followed by birth of a son foiled their hopes. According to rumors that spread following the death of Damodar Rao and according to our guide's narration, it was Lakshmi Bai's brother-in-law and sister-in-law who played an active role in poisoning the child to death.

Raja Gangadhar Rao fell ill thereafter. Upon Rani Lakshmi Bai's continuous request, the king, on his death-bed, adopted 5 year old Damodar Rao, a relative. Under the Doctrine of Lapse, the British annexed many kingdoms and principalities. Hence, to ensure that the adoption was proper and that Damodar Rao would be heir to the throne, three local British officials, namely Major Ellis, Captain Martin and a Political Agent, were called to witness the event. Gangadhar Rao died a day later in November 1853.

After the king's death, Rani Lakshmi Bai defied the norms of widowhood followed in the society. She neither broke her bangles nor dressed herself in white. Besides, she limited her official mourning activities to the minimum and stayed indoors for only 13 days.

The British under Lord Dalhousie rejected Damodar Rao's claim to the throne of Jhansi, as he was adopted. They applied the Doctrine of Lapse and annexed Jhansi to their empire. A year later, Rani Lakshmi Bai was entitled to a pension of Rs. 60,000 and allowed to stay in her palace at the fort.

In the early months of 1857, rumor about cartridges containing pork or beef fat being supplied by British sparked unrest amongst soldiers and the common men alike. And the first rebellion started in Meerut on May 10, 1857. The news reached Jhansi. The witty Lakshmi Bai pretended to seek permission from the British to raise a small force for her own protection. Her permission was granted.

Lakshmi Bai assembled the women of Jhansi and conducted a *haldi kumkum* ceremony, convincing them not to fear the British. She termed the British cowards. Nearly a month later, i.e. in June 1857, Indian soldiers of 12th Bengal Native Infantry seized Jhansi fort. They massacred the European officers of the garrison along with their wives and children. The soldiers left the fort after taking a large sum of money from the Rani. Immediately, Lakshmi Bai assumed administration of Jhansi.

Meanwhile, a group of mutineers, who were supporters of a rival prince claiming the throne of Jhansi, attacked the fort. Rani Lakshmi Bai foiled their attempt, defeating them. The rulers of Orchha and Datiya, both allies of the British, attacked Jhansi in August 1857. They wished to divide Jhansi amongst themselves. Moreover, the British considered Lakshmi Bai responsible for the massacre of Europeans at the fort. Hence, they did not object the attack of Jhansi by their allies.

The Rani assembled her forces. She set up a foundry to cast cannons within the premises of the fort. Yes! She successfully defeated the invaders. Thereafter, Rani Lakshmi Bai ruled Jhansi peacefully from August 1857 to January 1858. She laid a strong defence of the fort with guns.

Towards the third week of March 1858, the British forces, under Commander Hugh Rose, marched towards Jhansi. They ordered the Rani to surrender and threatened destruction of the fort and the town if she refused.

These were Lakshmi Bai's motivating words to her forces: "We fight for independence. In the words of Lord Krishna, we will if we are victorious, enjoy the fruits of victory; if defeated and killed on the field of battle, we shall surely earn eternal glory and salvation."

The battle between Rani Lakshmi Bai and the British forces began on 24th March 1858. Tatya Tope, the Rani's childhood playmate, marched towards Jhansi with 20,000 men to defend her, but he faced British troops on the way. The battle in Jhansi continued for 10 days until April 2nd. There were heavy casualties from both sides.

At last British forces were able to penetrate the walls of the fort and into the fort and the palace. Thanks to a traitor, who worked under Lakshmi Bai! He opened one of the gates of the fort for the British. Jhalkaribai advised Lakshmi Bai to run away from the fort to accumulate a force. The Rani thought the same so that she could arrange an army with the support of Tatya Tope and Rao Sahib (nephew of Nana Sahib). The witty Jhalkaribai (Lakshmi Bai's lookalike), disguised as the queen and galloped in her horse towards the enemy. With her adopted son Damodar Rao tied to her back, Lakshmi Bai jumped down several feet from the fort, riding on Badal, one of her favorite horses. Badal died, while mother and son survived.

In the darkness of the night, Lakshmi Bai with her adopted son and escorted by nine of her warrior guards marched towards Pali to join Tatya Tope. Her guards were Kashi Bai, Moti Bai, Deewan Raghunath Singh, Khuda Bakhsh Basharat Ali (commandant), Deewan Jawahar Singh, Lala Bhau Bakshi, Gulam Gaus Khan, Sunder-Mundar, and Dost Khan. Jhalkaribai was caught and hanged to death by the British.

An alliance of four leaders, viz. Rani Lakshmi Bai, Rao Sahib, Nawab of Banda, and Tatya Tope occupied the town of Kalpi. The British forces attacked Kalpi on 22 May. In the fierce battle that took place, the Rani, who led the battle, was defeated. The four leaders fled to Gwalior and joined Indian freedom fighters, who took hold of the city. Maharaja Scindia, an ally of the British, had fled to Agra.

Nana Sahib was made the Peshwa of Gwalior. Rani Lakshmi Bai persuaded the leaders to get ready against a possible British attack in the near future. But, basking in the newly acquired glory, they did not pay heed to her warning. On 16th June, the British attacked Gwalior.

While Rani Lakshmi Bai was leaving Gwalior, she confronted the British forces near Phool Bagh. It was 17 June 1858. The Rani had worn a cavalry horse soldier's (sowar's) uniform. In the battle that ensued, most of her soldiers were martyred. While fighting with an enemy soldier, an wounded Rani Lakshmi Bai was unhorsed. She was further hit with sword and gun shots. Badly wounded, she managed to flee the battlefield, as she did not wish the British to touch her body or capture her. Few British soldiers pursued her.

Lakshmi Bai reached a jungle near a village where she met a hermit in his hut. Hearing enemy soldiers rushing towards the hermit's hut, she requested the hermit to move out of the hut and set it on fire. She locked herself in the hut. The hermit gave in to her request. The enemy forces moved away after they were confirmed that the Rani could not survive the fire. Later, the locals poured water over the hut and prevented further burning. They rescued a badly burnt Lakshmi Bai. She had already attained martyrdom. The villagers cremated her body and performed her last rites. It was after three days that the British captured Gwalior.

Salute to Rani Lakshmi Bai! Jai Hind!!

33

Hemchandra Vikramaditya
From a Vegetable Seller to the Last Hindu Ruler of Delhi

Do you know Hemchandra Vikramaditya, also called Hemu, defeated the Mughal army of Akbar to become the ruler of Delhi? He was the Emperor of Delhi from 7th October 1556 to 5th November 1556, i.e. for a month. Had he not been wounded by a stray arrow during the Second Battle of Panipat, the History of India would have been different.

Hemu was born to a poor family in Alwar of Rajasthan and brought up at Rewari in the south-eastern part of Delhi. According to historian RC Mazumder, he was born in Alwar. As per Kanwal Kishore Bhardwaj's book *Hemu: Napoleon of Medieval India*, he was known as Basant Rai and also Hem Raj and Hem Rai. He was more popular as Hemu. He belonged to the Dhusar Baniya sect. This book mentions Puran Rai as his father, a spiritual and religious man and Rai Jai Pal Das as his grandfather who was a petty trader. Hemu learnt Hindi, Sanskrit, Persian, and Arabic. He was good in Mathematics. He could not continue his studies due to poor financial circumstances at home.

Hemu had an elder brother and his father was less interested in earning for a livelihood. To support his family financially, he started working from a very young age. He sold vegetables and saltpetre (potassium nitrate). According to 16th century Muslim historian Abd-ul-Qadir Bada'uni, Hemu was a greengrocer in the township of Rewari in Mewat. This was followed by his stint as a weighman in the Delhi market. Muslim historians did not glorify Hemu in their writings though he rose in rank and position in the Muslim court.

Why would they glorify a Hindu? According to Shaikh Abu al-Fazal ibn Mubarak, another 16th century Muslim historian, who wrote the *Akbarnama*, Hemu 'outwardly had neither rank (*hasb*) nor race (*nasab*) nor beauty of form (*surat*) nor noble qualities (*sairat*)'.

During this time, Hemu trained himself in the art of warfare. He became a known name in the market for his soldierly traits, use of weapons, and as a successful trader. Hemu also practiced wrestling and became an expert in horse riding.

Meanwhile, Sher Shah Suri established the Sur dynasty with his capital in Delhi after defeating Mughal Emperor Humayun in 1540. He ruled for 5 years until his death in 1545 during siege of Kalinjar Fort of the Rajputs in Bundelkhand. His son Islam Shah became his successor. Islam Shah made Hemu the superintendent of the market in Delhi followed by his appointment as Chief of Intelligence and Superintendent of Post soon after. He was also appointed as a surveyor of the imperial kitchens. He rose to power by dint of his loyalty, hard work, maintaining of relations, and improving the mercantile system that fell under his jurisdiction. Abu al-Fazal even poured venom on Hemu's success, writing thus that he rose to power by 'masterpieces of feline trickery' and by 'evil speaking and business capacity'.

Success kissed Hemu's destiny the big way. Recognizing his soldierly capabilities, Islam Shah appointed him as a high-ranking officer in his army. During that time, Humayun's half brother Kamran Mirza lived in Mankot in Jammu and Kashmir. Hemu was assigned the responsibilities of monitoring the movements of Kamran Mirza, who was a threat to the throne of Delhi.

Islam Shah ruled for only 8 years. After his death in 1553, his 12-year old son Firoz Khan became his successor. But his uncle Adil Shah Suri murdered him after three days and ascended the throne. Adil Shah, who was more interested in pleasure, was not serious about the affairs of the kingdom. He appointed Hemu as the Chief Minister and as general supervisor of the state. Hemu started undertaking all key responsibilities of the Sur Sultanate. According to Abu al-Fazal, Hemu "undertook all appointments and dismissals, and the distribution of justice".

Adil Shah had many enemies, especially Afghans, who waged war against him. Hemu led many battles to victory. He won 22 battles in totality. He never lost any battle; such was his prowess. Of the 22 battles, the last battle was fought at Chunar with Taj Khan Karrani, a loyal courtier of Islam Shah. Karrani fled the battlefield to Bengal. Hemu chased him all the way to Bengal.

Meanwhile, in 1555, Ibrahim Shah Suri, Adil Shah's brother-in-law from Agra, revolted. He dethroned Adil Shah after defeating him. Following this, the Sur dominion was divided into four parts. Delhi and Agra came under the rule of Ibrahim Shah Suri. Bengal fell in the hands of Shamsuddin Muhammad Shah. The area from Agra to Bihar remained under Adil Shah. Sikandar Shah Suri, another brother-in-law of Adil Shah declared himself the independent Sultan of the Punjab region. He later took possession of Delhi and Agra.

While Hemu was in Bengal, Humayun defeated Sikandar Shah Suri on 23 July 1555. The Mughals thus recovered Delhi and Agra from the Sur rulers. Sur dynasty lasted for 16 years in total.

Humayun died six months later, i.e. on 26 January 1556. Akbar, then aged 14 years, became his successor. As Akbar was a minor, Bairam Khan, the Mughal military commander, became his Regent. Humayun's death and succession of a minor boy to the Mughal throne gave Hemu an ideal opportunity to attack Mughal dominions.

Hemu marched from Bengal towards Delhi, capturing Mughal cities on his way one after another. Bayana, Etawah, Sambhal, Kalpi, Narnaul, and Agra came under his siege. Tardi Beg Khan was then the Mughal governor of Delhi. During this time Akbar and Bairam Khan were at Jalandhar. Bairam Khan sent Lieutenant Pir Muhammad Sharwani with an army as reinforcement to the Mughal forces led by Tardi Beg Khan to resist Hemu's attack in Delhi. Following Khan's orders, all the Mughal nobles in Delhi and adjoining areas met and strategized to fight against Hemu. The Mughal forces and Hemu's army met at Tughlaqabad, a village in the outskirts of Delhi. A fierce battle ensued. The Mughals divided into four wings with the left led by Iskandar Beg, Van by Abdullah Uzbeg, right by Haidar Muhammad, and the centre by Tardi Beg Khan.

The Mughal forces outnumbered Hemu's army and were far superior in arms and ammunition. Initially the Mughal army was winning and sensing overall victory, few of Tardi Beg's soldiers dispersed to attack Hemu's camps. This action weakened the governor's position. Meanwhile, Hemu had been holding a force of select horsemen and 300 choice elephants as a reserve in the centre. Grabbing the opportunity, he suddenly attacked Tardi Beg Khan. Such was his force of action in the battlefield with himself and his soldiers killing every Mughal that came their way that the Mughal army fled from the battlefield. So did Khan without offering a defence. It was 7th October 1556. The battle lasted only for a day. Hemu took possession of Delhi.

Hemu assumed the title of Vikramaditya, claiming royal status as an independent ruler. He thus came to be known as Hemchandra Vikramaditya. As per account by Abd-ul-Qadir Bada'uni, Hemu took on the title of *Bikramjit*. Another contemporary Muslim historian Khwaja Nizam-ud-Din Ahmad mentions the same. But no Muslim historians have described Hemu's coronation and rule in detail.

Akbar and Bairam Khan marched towards Delhi with a huge army. Only a month later after Hemu's kingship, i.e. on 5th November 1556, Akbar's and Hemu's forces met at Panipat. The First Battle of Panipat was fought between Babur and Ibrahim Lodi on 21 April 1526 where Mughals emerged victorious. At this Second Battle of Panipat, Hemu was at an advantageous position; his army outnumbered that of the Mughals. But he lacked artillery. 30,000 robust cavalry soldiers on horseback and a contingent of 500 elephants created ruckus in the battlefield, injuring and killing the enemy soldiers. Hemu himself led the battle sitting atop an elephant named Hawai. All elephants were protected by plate armors. Hemu was almost winning the battle when a stray arrow suddenly hit his eye. He became unconscious and collapsed on his elephant. This created panic among his soldiers, who then fled the battlefield. Hemu with his elephant was captured and taken to the Mughal camp. He was beheaded by Bairam Khan on Akbar's orders.

Do you know the cruel Mughals sent Hemu's head to Kabul while his body gibbeted on a gate in Delhi? The Mughals were not contended with this. They constructed a minaret with the heads of Hemu's 5000 plus dead soldiers. This was not the end of the cruel story. They captured Hemu's old father from Alwar. Pir Muhammad, the Mughal officer who captured him, offered to spare his life if he converted to Islam. Hemu's father refused to convert. He was then executed. Hemu's wife managed to escape.

According to an account by Satish Chandra in his book *Medieval India: From Sultanate to The Mughals, Part II: Mughal Empire (1526–1748)*, Abu al-Fazal praised Hemu, but on his death. The Muslim historian praised Hemu's 'lofty spirit, courage, and enterprise and wished that young Akbar or perhaps a wise member of his court had deigned to keep Hemu prisoner rather than executing him.'

Hemu was winning the battle until he was wounded. Had the stray arrow not injured Hemu, the story would have been different.

34

Alluri Sitarama Raju

Freedom Fighter Who Killed Several British Officers and Martyred at 26

He was born into a Telugu Kshatriya family at Bhimunipatnam *taluk*, Visakhapatnam. He played an instrumental role in India's freedom struggle in the early 1920s. He fought for the cause of the tribals of the Godavari-Rampa region of coastal Andhra Pradesh, leading the Rampa Rebellion. He was successful in killing several British army officers until he was caught and executed. He attained martyrdom at a young age of 26 years. Like many other unsung freedom fighters, his name is in oblivion in History text books! He was Alluri Sitarama Raju.

Alluri Sitarama Raju was born to Alluri Venkata Rama Raju and Suryanarayanamma on July 4, 1898. His father was an official photographer in the central jail at Rajahmundry. Alluri Sitarama lost his father during his childhood. He studied at different schools – Vullithota Bangarayya School in Rajahmundry, National School in Ramachandrapuram and PR High School in Kakinada. He grew up under the care of his uncle, Rama Chandra Raju, who was a *tehsildar* in Narsapur in the West Godavari district. He was then enrolled at Taylor High School in Narsapur. He studied Sanskrit, *Vedas* and Astrology in Kotananduru in Tuni *mandal*. Later he moved along with his mother, brother and sister to his maternal home town Vishakhapatnam at the age of 15. He enrolled at Mrs. A.V.N. College. Raju did not complete his college education.

Since his teenage days, Alluri Sitarama Raju nurtured hatred against the British. He was familiar with the problems of the tribal people of his region. 16 years before his birth, i.e. in 1882, the British passed the Madras Forest Act. Their objective was to use the forest lands of the Godavari region. The tribals of the area, numbering around 28,000 depended on shift cultivation for their livelihood. They followed the traditional method of cultivation in the hills and jungles whereby each year some areas of jungle forest were burned to clear land. It was known as the *podu* system.

The hilly Rampa area in the Godavari region comprised an approximate 700 square miles. The Madras Forest Act hindered the farming activities of the tribal people, putting restrictions on their shift cultivation and even objecting their movement in the forest area. Economically affected, they started looking for alternate sources of livelihood. While many worked as labour in the construction of roads in that area, a number of them started working as coolies. The British cleared the forests, using the timber for building railways and ships. They ignored the needs of the tribal people. British officials harassed the tribal people every other day.

According to a 1922 government memorandum that recorded an Agency Commissioner's opinion, "the country had suffered from too severe restrictions on jungle clearance, that various restrictions had been overdone and much population and food grains lost for the sake of forests of doubtful value."

The young Alluri Sitarama Raju was disheartened seeing the condition of the tribal folks. He could have led a peaceful life doing a job. But he gave up everything to fight against the British for the freedom of the country. Raju held meetings with the tribal leaders. He started devising plans to oust the British from the region. He was instrumental in uniting the tribals of the region and fight for a common cause. The British were superior in number, ammunitions, and in military tactics. Alluri Sitarama Raju suggested use of Guerrilla warfare techniques using bows and arrows and stolen guns and ammunition. He himself trained them.

At the age of 24, Alluri Sitarama Raju led the Rampa Rebellion, following Guerrilla warfare technique. The Guerrilla warfare involved involvement of a small group of combatants in ambushes, hit-and-run tactics, sabotage, raids, etc. using arms. He and his followers stole guns and ammunition from the British and used them against the enemies. The tribal volunteers under the leadership of Gam Mallu Dora and Gantam Dora and more leaders used bows and arrows.

Alluri Sitarama Raju heard a lot about freedom fighters from Bengal. Drawing inspiration from their activities, he with few of his followers raided several police stations. Few of the police station locations worth mentioning were Addateegala, Narsipatnam, Chintapalle, Rampachodavaram, Dammanapalli, Krishna Devi Peta, Rajavommangi, and Annavaram. The group stole guns and ammunition from the police stations and used these in ambushes against the British.

Rampa Rebellion continued for months. Alluri Sitarama Raju killed several British officers during a period of a few months. Soon he became a terror for the British forces. He also killed two British army officers namely Scott Coward and Hites. The British deployed forces to trap him, but in vain. He remained in hiding for some time, but again successfully attacked the British time and again. Alluri Sitarama Raju was eventually trapped by the British in the forests of Chintapalli on 7 May 1924. The British tied him to a tree and shot him dead. He was then aged only 26 years!

Following the martyrdom of Alluri, the Rampa Rebellion lost its momentum.

Salute to Alluri Sitarama Raju! Jai Hind!!

35

Rana Hammir Singh

Regained Mewar from Delhi Sultanate and Rajputana from Tughlaqs

Mewar had been a robust kingdom until Ala-ud-Din Khilji established his supremacy after sacking Chittorgarh. In less than 25 years, Rana Hammir Singh regained Mewar. He was a direct descendant of Bappa Rawal, who along with Nagbhat Gurjar and a confederacy of other North and South Indian rulers, had driven the Arabs out of India in around 738 AD. Hammir Singh also helped the Marwar Rajputs regain their supremacy. He defeated Muhammed Bin Tughlaq in the battle of Singoli, captured him, and released him against a huge ransom. He regained the entire Rajputana from the Tughlaqs.

Kingdom of Mewar

Mewar included several principalities — Udaipur, Pirawa, Neemuch, Bhilwara, Chittorgarh, Rajsamand, including parts of Madhya Pradesh (Mandsaur) and parts of Gujarat. Chittorgarh was the main base. Mewar's defense was the formidable and well fortified Chittor Fort, built during the 7th century. This fort, spread across 700 acres, had stood robust against the tides of time and attacks!

How Mewar Came under Delhi Sultanate

During the reign of the Delhi Sultanate under Ala-ud-Din Khilji, Mewar, ruled by Rana Ratan Singh, was the strongest Rajput kingdom. Ala-ud-Din Khilji, who proclaimed himself the Sultan of Delhi after killing his father-in-law and uncle Jalal-ud-Din Khilji, attacked Chittor Fort with a huge army in January 1303. Ala-ud-Din Khilji laid siege to Chittor Fort on all sides. The strong defense in and around the fort dampened his spirits.

On 26th August, 1303, Ratan Singh with his army, donning saffron turbans, made a suicide attack (*Saaka*) against the enemies. Their goal was to defend or die. In the battle that followed, they perished. Rani Padmavati and thousands of Rajputinis committed *Jauhar* to save themselves from disgrace at the hands of the enemies.

Hammir Singh's Ancestors

Lakshman Singh, a distant kinsman of Rawal Ratan Singh and a direct descendant of Bappa Rawal, had eight sons. His eldest son Ari Singh was married to Urmila from the Chandana Rajput clan from Unnava village. The couple had a son named Hammir Singh. During the siege to Chittor Fort by Khilji, Ajay Singh, the second son of Lakshman Singh took the infant Hammir to Kelwara in Kumbhalgarh for safety.

In the battle between Khilji and the Mewar Rajputs, all of the Raputs and Rajputinis present in Chittor Fort perished. The king of Mewar had died issueless. Only Ajay Singh and the infant Hammir Singh from the royal lineage survived.

Hammir Singh's Upbringing and as Head of Sisodia Clan

The people of Mewar banked upon Ajay Singh to continue their fight against the Delhi Sultanate and regain Mewar. Ajay Singh pursued a guerrilla campaign against the Muslims who occupied Chittor Fort. This continued for years together.

Meanwhile, Hammir Singh started growing up under the care of his uncle, who trained him in the art of warfare. While still young, Hammir Singh killed Munja Balecha, the king of a small neighboring kingdom called Kantaliya for creating chaos. This act of bravery led Ajay Singh bestow on Hammir with the claims of rulership.

Ajay Singh died in the mid 1920s. The people of Mewar then declared Hammir Singh as the rightful heir to the throne of Mewar.

Hammir's grandfather Lakshman Singh hailed from Sisoda of Mewar and thenceforth he was known as the head of the Sisodia clan.

Marriage and Claim to Mewar Throne

Ala-ud-Din Khilji, after occupying Chittorgarh, entrusted the administration of Mewar to Maldeo, ruler of a nearby Rajput kingdom. Maldeo had earlier sided with Khilji during his war ventures. Maldeo had a widowed daughter named Songari. Aware that Rana Hammir Singh was of royal lineage, he sent him a marriage proposal for his daughter.

Hammir Singh agreed to the proposal. After the marriage was solemnized, Hammir Singh overthrew his father-in-law Maldeo and ascended the throne of Mewar in 1326. He easily subjugated all from the Delhi Sultanate who opposed him. In a few years, Hammir Singh also helped the neighboring Marwars of Jodhpur regain their lost territory.

The Delhi throne was then no longer under the Khiljis. Ala-ud-Din Khilji had died in 1316. Four years later, i.e in 1320, one Khusro Khan killed Khilji's son Mubarak Khilji and claimed authority of Delhi. But the other nobles and ministers of the Khilji dynasty did not recognize his claim. They invited Ghazi Malik, the then governor of Punjab, recruited by Khilji, to overthrow Khusro Khan. Grabbing the opportunity, Ghazi Malik marched towards Delhi, killed Khusro Khan, and assumed power of Delhi under a new name — Ghiyasuddin Tughlaq, laying the foundation of the Tughlaq dynasty.

Battle of Singoli

Muhammed Bin Tughlaq, earlier known as Ullugh Khan, ascended the throne of Delhi in 1325 AD after getting his father Ghiyasuddin Tughlaq and brother treacherously killed. Ghiyasuddin Tughlaq was a cruel ruler but his son was many times crueler than him.

Muhammed Bin Tughlaq imposed heavy taxes on Hindus, 10 to 20 times more than those levied earlier. Farmers were forced to give half of the crop yields in addition to taxes. Many farmers left farming, left their lands and started living in the forests. Tughlaq's men pursued them and executed them. They also executed those who could not pay taxes or paid lower than the decided amount.

Muhammed Bin Tughlaq did not even spare certain sect of Muslims. He routinely executed Sayyids (Shia), Sufis, Qalandars, and other Muslim officials. Ziauddin Barni, his court historian wrote in *Tarikh-I Firoz Shahi* — 'Not a day or week passed without spilling of much Musalman blood'. Such was the atrocities committed by Muhammed Bin Tughlaq. The list of more atrocities committed by him is unending.

Tughlaq was also on an empire expansion spree soon after he ascended the throne of Delhi. He even dreamt of advancing beyond the Himalayas and conquering China. He laid attacks on kingdoms on the way to China. But his dream of conquering China was shattered after he was defeated by the Katoch Rajputs of Kangra.

Muhammed Bin Tughlaq then set his eyes on Rajasthan. He wished to subjugate the whole of Rajasthan under his dominion. Ajmer, Ranthambhore, Nagor and Shivapuri — all Rajputana kingdoms were under his siege. He then advanced towards Mewar with a huge army.

A fierce battle took place between Muhammed Bin Tughlaq and Hammir Singh in 1336 at Singoli in Neemuch (currently Madhya Pradesh). Hammir Singh had the support of Charans, who were known for their preference to die rather than break a promise, and neighboring Rajput forces. The combined Rajput army was a disaster for Tughlaq's forces. Muhammad bin Tughlaq was badly defeated and taken captive.

Following the rules of Dharma, the Mewar Rana did not kill the Tughlaq Sultan. The Tughlaqs came forward with a proposal agreeing to pay ransom against their ruler's release. Hammir Singh agreed. He released Muhammed Bin Tughlaq against a ransom amount of 5,000,000 *tankas*. Besides, Hammir Singh annexed the territories of Ajmer, Ranthambhore, Nagor and Shivapuri which were subjugated by the Tughlaqs, into the Mewar Empire. Entire Rajputana was regained.

Such was the humiliating defeat of Muhammed Bin Tughlaq at the hands of Hammir Singh that the Tughlaqs left the idea of attacking Rajasthan again. So did the next two successive Muslim dynasties in Delhi. The Lodis did try to subjugate the Mewar Rajputs but were defeated.

36

Kakatiyas and Kapaya Nayaka

Telugu Chieftain Who Reconquered Warangal from Delhi Sultanate

Kapaya Nayaka! His name is familiar only amongst a few in South India. He was the leader of a confederation of Telugu nobles who united to liberate the South Indian kingdom of Warangal from the Delhi Sultanate. Delhi was then under the Tughlaqs. He drove the Tughlaqs out of the Warangal (then Telangana) territory in 1336. He ruled Telangana for the next 30 years.

Kapaya Nayaka was a Musunuri Nayak, a group of warrior chieftains in the army of the Kakatiya dynasty. The Kakatiyas, who trace their origin to a chief named Durjaya, a Suryavamshi, were initially feudatory chiefs under the Chalukyas. Beta Raja I was the first Kakatiya chief, who ruled as a feudatory chief for 30 years with capital at Hanamkonda near Warangal. During the reign of Prataparudra, the 6th Kakatiya chief, the Kakatiyas asserted their independent rule. It was 1163. Thus started the sovereign rule of the Kakatiya dynasty. Prataparudra ruled from 1158 to 1195 with capital at Orugallu, which later came to be known as Warangal and then Telangana. One of the well known Kakatiya rulers was Rudramadevi who ruled from 1262 to 1289. She was the only woman to rule over Telugu region.

Meanwhile in 1320, the Delhi Sultanate which was hitherto under the Khiljis, fell in the hands of Ghazi Malik, the then governor of Punjab. He overthrew and killed Khusro Khan, the temporary Sultan of Delhi, and assumed power of Delhi under a new name —

Ghiyasuddin Tughlaq, laying the foundation of the Tughlaq dynasty. Ghiyasuddin Tughlaq tried to subjugate kingdoms and annex them to his empire. He also sent his generals to many a kingdom to collect tributes; those who paid tributes were spared from being attacked.

Warangal was first attacked in 1310 by Malik Kafur on the orders of Ala-ud-din Khilji. After a four-month siege of the Kakatiya capital, the Sultanate forces obtained much booty and a promise of tribute in the years to come. Prataparudra II was then the Kakatiya king. Later he stopped paying tribute to the Delhi Sultanate.

Ghiyasuddin Tughlaq sent his messengers to Warangal to collect tribute from Prataparudra II. The Kakatiya king refused to pay any tribute. The Tughlaq Sultan sent his son Ulugh Khan to plunder and loot Warangal in 1323. Ulugh Khan was also called Juna Khan, who later christened himself as Muhammed Bin Tughlaq after ascending the throne of Delhi. By the time Ulugh Khan reached Warangal, he heard a rumor that his father Ghiyasuddin Tughlaq died and there was rebellion for the succession to the throne. It is believed Ulugh Khan himself created the false rumor to create chaos and gain the throne of Delhi. Ulugh Khan retreated but returned again after 4 months. This time he brought along a huge army.

Ulugh Khan upon reaching Warangal first besieged and captured the outer mud fort. He and his army then surrounded the core fortified area of the city. Prataparudra and the Kakatiya army gave a stiff resistance. The siege continued for five months, but Ulugh Khan and his army could not subjugate the brave Kakatiyas. They were unable to penetrate into the fort.

During the five month long siege, the Kakatiyas could not bring fresh provisions into the fort. Scarcity of provisions led Prataparudra II open the gates of the fort and surrender. The Tughlaq army ransacked and plundered the houses. They razed temples to the ground and destroyed heritage structures. While many were killed many were spared after they converted to Islam.

The Tughlaq prince Ulugh Khan sent Prataparudra and his family members to Delhi. They were escorted by his generals Qadir Khan and Khawaja Haji. During a halt at the banks of the Narmada

River on the way, Prataparudra committed suicide. The Kakatiya dynasty thus came to an end. Warangal fell under the reign of the Delhi Sultanate under Tughlaqs under a new name – Sultanpur.

Cynthia Talbot wrote in *Precolonial India in Practice: Society, Region, and Identity in Medieval Andhra*, 'The seizure of the Kakatiya capital and king in 1323 had a devastating effect, for nothing of the Kakatiya political system survived, at least in recognizable form. There were no subsequent claimants to the Kakatiya throne nor do any attested Kakatiya subordinates figure in later epigraphic records'.

Ulugh Khan remained as the governor of the Warangal region for a year. He was recalled to Delhi by his father. The administration of Warangal was entrusted upon Malik Maqbul, a convert, who was actually Nagaya Ganna Vibhudu, a former Kakatiya commander.

Ullugh Khan ascended the throne of Delhi in 1325 AD after getting his father Ghiyasuddin Tughlaq and brother treacherously killed. He assumed a new name — Muhammed Bin Tughlaq. Besides Warangal, the Tughlaq prince had also conquered other South Indian kingdoms encompassing Malabar, Madurai, and areas up to the southern tip of Karnataka. Tughlaq entrusted revenue officials to collect revenues from the South Indian kingdoms and stationed military forces to check any rebellions.

Most South Indian kingdoms were subdivided into palayams or regions with each region under the chieftainship of a Nayaka. The Nayakas were generally military governors. They were entrusted with the role to administer their respective territories, collect taxes, run the local judiciary, and maintain an army for the key king under whose aegis the principalities were run.

The concept of a kingdom where a ruler shared sovereignty with his carefully selected set of subordinates was a paradigm associated with the Kakatiyas. During the reign of Prataparudra, there were 75 Nayakas. One was Musunuri Prolaya Nayaka, who published the Vilasa copper-plate grant near Pithapuram in 1330 that speaks volume about the devastation caused by the Tughlaqs in the Telugu country. The inscription also mentions him as the rightful restorer of order. It depicts the Muslim invaders of Warangal as demonic barbarians.

According to Tripurantakam inscription of 1290 published by Ambadeva, a rebel Kayastha chief who fought against the Kakatiyas, Ambadeva won a battle against 75 kings. This inscription corroborates the existence of the 75 Nayakas, who were termed 75 kings by Ambadeva. The Kaluvacheru grant of 1423 portrays the Musunuri Nayakas as legitimate successors to the Kakatiyas. All of these inscriptions are in Sanskrit.

Muhammed Bin Tughlaq imposed heavy taxes on Hindus, 10 to 20 times more than those levied earlier. Farmers were forced to give half of the crop yields in addition to taxes. Many farmers left farming, left their lands and started living in the forests. Tughlaq's men pursued them and executed them. They also executed those who could not pay taxes or paid lower than the decided amount.

The nobles or Nayakas rebelled against the Tughlaqs under the leadership of Prolaya Nayaka. They were able to assert control in the Godavari area in 1325. Prolaya Nayaka declared himself the ruler of this region. He ruled until his death in 1333. As he was issueless, he was succeeded by Musunuri Kapaya Nayaka.

After assuming power in the Godavari area, Kapaya Nayaka decided to drive away the Tughlaq Muslim invaders from Warangal. He held meetings with all the Nayakars and strategized effective plans. Accordingly, a series of battles were fought between the Tughlaq army and the combined forces of the Nayakas led by Kapaya Nayaka.

In 1336, Kapaya Nayaka was able to defeat Malik Maqbul, the governor of Warangal appointed by the Tughlaqs. According to the Kaluvacheru inscription of a female member of the Panta Reddi clan in 1423, Kapaya Nayaka had the support of 75 subordinate Nayakas in this battle. One of the chiefs was Vema Reddi, the founder of the Reddi dynasty.

Kapaya Nayaka thus reconquered Warangal from the Tughlaqs. Majority of the Muslims were driven out of Warangal. He also annexed a wider swathe of eastern Telangana from the Tughlaqs. He rechanged the name of Sultanpur to Warangal and reestablished Hindu supremacy in the region. Kapaya Nayaka also helped neighboring kingdoms end Muslim rule in respective areas.

The chieftain ruled over Telangana until 1368 and brought stability in his kingdom. A contemporary inscription compared Kapaya Nayaka in majesty to Prataparudra, the last Kakatiya ruler. Kapaya Nayaka died during a battle with the Velamas, another Andhra dynasty, also called Recherla Nayakas who were warriors under the Kakatiya army, at Bhimavaram in 1368. And with him ended the period of the Musunuri Nayaka family as rulers.

37

Matmur Jamoh

Arunachal Pradesh Freedom Fighter Who Killed British Officer; Jailed at Kalapani

Matmur Jamoh! He is hailed as a hero in the Yangrung village of Pasighat in Arunachal Pradesh. The state pays him tribute every year for his martyrdom for the nation. But does the rest of India know about this brave warrior from the Northeast? No! A pity that we grow up reading more about the glories of invaders rather than the heroic exploits of warriors from east to the west, north to the south.

Pasighat in the East Siang district of Arunachal Pradesh at the eastern foothills of the Himalayas is home to Adi tribesmen. It is the northeastern state's oldest town. The Adis are also known as Abors or Abhors, meaning 'barbarous', a term coined by neighbouring communities of the plains. After Independence, they appealed to the government to be termed as Adis. This place is home to few brave warriors of Bharat Mata who fought valorously against Britishers. Matmur Jamoh and a group of Adi warriors collectively killed two British officers and their attendants in 1911. Though Pasighat has an ancient origin, the British established it as a colonial outpost in 1911 as gateway to the greater Abor hills and northern area of Arunachal Pradesh.

The British established their supremacy in parts of the northeastern states after the Treaty of Yandaboo signed in 1826 with Burma. As per the treaty, the British would occupy Assam, Manipur, Rakhine (Arakan), and the Taninthayi (Tenasserim) coast south of the Salween River besides supremacy in Cachar and the Jaintia Hills district. After the treaty was signed, the British planted tea gardens in most of these places and stationed British planters and forces. Besides, they established bazaars or trade marts where they sold products to the tribals and locals and minted money. Soon the British started establishing their supremacy in the Northeastern kingdoms. Since 1875 the British India government firmly decided to push the outer line to further north. It was in the 1900s that the British moved inwards towards the hill regions of Arunachal Pradesh.

Most of Adis and other tribes raided the neighboring lowlands including those annexed by the British. Few Adi communities worth mentioning are Pasi, Padam and Minyong. This led to three Anglo-Adi wars in 1858, 1859, and 1894. During the process, the British burnt down villages, destroyed crops and granaries, razed houses to the ground and killed hundreds of tribals who offered resistance. Though their tribal weaponry were no match to the advanced artillery of the British, yet the latter could not crush the indomitable spirits of the Adis until 1911. It was in 1911 after the last Anglo-Adi war that Pasighat entered into the map of British colonial rulers.

Matmur Jamoh was an Adi warrior. He was the Kebang Abu, the headman of Yangrung village where he was born. Sucheta Sen Chaudhuri wrote in *Pasighat: Post-colonial Geography and History in Interface in Glocal Colloquies* journal, "Matmur Jamoh was middle aged with medium stature figure and was appreciably a good orator. He had an adamant attitude…"

Captain Neol Williamson was then the Assistant Political Officer of the British at Sadiya in Assam in the beginning of the 1900s. Soon after his appointment, he started a tour expedition with Colonel D.M. Lumsden, W.L.B. Jackman and more Britishers into the interiors of the north eastern hills beyond his jurisdiction. They entered Pasighat in 1908 without sanction from the British govt. to enter the Adi territory. Their objective was to gather detailed knowledge of the tribal land in addition to exploring the possibilities of a trade route through these hills to Tibet. One of their objectives was to find influence of China if any in the hills of Arunachal Pradesh. The British employed local tribesmen as porters and collected ration supply for themselves without making any substantial payment. Besides, they interfered into the freedom of the Adi tribesmen and humiliated them often.

Do you know the Adi tribes follow the Donyi-Polo religion, an indigenous faith? Donyi represents the Sun and Polo the Moon. They call themselves *Donyi O, Polo Ome*, meaning children of the sun and the moon or children of truth.

The Adis termed the British as Milun, meaning Whites. In 1908, the British toured the Pasi, Gallong and Minyong villages. They returned again the next year and then in 1911. In 1909, Neol Williamson had humiliated Matmur Jamoh. In 1911, Williamson was accompanied by Dr. J.D. Gregorson, a doctor employed by the British as medical in charge of Tinsukia and Lakhimpur tea gardens. They were further accompanied by 34 Gurkhali coolies, 10 Miris, 2 orderlies and three servants.

Matmur Jamoh did not like the advancement of the Britishers into the interior of the Adi lands. For a better journey, the British employed Adi people as labor to clear the paths. They also forced them to carry loads and supply of ration. They tried to prove their superiority over the Adis. Matmur Jamoh did not like this behavior of the British meted out to his tribal folks.

There were more than score villages in Pasighat. On 18th March 1911, this group reached Rottung in Pasighat and halted there for the night. During the night some provisions of the group went missing. Neol Williamson demanded the villagers that the guilty were to be presented before him till he returned back. The next day the party marched up to Pangi village and stayed there waiting for the arrival of the porters. The British captain's guts to threaten the Adis in the Adi land angered the latter. On 30th March, Williamson marched further to Yangrung, leaving Dr. Gregorson and three coolies in the camp in Pangi.

Willamson and his men camped at Komsing in Yangrung. Matmur Jamoh organised a council of village headmen and discussed about stopping the British from advancing further into the Adi territory. They devised plans of killing all the Britishers and their men in the expedition and also strategized about stopping Britishers from entering the Adi hills in future.

Matmur Jamoh led by few Adi warriors attacked Williamson's camp the next day, i.e. 31st March at 10:00 a.m and killed all of them. Following the instructions of Matmur Jamoh, another group of the Adi tribesmen went to Pangi camp and killed Dr. Gregorson and his group. Only a few managed to escape to relay the news of this assassination at the British post at Sadiya.

The British immediately set to action. They sent a force of 1000 soldiers and military police led by Major General Hamilton Bower to Pasighat to arrest Matmur Jamoh and his men who were involved in the killing of Noel Williamson, Dr. Gregorson and their attendants.

On 18th December, the British army reached Yangrung village and camped there. They set fire to the nearby Kebang village and demanded that the Adi tribals cooperate to arrest Matmur Jamoh to avoid further destruction. The Adi tribesmen retaliated bravely, but in vain. This war took place at a mountain cliff near Rottung.

To avenge the British killings, Bower attacked more Adi habitations, destroying houses and crops and torturing the Adi people. He tortured Matmur Jamoh's wife Yasi and son Matkep. The Abor Expedition continued for a few months until Matmur Jamoh along with few others surrendered to stop British atrocities in the Adi villages in Pasighat. The brave freedom fighters were arrested and taken in chains to Kalapani (Cellular jail). There are hardly any records about Matmur Jamoh's last days in the jail. He died in obscurity.

According to a *Telegraph India* report, Bosiram Siram, Arunachal Pradesh education minister visited Cellular Jail in the Andamans in 2005. He searched in the records where political prisoners from the mainland were interned. But the authorities were unable to provide any records about Matmur Jamoh.

Salute to Matmur Jamoh and the brave Adi warriors.

38

Kalyan Singh Gurjar

Terrorized the British by Killing Many Britishers in 1822-24

Kalyan Singh Gurjar! He was also nicknamed Kalua Gurjar. He was a *pehelwan* and a general under the *riyasat* of Gurjar Raja Vijay Singh during the beginning of 1820s. Such was the level of his atrocities against the British during their transit in the Saharanpur Meerut area that he was termed a 'Dacoit' by the colonials. He played an instrumental role in fighting against British forces in 1824 at Koonja Bahadurpur, a principality located in present Roorkie, bordered by Haridwar, Saharanpur, and Dehradun. Sadly, we don't get to read in History books about the heroic exploits of this brave son of Bharat Mata.

There is not much evidence available about the childhood of Kalyan Singh Gurjar. Cassell's *Illustrated History of India by James Grant* contains a detailed account of this brave Gurjar warrior and an entire Gurjar clan numbering over 800 in the Sharanpur-Meerut belt dated 1822-24.

The British had established their supremacy in almost all major parts of India in the beginning of the 1800s. They established direct rule in many princely states while in few places they allowed the rulers to continue their rule against payment of tax and certain terms and conditions. In 1857, there were major revolts across the country. But before this there were several major uprisings and wars which don't find a place in history books. One is the Uprising of 1822-24 in the Saharanpur Meerut belt. It was led by Raja Vijay Singh and his general Kalyan Singh Gurjar.

Raja Vijay Singh was the ruler of Koonja Bahadurpur. His *riyasat* extended as far as Saharanpur and Meerut. The raja declared his independence and held seize of Koonja Bahadurpur fort. He made Kalyan Singh Gurjar his general.

The British had stationed forces in colonial outposts across the country. One of their outposts in the Northern belt was located at Saharanpur (British termed it as Saharanpore). Mr. Grindall was then the local magistrate of this region. According to an account by Mr. Grindall, as described in *Cassell's Illustrated History of India* that finds mention of Raja Vijay Singh as 'kower', "part of the district has risen in rebellion that upwards of 800 men principally Goojurs, headed by a notorious freebooter named Kower, had taken possession of the ghurry of Koonja, in that neighborhood and was committing every species of atrocity. He announced his advent as Kali, the last of the Hindoo avatars, for the purpose of putting an end to the reign of foreigners."

On one instance, when the British were transporting their treasury from Jawalapur to Saharanpur, escorted by 200 British soldiers, Kalyan Singh Gurjar, led by his men, attacked them. The Gurjars looted the treasury and killed a number of the British forces. The colonial rulers immediately set to action, but in vain. In between 1822-24, Kalyan Singh Gurjar following the advice of the Raja committed more atrocities against the British, looting them and butchering them. And then no British soldier or officer dared to trespass Raja Vijay Singh's territory. Such was the terror stamped in the British minds!

The British branded the Gurjars as 'dacoits' and 'criminals'. British soldiers stationed there could not curb the rising rebellion of the Gurjars in the Saharanpur-Meerut region. They needed a robust armed force.

It was the year 1824. British forces employed Gurkhas for this task and marched towards Koonja Bahadurpur. According to *Cassell's Illustrated History of India*, "Mr. Grindal solicited the aid of 200 rank and file of the Sirmoor Battalion, which had been formed of disbanded Nepaulese in 1815; and this detachment instantly marched, under Captain Young (commanding the corps) accompanied by the Hon Frederick Shore, of the Bengal Civil Service, who with his accustomed zeal and love of enterprise, marched with the little band. Mr. Grindall joined the detachment at Secunderpore with 150 men of the Sirmoor Battalion, attended by Lieutenant Debude, of the Engineers and Dr. Royle, as volunteers."

Learning about the approaching army of the British towards Koonja Bahadurpur, Raja Vijay Singh, Kalyan Singh Gurjar, and the other Gurjar warriors were all ready to fight. Along the skirts of the village outside the fort, a section of the Gurjar warriors stationed themselves in fighting order. They struck at the advancing British army. A fierce fight ensued between the Gurjars and the British army outside the fort. Many Gurjars were martyred. This was because the British were superior in terms of advanced weaponry and artillery.

Captain Young's target was to enter the fort. But the walls of the fort were high, which was a hindrance. Climbing up the walls of the fort was impossible, as there was neither detachment nor ladders. And they had no gun to blow open the gate. On Mr. Shore's suggestion, a large tree was cut and its branches were lopped off by the Gurkhas using their sharp kookeries. They obtained ropes. Using the ropes and the tree, they rammed against the gate. They made several attempts. At every attempt the Gurjars attacked, thrusting long spears through the opening of the iron gate of the fort. The British opened fire. In the fifth attempt, the British succeeded in making an aperture in the gate, but only large enough to admit of entrance in a stooping posture.

Captain Young dashed through the opening attended by two soldiers and followed closely by Shore and others. As Young rushed on through the opening, a Gurjar warrior, sprang from a corner and was about to strike a desperate blow at the back of the Captain's neck when Shore came to his rescue. Shore took out his sword and struck at the Gurjar warrior when the latter's sword just touched Young's neck. The lifeless trunk of the brave freedom fighter bound past Young. Due to the effect of the blow by the Gurjar mutineer, Young's neck turned blue.

Soon the British forces penetrated into the fort. A fierce fight ensued thereafter. 150 Gurjars were slain by the British forces inside the fort. Kalyan Singh Gurjar has been described by the British author as a "gallant, athletic and gigantic *pehelwan*'....who was perfectly naked, with the exception of a middle cloth…he was gaily and fantastically painted, 'for this, his last battle'. He was armed with a sword and a shield…"

Kalyan Singh Gurjar scornfully addressed Frederick Shore as they advanced towards each other at the flat roof of a house adjoining the ramparts of the fort. The brave Gurjar warrior by then had killed seven soldiers of the British forces using his sword and shield.

A fight ensued between Kalyan Singh Gurjar and Shore. Their swords flashed in the setting sun. Such was the might of the Gurjar *pehelwan* general that Shore's shield was rendered nearly useless by the loss of its corded handle. Shore could only grasp the two rings to which the shield had been attached. Singh hit several blows with his sword on Shore's chest. He was about to hit the final death blow to the heavily wounded Shore with his sword when Captain Young, who turned up by then, opened fire at him.

In the British author's own words, "Captain Young…levelled his 'Joe Manton' at the Goojur's breast; the first barrel flashed in the pan, but a ball from the second pierced his chest just as he was making a desperate cut. The sharp blade swept under Shore's unsteady shield and gashed his side at the moment his antagonist fell back dead."

The bullet hit Kalyan Singh Gurjar but such was his aim that his 'sharp blade swept under Shore's unsteady shield and gashed his side' before he fell dead to the ground.

150 Gurjars and 37 British forces lost their lives and several were wounded in the battle within the fort. The British captured Raja Vijay Singh. The king was later hanged at Saharanpur. Raja Vijay Singh's head and Kalyan Singh's waist (*dhad*) were hung on the main gate of Dehradun Jail. Later the head was transferred to Thomson College (University of Roorkee).

The British captured the local Gurjars, especially men, of Koonja Bahadurpur. In a single day, 100s of them were hung by neck until death on a huge tree. This tree still contains the iron rings (*kunde*) where they were hung. The British razed the fort to the ground and destroyed the standing structures within.

Do you know Frederick Shore never recovered from his wounds? In the words of the author, "His originally robust constitution never recovered the wounds received at Koonja, though he survived till 1837, when he died at Calcutta, in his thirty-eighth year."

Salute to Kalyan Singh Gurjar and the brave sons of the soil, who sacrificed their lives for the freedom of the motherland.

39

Sambhudhan Phonglo

Dimasa Freedom Fighter Who Raised an Army for
War against British

Sambhudhan Phonglo! Not many, except from the Dimasa tribe, have heard about him. We know how Subash Chandra Bose established the Azad Hind Fauz and raised a huge army of 60,000 soldiers in foreign lands. His objective was to involve in war against the British and free India. Do you know Sambhudhan Phonglo raised a huge army in the Dimasa territory of the Northeast for war against the British? He was driven by the same objective – drive out the British by involving in war. It is an irony that we know nothing about this brave warrior of Bharat Mata from the Northeast! Likewise, the saga of a thousand and more warriors from the east to west, north to south, is in oblivion.

The British established their supremacy in parts of the northeastern states after the Treaty of Yandaboo signed in 1826 with Burma. As per the treaty, the British occupied Assam, Manipur, Cachar and the Jaintia Hills district. They annexed the Dimasa territory in 1832 and 1854 in two phases. The Dimasa territory included parts of Cachar and Nagaon in Assam, ravines of the Jatinga valley, lower part of Karbi Anglong district, parts of Dimapur of Nagaland and Jiribam in Manipur.

Initially, the British appointed a Junior Political Officer with headquarters at Asalu to handle the Dimasa region. Later, in 1866, they sliced away parts of the Dimasa territory and brought them under Nagaon and Naga Hills. This was part of the divide and rule policy of the British to weaken the natives and facilitate enmity between tribes. Sambhudhan Phonglo became aware of this policy of the British, which culminated in his firm resolution to fight for the freedom of the motherland until death.

Sambhudhan Phonglo was born into a Dimasa Kachari tribal family to Khasaidi and Deprondao Phonglo at Maibang in 1850. He was also known by the surname Phonglosa. Though his exact date of birth isn't on record, he was said to have been born at dawn on a *Falgooni Purnima*, which may correspond to March or April according to the Gregorian calendar. He was the eldest amongst five siblings.

Dimasa people, also called Dimasa Kachari, are one of the Kacharis — a group of ethnic tribes from Assam. Sambhudhan Phonglo has been described as well-built, tall, fair, and handsome. He was married to Nasadi after he shifted base to another Dimasa village called Semdikhor.

According to Dimasa mythology, the Dimasa Kacharis trace their origin as the children of the Earthquake God Bangla Raja and divine bird Arikhidima. They suffered from severe drought in their ancestral land sixty thousand lunar months ago and migrated to the foothills of the Himalayas and the now so-called Dimasa territory. They are one of the oldest inhabitants of the region. Few historians are of the opinion that the 'Kiratas' mentioned in the *Mahabharata* are actually Kacharis of the Northeast. The Kacharis are also termed descendants of Ghatotkacha, the son of Pandava prince Bhim and Hidimbi. The Dimasa Kachari kings ruled for a long period with one of their capitals in Dimapur. Few kings worth mentioning of different Dimasa kingdoms are Virochana, Nirbhay Narayan, Harischandra II, Krishnachandra Narayan Hasnusa, and the list goes on. Kachari Rajbari fort in Dimapur, which is in ruins, has stood the ravages of time. This fort and more historical relics prove that the Dimasa Kacharis were experts in brick making dating back to several hundred years. Another existing historical monument is the Baroduwar Dimasa Kachari Palace in Khaspur in Cachar. Today, the Dimasas of Cachar who have adopted Hinduism, are called Barmans and this tribal group from Assam who adopted Vaishnavism are called Hojai Kachari. Other Kachari tribes worth mentioning are

Sonowal Kachari, Bodo, Kirata Kachari, Saraniya Kachari, Thengal Kachari, Mech Kachari, and more. Their common ancestral kingdom was at Dimapur.

The British introduced a set of new revenue rules and taxation policy in the Dimasa territory. They did not vest any administrative power to the Dimasa nobility. The people found it difficult to cope up with the new regulations and new administrative system of the British. Moreover, the colonial forces looted and drained the resources of the people forcefully in the name of tax. Most Dimasa Kacharis lost their lands to the British. Besides, the British forcefully employed the tribals in large numbers as porters for various manual jobs and hard labor. According to one historical account, Captain Francis Jenkins and R B Pemberton with a team of 83 Britishers employed 1400 porters during a survey in the North Cachar hills. Those who failed to carry out their duties with devotion were punished. Many of the men were abducted and forced to work as labors. Such was the brutality of the British!

Here is a Dimasa Kachari folk song from the mid 1800s:

"What a disgraceful incident has happened in our village / the chicks are captivating the mighty Eagles / The white men are gradually occupying our land and river / Will nobody be born in our golden land that will save our country? Will our legendary heroes Demalu, Halodao, Rangadao Degadao and Delai Mailai not reincarnate?"

There were no resistance against the British occupation of the Dimasa territory and their exploitation of the tribal folks until Sambhudhan Phonglo raised his voice. Under his leadership, the Dimasa Kacharis of the North Cachar Hills started preparing for war against the British. Sambhudhan Phonglo moved from place to place, visited almost the entire Dimasa territory and inspired the folks to rise in revolt against British and free the region from their rule. He also approached people from neighboring regions and motivated them to rise up in rebellion.

Sambhudhan Phonglo could not witness the terrible condition of the Dimasa Kacharis under British rule. He felt restless. He saw his people lose their freedom to the British. Why support the British consolidate their position? Why lose freedom? Why embrace slavery? Was it worthwhile to live in peace under foreign rule? These questions arose in his mind. Losing freedom was embracing slavery! He felt it was easy to endure hardships but impossible to endure slavery. He felt the British had only annexed their lands but not the heart of the people. He felt confident that united, the Dimasa Kacharis could drive away the British.

And then started his tour from one village to another in the Dimasa territory, especially the North Cachar Hills! Sambhudhan Phonglo gave lectures to the villagers who assembled in groups and motivated them to rise up in rebellion. Within a short span of time, he was able to recruit a great number of the Dimasa Kachari youth and formed a revolutionary force. He appointed Mann Singha as his principal adviser, and Molongthong as subordinate commander. He himself started training them in batches in the art of warfare including Guerrilla warfare techniques.

Do you know Sambhudhan Phonglo was an ardent devotee of Mahadev? Though his residence was at Semdikhor in the Mahur valley, he chose Maibang, which was once the capital of the Dimasa Kachari Kingdom, as his base for training the youth. It was 1881. Maibang, located in the now Dima Hasao disctrict of Assam, has several historical monuments of the Dimasa Kachari kings, dating from the 12th century. Sambhudhan Phonglo established a training center at Maibang.

The Dimasa Kachari people came forward to help for the establishment of the training centre. They donated for the production of weaponry. And then the training started. Sambhudhan Phonglo started training the youth in batches with each batch consisting around 40 Dimasa Kacharis.

The British came to know about Sambhudhan's activities. The British Sub-Divisional Officer at Gunjung issued orders to Sambhudhan to appear before his court. Such was the strong influence of the brave warrior amongst his people that they supported him and resisted his visit. They paid no heed to the official order. The British then sent an arrest warrant to arrest Sambhudhan Phonglo but in vain. Sambhudhan stood defiant.

CA Soppit was then the SDO of North Cachar and Major Boyd the Deputy Commissioner of Silchar. On January 15, 1882, Boyd along with CA Soppit and 40 Kuki forces reached Maibang to arrest Sambhudhan Phonglo and his men. Phonglo knew beforehand that the British would arrive at Maibang with an army and about their intended operation. Hence, he asked the villagers to move out of the village until the British would return back. The British found the place deserted!

The same day, i.e on January 15, 1882, Sambhudhan Phonglo attacked the British sub-divisional headquarters at Gunjung. The British forces stationed there fled without giving any resistance. Phonglo and his men were able to kill three of the British forces during the attack and wounded many. The Dimasa Kachari warrior then set the British headquarters on fire.

After this successful attack of the British post at Gunjung, Sambhudhan Phonglo advanced with his men towards Maibang to fight against the British. The Dimasa Kachari troops involved in war dance with the accompaniment of *maduli* (a drum) as they marched speedily forward through the jungle towards their next target attack. They reached Maibang.

A war between the Dimasa Kachari troops and the British forces ensued at Maibang. Major Boyd received serious injuries during the fight. Several Dimasa soldiers attained martyrdom, as their tribal weaponry were no match to the advanced British artillery. An wounded Sambhudhan Phonglo and the remaining tribal warriors retreated into the jungle and waited near the Sainyader hill for the British troops to follow them. They strategized to attack them in the hill stretch. More Dimasa warriors joined Phonglo at the hill. But the British troops retreated, as Major Boyd was seriously wounded. Boyd succumbed to his injuries at Silchar, fifteen days later, i.e. on January 30, 1882.

Sambhudhan Phonglo was all the more determined to wage war against the British. But for his mission to be successful, he needed more people and weaponry. Hence, he strategized to seek help from the Tripura king. He sent his chief adviser Mann Singha to Tripura. The British somehow came to know about this. They arrested Mann

Singha in Tripura. He was brought to Silchar and sentenced to life imprisonment in Silchar jail. The brave warrior went on a hunger strike inside the jail, refusing to take even water from the British. He attained martyrdom in the jail cell. Phonglo continued training the youth and waited for an opportune moment to attack the British.

On 12 February 1883, Sambhudhan Phonglo died of an injury. Without a leader, the Dimasa Kacharis could not lead any rebellion against the British after this.

Salute to Sambhudhan Phonglo and the brave Dimasa Kachari warriors who sacrificed their lives for the freedom of the motherland. Jai Hind!

40

Banda Singh

Sikh General Who Led 5 Battles to Victory against Mughals and Established Supremacy in Punjab

A multi-faceted energetic child who was an expert in the art of warfare and hunting. An ascetic from his 15th to his 38th year. A Sikh at 38. A general of Guru Gobind Singh's Khalsa army at 38. Led five battles to victory against Mughals and other Islamic forces. Established his authority in the Punjab region east of Lahore putting an end to Islamic rule. Ended the *zamindari* system. Martyrdom at 45. A name that should be immortalized in golden letters in the pages of History. He was Baba Banda Singh Bahadur.

Baba Banda Singh was born on 27 October 1670 at Rajauri, Poonch, present-day Jammu and Kashmir. According to the *Encyclopaedia of Sikhism*, published by the Punjabi University, Patiala, his father was Ram Dev, a ploughman of the Sodhi sub-caste of Khatris. Lachman Dev was his birth name. His other names were Madho Daas Bairagi and Gur Bakhash Singh (named by Guru Gobind Singh).

His Expertise

- Horse riding
- Martial art
- Use of bows and arrows
- Use of all weapons used in wars during his time
- Art of warfare
- Hunting.

Why Banda Singh Bahadur Became an Ascetic at Age 15?

At a very young age, Banda Singh developed fondness for hunting. It became one of his major hobbies. An active and energetic child, he often practiced hunting in the nearby jungles. An incident changed his very perception of hunting and he stopped practicing this hobby all throughout his life. He was then 15 years of age.

As usual, he went to the forest and aimed at a she-deer that caught his attention. His arrow tore the belly of the deer. When he went near it, he saw it was pregnant. The sight of the deer and her wounded twin offsprings writhing in pain and dying in front of his eyes deeply disturbed him. He was so much moved of this happening that he couldn't sleep for days together. It was then that he decided to become an ascetic. He left his home and started walking towards an unknown destination.

Banda Singh Bahadur's Initial Gurus

Banda Singh had grown up watching his father providing food and shelter regularly to saints, *sadhus* and holy persons who visited their abode. As a recluse, he reached Lahore (now in Pakistan). He became a disciple of Sadhu Ram Daas of Ram Thamman near Lahore. Later he became a disciple of Janaki Daas. Hereafter, he came to be known as Madho Daas. But he could not get peace of mind.

Under his new identity as Madho Daas, he moved from place to place until he reached Punchvati near Nasik in Maharashtra. There he met Sadhu Aughhar Nath. A satisfied Madho Daas became his disciple and served him for 5 years. Pleased with his services, the Guru bestowed him with all his virtues, occult powers and even his own created holy book. Banda Bahadur was then only 21 years of age. Meanwhile, Aughhar Nath expired in 1691.

Banda Singh Bahadur set up his own *ashram* at Nander. Over time, his *ashram* expanded. Many people became his disciples. His name and fame, especially for his miraculous powers, spread far and wide. Soon, he became proud and arrogant.

Banda Singh Bahadur's Ultimate Guru — Guru Gobind Singh

Banda Singh Bahadur met Guru Gobind Singh at the age of 38, i.e. in 1708. Guru Gobind Singh happened to come with his followers to his *ashram* at Nander. Banda Singh wasn't in the *ashram* then. The Guru arranged for himself a seat. His followers started arranging food without the permission of the *ashram*'s head, i.e. Madho Daas. Enraged followers of Madho Daas informed the latter. Using his occult powers, Daas tried to humiliate the Guru, but in vain. It was then that he fell at the Guru's feet and offered himself as his '*banda*' (*sevak*).

Guru Gobind Singh stayed at the *ashram* for a few days. Both the Guru and Madho Daas engaged themselves in long conversations. Guru Gobind Singh named Madho Daas Gur Bakhash Singh, gave him *amrit* to drink and baptized him to Sikhism. Later, Gur Bakhash Singh became popular as Baba Banda Singh Bahadur.

How Baba Banda Singh Got Inspired to Fight Against the Mughals

In 1699, on Vaisakhi at Anandpur, Guru Gobind Singh created the Khalsa, a warrior community, involving a group of six warriors including himself, the other five being known as the Panj Pyare. He prepared nectar mixing water and sugar into an iron bowl and stirring it with a double-edged sword. Amidst recitation from the *Adi Granth*, the baptism ceremony took place with all six taking the surname 'Singh', connoting lion. Guru Gobind Singh's father Guru Tegh Bahadur was executed by Aurangzeb; Muslim Sikh conflicts increased thereby. Guru Gobind Singh led several wars against the Mughals and neighboring kingdoms.

In December 1704, the Guru had to temporarily leave Anandpur as a condition for peace. Aurangzeb died in 1707 AD following which a fight ensued between his sons for emperorship. His eldest son Bahadar Shah, a Shia Muslim, sought Guru Gobind Singh's help. With the Guru's help and against a promise, Bahadar Shah became the next Mughal emperor. The promise was that as king he would do justice in Punjab by punishing the Governor of Sirhind, Nawab Wazir Khan and his accomplices for their crimes against the common people and for killing the Guru's mother Mata Gujri and two younger sons Zorawar Singh and Fateh Singh. His sons, aged 5 and 8, were buried alive into a wall after they refused to convert to Islam. But after becoming emperor, Bahadur Shah did not keep his promise.

A year later, i.e in 1708, Guru Gobind Singh along with his family and followers reached the Nander *ashram*. Knowing about Banda Singh Bahadur's expertise in the art of warfare, he appointed him his general. The Guru appointed five Sikhs for counseling – Daya Singh, Binod Singh, Kahan Singh, Bijay Singh, and Ram Singh as his counselors. The Guru ordered him to go to Punjab and fight the Mughals.

Death of Guru Gobind Singh at Nander

Meanwhile, Wazir Khan, the Nawab of Sirhind who killed Guru Gobind Singh's two younger sons, came to know about the Guru's whereabouts. He sent two Pathan spies to Nander. They were entrusted to kill the Guru. By this time Banda Singh Bahadur had already left for Punjab with a small force of Sikh men. The two spies reached Nander; they were successful in stabbing Guru Gobind Singh while he was taking rest. The Guru retaliated bravely, killing one of them. His followers, alerted after the uproar, attacked and killed the other spy. The deep wounds of the Guru were operated and stitched. But he could survive only for one and a half month. The injuries led him breathe his last. It was 7th October 1708.

Banda Singh's Troops

Reaching Punjab, Banda Singh Bahadur managed to garner support from both Hindus and Sikhs for fighting against enemy forces in battle. The Sikhs, who had fought under Guru Gobind Singh and others who were waiting to take revenge, aligned themselves with Banda. The Guru had prophesized about Sikh sovereignty in Punjab. Supporting Banda Singh, they decided to fulfill the Guru's prophecy.

Jats, Gurjars, Rajputs, and people of other communities joined him. Though his followers were armed with matchlocks, spears, swords, bows and arrows in battle with no elephants, no good horses and no guns yet it was their zeal and determination that helped him win numerous battles.

Victorious Battles Fought by Banda Singh Bahadur

Battle of Sonepat in 1709: Banda Singh with his army marched towards Khanda, Sonepat, which was under Mughal rule. He successfully attacked the town, defeated the *faujdar* and his army and looted the state treasury. Later, he distributed the treasury wealth amongst the poor.

Battle of Samana in 1709: This battle took place at Samana in Patiala against Wazir Khan, who was badly defeated. 10,000 Muslims were killed in the aftermath. This battle shook the Mughal administration of Delhi.

Battle of Sadhaura in 1709: With only a few Sikh army, Banda Singh Bahadur attacked Sadhaura in Haryana ruled by the Sayyids and Shaikhs. He defeated them and killed its ruler Osman Khan.

Battle of Chappar Chiri in 1710: This battle was fought at Chappar Chiri near Sirhind Fatehgarh. Though the Mughals gained an advantage with artillery which the Sikh forces lacked yet they faced defeat. The Sikh forces led by Baba Banda Singh Bahadur gave a crushing blow to the Mughal army. Wazir Khan (Sirhind) was killed in the battle. Following victory in this battle, the Sikhs established their first rule in Punjab.

Battle of Rahon in 1710: By this time, Banda Singh Bahadur had captured almost entire Punjab in the east of Lahore. He then advanced towards Jallandhar. On the way, a battle took place against the Mughals at Rahon. The Sikhs emerged victorious.

Banda Singh Bahadur lost three battles, viz. at Lohgarh in 1710, Jammu in 1712 and Gurdaspur in 1715. In another battle against the Mughal forces in 1710 at Jalalabad, Muzaffarnagar, Banda Singh Bahadur lost and withdrew after four days. Sikh prisoners captured were executed by the Mughals.

What Banda Singh Bahadur Did for the People of Punjab

After his victorious win in battles against the Mughals and other Islamic rulers, Banda Singh Bahadur established his authority in

Punjab from the Sutlej to the Yamuna. He developed the village of Mukhlisgarh, and made it his capital, which he later named Lohgarh, which meant 'fortress of steel'. Though he ruled only for 6 to 7 years, he broke the yoke of 700 years rule of Islamic invaders. He married the daughter of one of the hill chiefs. The couple had a son named Ajai Singh.

Soon after, he abolished the *zamindari* system, and granted property rights to the tillers of the land. Farmers under him started living in dignity and self-respect. He removed corrupt officials and replaced them with honest ones. The liberal offerings he received were distributed amongst the poor and the needy.

His Last Days and Brutality of Mughals

In 1713, the Sikhs left Lohgarh and Sadhaura and went to the remote hills of Jammu. They established a Dera there. In March 1715, the Mughal army drove Banda Bahadur and the Sikh forces into the village of Gurdas Nangal, Gurdaspur, Punjab. Later, the enemy forces laid siege of the village. For eight long months, the Sikhs defended the fortress at Gurdas Nangal. On 7 December 1715, the Mughals could manage entry into the fortress; they captured Banda Bahadur and other Sikhs besides slaughtering thousands of others.

The Sikh leader was put into an iron cage and the rest, 780 in number, were chained. To terrorize the people, the Mughals hung 2000 slaughtered Sikh heads on spears, loaded 700 cartloads of the slaughtered heads and brought them to Delhi in a procession along with the leader and the prisoners. Once they reached Delhi, the Mughals pressurized Banda Singh and the 780 Sikh prisoners to convert to Islam, but in vain. Following this, on firm refusal, everyday 100 Sikh soldiers were executed in public until everyone faced martyrdom except their leader and his son. Banda Singh Bahadur was confined in prison for three months along with his four-year old son Ajai Singh. Every day he was pressurized to convert to Islam.

On 9 June 1716, a Mughal executioner gave Banda Singh a dagger to cut his son Ajai Singh, who was then seated on his lap. He refused. Immediately, the executioner pierced the chest of the little boy, violently took out the vibrating heart and tried to push it into the mouth of the father. A shackled Banda Singh furiously refused. Following the orders of the Mughal ruler, the executioner offered to spare his life if he converted to Islam. Upon refusal, his flesh was notched out with pliers and hot sharp rods were inserted into his flesh. His eyes were gouged out and his limbs severed. Yet he refused to give up his faith. The Mughals then went to the extent of having his skin removed. Yet he remained firm, refusing to convert. He was then killed. Banda Singh Bahadur was only 45 years old then. Such was the brutality the Mughals showcased!

Baba Banda Singh Bahadur's martyrdom will inspire generations to remain fearless against all odds and the extremes of circumstances.

41

Mula Gabharu

Ahom Warrior Who Killed Two Lieutenants of Muslim Army in 1533 Battle

Have you heard about the brave and valiant Mula Gabharu of Assam? Except few from Assam, not many have even heard her name! She was one of the few warriors who fought bravely in battlefield against Muslim invaders. She killed two Mohammedan Lieutenants in battle until she was treacherously killed by the enemy in the same battlefield. Like many other unsung warriors of India, she finds no place in Indian History text books.

Islamic invaders from Bengal made several attempts to conquer Kamrupa, now called Assam. In 1206, King Prithu of the Khen dynasty that drew their lineage from Narakasura, badly defeated Bakhtiyar Khilji. Do you know Khilji was the first Islamic invader to attack Assam? In 1527 A.D., Rukunuddin Rukun Khan, the general of Nasiruddin Nasrat Shah, the Sultan of Bengal invaded Kamrupa only to be defeated by the Ahoms. Viswa Singha was then the Ahom king of Kamrupa. Hearing about the defeat of Rukun Khan, the Sultan dispatched his general Mit Manik with an army of one thousand horsemen and ten thousand foot soldiers. In this battle, the Ahoms won. Mit Manik was taken prisoner while Rukun Khan fled from the battlefield. The Ahoms captured a large booty including some fire arms.

Nasiruddin Nasrat Shah was the son of Ala-ud-din Husain Shah, founder of the Hussain Shahi dynasty in Bengal. Husain Shah usurped the throne of Bengal after assassinating Shams-ud-Din

Muzaffar Shah, an Abyssinian Sultan. After his death in 1519, he was succeeded by his son Nasrat Shah. After the failed attempt of invading Assam in 1527, Nusrat Shah again sent a huge army under the commandership of Turbak Khan, an Afghan in 1532 AD.

The Mohammedan army, comprising of both land and naval forces, were armed with guns and cannons besides other weapons used in battle during that time. According to the book *War Drums of Eagle King* written by P.W. Ingty, "The forces led by Turbak Khan were well equipped with sufficient rations and armaments; their soldiers were well trained and seemed unbeatable as they moved steadily on the north bank of the Brahmaputra towards the core of the Ahom-held territories."

Ahom king Suhungmung was then the ruler of Assam. The 14th Ahom ruler, he ascended the throne of the Ahom kingdom under the title of Swarganarayan Dihingia Raja in 1497. Under his rule, the Ahom kingdom expanded beyond the previous borders.

A series of battles between the Ahoms and the Mohammedan forces were fought between 1532 and 1533 AD. The first battle was fought between Turbak and Ahoms at Singri. This battle was commandeered by Suklen, the son of Suhungmung. Suklen was defeated and wounded in this battle. The Ahom forces retreated over to the south bank of the Brahmaputra. The Mohammedan forces followed. Several more battles followed at different places with neither party at the winning end.

In 1533 AD, the Ahom forces in one of these battles were led by Ahom commander Phrasengmung Borgohain. The title Borgohain is the 2nd in rank in the Ahom court of ministers conferred by Sukaphaa, the founder of the Ahom dynasty. Burhagohain was the 1st in rank, conferred by the same Ahom king. Later, Suhungmung added three more ranks, the descending order of which, were Borpatrogohain, Sadiakhowa Gohain, and Marangikhowa Gohain. All of the five ministers were entrusted with supervising certain Ahom territories and of leading armies in battle.

Turbak Khan treacherously killed Phrasengmung Borgohain in battle. The death of the commander demoralized the Ahom forces.

Meanwhile, the slain Ahom general's wife Mula Gabharu heard the news about her husband's death. Like Goddess Shakti, Mula Gabharu immediately set to action, marching towards the battlefield in a horse with a flashing sword in hand, all ready to strike!

Mula Gabharu was trained in the art of warfare. Right from riding a horse in battlefield to use of sword and other arms used in warfare, she was an expert.

To defend her motherland from the Muslim forces and to avenge the death of her husband, Mula Gabharu rode into the large Mughal forces, striking hard on either side as she marched ahead like lightning amid the dark clouds. Many a soldier was slain. The Ahom forces were greatly motivated and inspired by her feat and they fought with renewed vigor. She came face to face with one of the Lieutenants of Turbak Khan. Without much effort, she struck him with her sword and killed him. Mula Gabharu confronted another Lieutenant of the Mohammedan forces. She struck him and killed him too. And then she confronted Turbak. The Afghan commander treacherously killed her. Neither party won.

The Ahoms, now commandeered by Tonkham Borpatra Gohain, another general, made a change of their war tactics. They positioned themselves in such a way so as to cut off all supply and communication lines of the army of Turbak Khan with their homeland and headquarters at Gauda, Bengal. The final battle took place at Duimunisila along the banks of the mighty Bharali (tributary of Brahmaputra) river a few days later. Tonkham Borpatra Gohain defeated the Mohammedan forces and killed Turbak Khan. In the words of Leslie Shakespear from his book *History of Upper Assam, Upper Burmah and North-Eastern Frontier,* the Ahom Raja "sent large reinforcements by land and river. Turbak's forces were defeated, he himself killed, and his head, as was customary, was sent for burial on Charaideo hill. The beaten and disorganized forces were pursued by the victorious Ahoms through Koch territory to the Karatoya river."

After Turbak was killed, the Ahom forces of Suhungmung pursued the Mohammedan army till the Karatoya river in present day North Bengal.

Mula Gabharu's brave participation in the war and her sacrifice had raised the spirits of the Ahom forces to fight for victory. They won. Thus Mula Gabharu won! India salutes the valor and sacrifice of Mula Gabharu. Jai Hind!

42

Chain Singh

24 Year Old Rajput Who Led an Army of 50 against Huge British Force in 1824

"Kunwar Sahib, why do you wear two swords?" asked Maddock, the in-charge of British cantonment in Sehore near Narsinghgarh in Madhya Pradesh.

"One of the swords is for cutting down the throats of those Indians who prove to be traitors and the second is for severing the heads of the Britishers who are treacherous," replied Kunwar Chain Singh.

A startled Maddock looked at the prince. The reply was harsh for the British officer. He pretended not to be offended. But his intentions were dire.

Who was Kunwar Chain Singh? What was the occasion of the meeting between Maddock and the Rajput prince? History text books will not enlighten you with the valorous saga of this brave Rajput warrior who led an army of 50 soldiers against a huge British force at the battle of Sehore in Madhya Pradesh in June 1824! He never surrendered to British supremacy and always held his head high in front of them. At a young age of 24, he fought until his last breath killing 25 British soldiers while fighting lonely after all of his 50 accompanying soldiers were martyred.

It was the year 1824. There were uprisings against the British across India. James Grant in his book *Cassell's Illustrated History of India*, has given a detailed description about the War of Independence of 1824. According to this book, the major areas of revolt were the

Bundelkhand region, Rajpootana, Kutch, Saharanpur, Roorkie, Dehradun, Kittoor, and Kolhapur. Grant writes, "At this time a strange impression prevailed in the upper provinces of India that the British were preparing to evacuate the whole country." During this time, Chain Singh, the prince of Narsinghgarh secretly held meetings with the rulers of neighboring princely states, strategizing to drive away the British.

Narsinghgarh, located near Bhopal in Malwa region of Madhya Pradesh, was a princely state. The rulers, who established this kingdom in the 17th century, were descendants of Raja Bhoj of the Parmar clan of Rajputs. Before the principality was founded, it was a part of a bigger Rajgarh kingdom. The rulers of Narsinghgarh were famous for their Rajput pride, valor and honor.

Kunwar Chain Singh, aged 24, took a lead in the administrative affairs of the kingdom of Narsinghgarh after his father Rawat Sobhag Singh fell ill. His mother was from the royal family of Mewar. The prince was married to Rajawati, daughter of the Rajput chief of Muvaliya, a *jagir* of Narsinghgarh.

During that time, while few of the princely states were directly under British dominion, respective rulers of few kingdoms continued their rule against certain terms and conditions laid down by the British. Few kingdoms were independent though the British interfered in the internal affairs. Narsinghgarh belonged to the third category. The British were looking for ways to annex Narsinghgarh to the British Empire.

The above conversation took place between Maddock and the prince in a meeting at Sehore in the British cantonment. It was their second meeting. Date: 24th June 1824. The first meeting took place a few days ago at Bairasia, another place near Narsinghgarh.

It is but a fact that during Mughal and British rule, many Indians themselves were traitors. Had these traitors not existed there would have been no Mughal or British rule. It is because of these traitors that Mughals and British ruled India for a long time. And traitors led to the interference of the British in the internal affairs of Narsinghgarh, further leading to a battle between the two forces and martyrdom of the prince and 50 Rajput soldiers. Even after independence, the legacy of traitorhood continues till today with many joining the break India forces to divide and break India!

Chain Singh held regular secret meetings with neighboring kings and princes. They strategized and planned to collectively drive away the British. Anand Ram Bakshi, the Chief Minister of Narsinghgarh court secretly leaked the information to the British. When Chain Singh came to know of this treason, he killed Anand Ram Bakshi despite his father's repeat requests to spare him.

For the Rajput prince, traitors had no place in his kingdom. Meanwhile, another minister Roop Ram Bohra also sided with the British, providing all information about the secret meetings and future plans of Narsinghgarh. Chain Singh, who kept spies to check traitors besides himself keeping a strict eye on treacherous activities in his kingdom, came to know of this. He immediately killed Roop Ram Bohra.

The members of the families of the dead ministers approached the British Governor General for help. The general entrusted Maddock to investigate and solve the matter. In this context, a meeting was organized at Bairasia.

Maddock laid three conditions for Chain Singh at the meeting:

1. He should leave Narsinghgarh for good.
2. The state of Narsinghgarh to be subjected to British rule for three years
3. Only the British will have the right to buy opium in Narsinghgarh.

Chain Singh did not agree to any of the three conditions. A prolonged argument broke out between the Rajput prince and Maddock. Ultimately, Maddock proposed for another meeting scheduled for 24th June 1824 in Sehore to which Chain Singh agreed. Maddock agreed that he would moderate his terms.

It was in the second meeting that the conversation, aforementioned in the beginning, took place. Chain Singh came wearing an armor and well prepared for any possible fight. He wore two swords. He was accompanied by fifty of the bravest soldiers and his faithful dog Sheru.

Responding to the harsh reply by Chain Singh, Maddock said that the British and the rulers of Narsinghgarh were friends and that no question of treachery by the British would arise.

"Will you show me the sword that you are carrying to severe the heads of the British?" asked Maddock.

Chain Singh had confidence in his abilities as well as those of his soldiers present at the meeting. Though he smelt something fishy and could read the secret intentions of Maddock, he gave one of his swords to the British officer. Maddock started inspecting the temper of the sword. He waited for an opportunity to strike at Chain Singh as soon as the latter's eyes would fall elsewhere. But Chain Singh's eyes were fixed at Maddock and the sword. For not a single instance did he divert his attention.

This time, the clever Maddock asked for the other sword that Chain Singh was carrying. The Rajput prince understood that this was Maddock's trick of disarming him completely.

"The waist of a Rajput is never left unadorned. I cannot give you my second sword," retorted Chain Singh.

"You have given me the sword which severs the heads of the British. I will show you how it severs the head of an Indian," replied a vexed Maddock.

The British officer was about to strike when Chain Singh moved back to a safe distance. He drew out his other sword from the scabbard to strike at Maddock. But before the Rajput price could attack, Sheru, his dog jumped towards the British officer. The dog's blood-shot eyes and sharp teeth frightened Maddock and he ran for his life out of the room. Sheru pursued him. Meanwhile, the British soldiers at the cantonment were alerted. While swords of both the forces clashed, Chain Singh ran after Maddock to save Sheru. He feared the British shooting at his loyal dog.

Both parties reached a crossing while continuing to fight. The British had fixed some of their cannons there. In the words of Srikrshna Sarala, author of *Indian Revolutionaries A Comprehensive Study, 1757-1961*, Volume 1, "When Kunwar Chain Singh saw that an artilleryman was about to put the fuse to the cannon, he sprang forward and struck a fierce blow on his neck. It was completely severed and his neck fell off. After cutting off the artilleryman's head, Kunwar Chain Singh's sword struck the cannon and a part of it was also chopped off."

A fierce battle ensued between the huge British forces and the Rajput army of fifty soldiers led by Chain Singh. Sheru injured many of the British forces in this battle until it was martyred. In the course of the battle, Chain Singh lost all of his soldiers except two until they reached the Dussehra Garden while fighting. At last only the Rajput prince was left and the rest were martyred. Before breathing his last, a heavily wounded Chain Singh could kill 25 British soldiers!

It is said Maddock took away Chain Singh's swords to England. Rulers of Narsinghgarh later built cenotaphs in memory of Kunwar Chain Singh at Dussehra Garden in Sehore. Today, Sehore is a tourist spot and people from all over the country visit Sehore to relive the valor of the brave Rajput prince Chain Singh.

Do you know Rani Lakshmibai of Jhansi sought help from the king of Narsinghgarh to fight against the British? Lakshmibai had heard about the valorous saga of Chain Singh and she was confident of getting help. The ruler of Narsinghgarh sent a force to Lakshmibai's aid towards Gwalior but before they could reach her, the Rani breathed her last.

43

Kaneganti Hanumanthu

Revolted Against British Tax Policy Imposed on Farmers; Martyred at 30

'Neeru pettava, Natu vesava Kota kosava, Kuppa nurchava Endhuku kattali ra sisthu?'

'Have you ever irrigated the land, or planted a seed in your life? Ever harvested or trashed a field? Why would I pay you any tax for what is mine?'

This was the slogan, the rebellion cry of Kaneganti Hanumanthu against the British against paying of taxes.

Who was Kaneganti Hanumanthu? What was the Pullari Rebellion? Why was he shot at by the British?

Not much information is available about Hanumanthu's birth, childhood, and education. He was born around the year 1891 in Minchalapadu in Durgi mandal of Palnadu in Guntur district of Andhra Pradesh. Palnadu has a rich historical legacy dating back to several thousand years.

India was and is primarily an agricultural country with majority of the population involved in farming for sustenance. Before the British established their rule in India, Indian cottage industry flourished overseas owing to good agricultural output. The British destroyed India's cottage industry and crippled the prosperity of farmers by levying heavy taxes irrespective of whether the yields were good or bad. They introduced new systems of land tenures and policies of tax collection, which were against the farmers.

Besides collection of heavy taxes, the British also tortured the farmers. Many farmers lost everything they had to the Britishers. Besides, the British also imposed draconian forest laws on forest produce. Kaneganti Hanumanthu grew up watching the atrocities of the British on the peasant community in Palnadu.

Kaneganti Hanumanthu started holding secret meetings with the farmers of Palnadu. He started revolting against the British in small groups and refused to pay tax. He influenced the farmers to stop paying taxes. In this context, the British arrested him several times and warned him of dire consequences if he led any future revolts. But Hanumanthu did not pay heed to the warnings. He continued with his activities.

He led two key movements against the British:

1. Pullari Movement

2. No-Tax Campaign.

The British collected taxes even on forest produce. Under the draconian law, farmers of the forest villages were forced to pay tax to use the forest produce and even to collect fodder. Free cattle grazing in the fields and forest was prohibited by the British. They collected tax for it too. Kaneganti Hanumanthu with the help of his associate Ellampalli Seshu started visiting the farmers in the forest villages regularly and asked them to stop paying taxes on forest produce and on cattle grazing.

The farmers, following the advice of Kaneganti Hanumanthu, resisted the British laws and revolted. They openly and socially boycotted all the government officers including the collector of the district. The farmers also stopped providing milk, vegetables and other crop produce to the District collector and other British officials who were on tour or residing in that region. The farmers also stopped supplies to revenue and police officials. Villagers employed by the British for tax collection stopped doing their duties. It was termed the Pullari rebellion.

Alongside the Pullari rebellion, Kaneganti Hanumanthu also started a no-tax campaign. He was able to convince the farmers of the region to stop paying taxes on farm produce. He openly questioned the British when they came to collect taxes, "Have you ever irrigated the land, or planted a seed in your life? Ever harvested or trashed a field? Why would I pay you any tax for what is mine?" Every farmer started giving a similar statement.

More people joined the cause. Kaneganti Hanumanthu, Ellampalli Seshu, and more leaders and farmers were arrested and put behind bars. This led to *hartal* by the farmers condemning the arrest as well as demanding their release. Kaneganti Hanumanthu was let free with a warning.

The agitation took a serious turn within months. There were regular scuffles between the tax collectors, police officials and farmers. The British forcibly tried to snatch away the grazing cattle to which the farmers led by Kaneganti Hanumanthu strongly resisted. It was then that the British decided to use brutal force.

The police seized a large number of cattle in Minchalapadu village on 16th February, 1921. Few peasants keeping guard of the cattle alerted the other farmers and Kanneganti Hanumanthu. They immediately marched forward and tried to resist. In retaliation, the British opened fire. Few bullets hit Kanneganti Hanumanthu and he breathed his last in the grazing field. He was only 30 years old. It was British General Rutherford who shot at him. Many peasants were martyred.

The next day the District Collector raided the forest villages with a huge force. He arrested every male member and took them into custody. The accompanying British police looted all the movable property of the farmers in this raid.

Salute to Kaneganti Hanumanthu! Jai Hind!

44

Avantibai

Ramgarh Rani who Won 1st Battle against British and Martyred in 2nd at 27 Years

She was the queen of Ramgarh. She raised an army of 4000 soldiers, trained them, and herself led them in battlefield against the British forces. She won. She is one of the few Indian rulers who won a battle against British in 1857. Did the British stop after their defeat? No! They attacked her kingdom with additional forces and destroyed many a standing structure besides killing many. The Rani remained in hiding and started reciprocating following guerilla warfare techniques in several successful attempts until she was surrounded by the enemy forces. Sensing defeat and her capture certain, she struck herself with her sword and attained martyrdom. Until death she did not let the enemy capture her or touch her! She was Avantibai.

But how many of us have read about Avantibai in our history text books? I never read nor heard about her in school or college. According to a *dailymail.co.uk* report, "following an uproar engineered by MPs of the Bharatiya Janata Party and Bahujan Samaj Party in the Rajya Sabha during the monsoon session" in 2011, the HRD ministry had advised NCERT to consider the inclusion of Avantibai in text books. "The protest had led to two adjournments in Parliament." This political pressure led NCERT mention the brave 19th century freedom fighter's name in "NCERT's Social Science textbook for Class VIII — on pages 58 and 59 under chapter five called 'When People Rebel' — from the new academic session." Though the inclusion does not contain a detailed historical account of the valorous warrior, it was indeed a welcome step by NCERT. The valorous saga of hundreds of our unsung warriors should be included in the school curriculum too.

Avantibai was born on the 16th of August 1831. Not enough sources are available about her childhood. She belonged to the Lodhi community of agriculturists from Madhya Pradesh. She was married to Vikramjeet Singh, also known as Vikramaditya Singh, the ruler of Ramgarh state in present day Sikar, Rajasthan. The couple was blessed with two sons — Aman Singh and Sher Singh (though few historical records say that they were adopted). Ramgarh was founded by Maharaja Ramchandra Singh in 1830 with the help of Poddars, a business clan.

Vikramaditya Singh fell seriously ill. He was unable to take part in the administrative and other affairs of his kingdom. The young Avantibai in her early twenties took over the reins of Ramgarh. She started ruling wisely. She trained herself in the art of warfare to lead from the front in possible future battles.

During that time, while few of the princely states were directly under British dominion, respective rulers of few kingdoms continued their rule against certain terms and conditions laid down by the British. Few kingdoms were independent though the British interfered in the internal affairs. Meanwhile, from 1848, Lord Dalhousie applied the Doctrine of Lapse and started annexing kingdoms to the British Indian Empire. This doctrine included those kingdoms whose kings were 'incompetent' or 'died without a male heir'.

The British started interfering in the affairs of Ramgarh when they learnt that the king was bedridden for several days. They declared him as unfit to be a ruler and forcefully tried to annex Ramgarh. It was 1851. The British declared Ramgarh as 'Court of Wards' and appointed their own administrator. But Avantibai did not recognize the supremacy of the British. She rose to the occasion and took charge of the administration, throwing out the administrator. Meanwhile, the king died. The British did not accept Aman Singh and Sher Singh, the heirs to the throne, as they were minors (also amid rumors that they were adopted).

Six years passed by amid bitter relations between Avantibai and the British, who forcefully employed British officials in her territory.

She did not let them enter Dindori Ramgarh fort. Meanwhile, the War of Independence in 1857 started in Meerut cantonment on May 10 where Indian sepoys with the help of local civilians killed 50 Britishers. This news spread like wild fire influencing freedom fighters to rise in revolt against the British across the country.

Avantibai joined this movement independently. Her objective was – the British should leave Ramgarh and the Indian soil. She raised an army of 4000 warriors with the help of neighboring rulers and local *zamindars*. In association with many *Thakurs* and *Malguzars* of the area, she first forced the British officers to leave Ramgarh and occupied the treasury. It was 26th September, 1857. This enraged the British. They attacked Ramgarh with a huge force.

The first battle between the British forces and Avantibai took place in the village of Kheri near Mandla in Ramgarh. The queen herself led her army. She fought like an angry goddess in the battlefield. The British lost the war. Avantibai is one of the few Indian rulers who won a battle against British in 1857.

Stung by the defeat, the British came back with vengeance and launched an attack on Ramgarh after a few days. Avantibai moved to the hills of Devharigarh for safety. The British forces set fire to the city of Ramgarh besides destroying crops and standing structures. They pursued the queen to Devharigarh.

Avantibai resorted to guerilla warfare techniques as an open battle would mean her defeat given the superiority of the British forces in terms of military strength and ammunition this time. The guerrilla warfare involved involvement of a small group of combatants in ambushes, hit-and-run tactics, sabotage, raids, etc. using arms. This went on for some time until she was surrounded by the enemy from close range. The British asked her to surrender.

The valorous queen thought it better to sacrifice her life rather than to surrender and get captured. She would not let the British touch her! She drew out her sword from the scabbard tied to her waist. With one blow she struck herself hard and attained martyrdom. It was 20th March 1858. She was only 27 years old!

Naman and Salute to the brave Rani Avantibai! Jai Hind!

45

Mahabiri Devi

How Mahabiri Devi and 22 Village Women Killed Many British Soldiers in 1857

They are the symbols of bravery and patriotism. Their names are in oblivion — unknown and unheralded in the pages of History. Mahabiri Devi, a Bahujan woman in her twenties, hailing from Mundbhar in Mujaffarnagar, Uttar Pradesh, inspired women in her village to fight for the freedom of India. 22 village women led by her formed a group and strategized to attack British soldiers. Their motto was kill the British or perish! They succeeded. They killed several British soldiers until all of the 22 freedom fighters were shot at by the British and martyred. No one propagated their stories of unprecedented valor.

Mahabiri Devi raised voice against the social custom of manual scavenging done by a particular section of the society. She was uneducated but opposed exploitation of any kind since her childhood. She hated the British from an early age and openly spoke hatred against them. People in her village revered her.

When the War of Independence broke out in 1857, many a son and daughter of Bharat Mata were inspired to rise in revolt. The news reached Mundbhar village in Mujaffarnagar. This village was not far from Meerut cantonment, the nucleus of the uprising. On May 10, Indian sepoys with the help of local civilians had killed 50 Britishers at Meerut cantonment. Mahabiri Devi decided to attack the British with the help of local village women.

The uprising in Meerut cantonment inspired many women in the Muzaffarnagar area in western UP to rise in revolt. Few historical records find mention of few brave women in their twenties who were successful in killing Britishers. They are Indra Kaur, Man Kaur, Rahimi, Raj Kaur, Shobha Devi, Asha Devi, Bakhtavari, Habiba, Bhagwati Devi Tyagi, Umda, and many others, who actively participated and attained martyrdom while fighting. While few were shot dead, few were hanged, and few burnt alive by the British.

According to an account by Charu Gupta in a piece titled *Dalit 'Viranganas' and Reinvention of 1857* published in *Economic and Political Weekly*, Mahabiri Devi and her group of 22 women revolted against the British two days ahead of the uprising in Meerut cantonment, i.e. on 8 May 1857.

According to another account, the conspiracy for attacking the British in Meerut cantonment was planned days ahead and the plan was given shape on May 10th. It was possible that the news about the conspiracy might have spread to adjoining areas including Mujaffarnagar. Charu Gupta mentions Mahabiri Devi and other women attacking British soldiers on 8 May, 1857 and themselves getting martyred during the course of action.

Such was the inspiring speech of Mahabiri Devi that 22 women in their twenties, who never used arms and who were involved only in household chores, joined her. This group started training themselves in the use of swords and sticks so that they emerged victorious fighting the enemy. They were fearless and were ready to sacrifice their lives for the motherland.

In the words of Crispin Bates, Editor of the book *Mutiny at the Margins: New Perspectives on the Indian Uprising of 1857*, they emerged as "physically commanding and armed, infused with power, strength, bravery, activism, and sacrifice, locked in violent conflict with the British."

Mahabiri Devi and the 22 women rose in arms against the British. They attacked British soldiers stationed in Mujaffarnagar. They were able to kill many British soldiers until all were martyred.

It is unfortunate that not much information about Mahabiri Devi and the 22 village women are available on records. Salute to the 22 women warriors and the brave sons and daughters of Bharat Mata who sacrificed their lives for the freedom of the motherland. Jai Hind!

46

Suhaldev

Shravasti Raja who Defeated and Killed Ghaznavid General Salar Masud in 1034 AD

Most modern historians have designed history text books in line with secularism avoiding depiction of the feats of hundreds of thousands of warriors who resisted Muslim invasion and British aggression. They consider the glory of Raja Suhaldev as 'semi-legendary'. Muslim historical records find mention about Suhaldev. These records didn't glorify Suhaldev, but they did glorify 'Ghazi' Salar Masud and his *dargah* at Bahraich. Salar Masud earned the title of 'Ghazi' because he was killed in a battle. The title denotes him as a religious warrior. He was killed in battle at Bahraich by Suhaldev, the king of Shravasti.

A detailed description of Suhaldev is found in *Mirat-i-Masudi*, a historical biography on Ghaznavid general Ghazi Saiyyad Salar Masud. The book was written in Persian by Abd-ur-Rahman Chishti in the 17th century. Chishti wrote the historical drama based on the book *Tawarikh-i-Mahmudi* written by Mulla Muhammad Ghaznavi, who belonged to the court of Sultan Mahmud of Ghazni.

Suhaldev was the king of Shravasti, now in Devipatan division of Uttar Pradesh. According to Alexander Cunningham, archaeological surveyor of India in the 1860s and founder of the Archaeological Survey of India, Suhaldev's predecessors from the period of 900 AD find mention in the traditional accounts of Tharu Rajas of Gonda of UP. According to Cunningham, Suhaldev, also called Suhridal-dhaj, ascended the throne of Shravasti around 1000 AD. Suhaldev was known by various names such as Sohal Deo, Suhildev, Suhar Deo, etc.

The ancient city of Shravasti carries forward a legacy of several thousand years. King Shravasta from the Vedic period founded this kingdom. It was one of the major cities that flourished during the time of Gautam Buddha. It was the capital of the Kosala kingdom that drew its lineage from Shri Ram. Shravasti was the place where Buddha first came, 2500 plus years ago, at the invitation of Sudatta, a rich merchant, who was also known as Anathapindika. Sudatta bought a piece of land from Jeta, the then king of Shravasti, for building a vihara. The king donated valuable wood for the construction of the vihara; hence the place where the vihara was built was also called Jetavana Vihara. It was here where Buddha spent the longest period of time. Over time, Buddhist followers from Myanmar, Thailand, Sri Lanka, South Korea and other countries donated for the construction of stupas, viharas, and monasteries in Shravasti. Today, Shravasti is an important Buddhist pilgrimage centre and home to ancient Buddhist monuments.

Raja Suhaldev ruled the kingdom of Shravasti wisely. He was the emperor of the region with several small kingdoms each under a chief under his emperorship. He was known far and wide for his skills in warfare and leading armies to victory. Like Krishn's Mathura, Shravasti and neighboring kingdoms were home to great number of cows. Suhaldev initiated measures for the protection of cows. He was a patron of saints and staunch follower of Vedic rituals.

Ghazi Saiyyad Salar Masud, also known as Ghazi Miyan, was the nephew of Sultan Mahmud of Ghazni. During Mahmud's conquest of parts of India in early 11th century, Salar Masud accompanied him in the expeditions. He was with Sultan Mahmud when the latter destroyed the Somnath temple, looted the temple treasury, and killed hundreds and thousands of Hindus.

Ghaznavid campaigns in Indian subcontinent were a success in Multan, Delhi, and Meerut under the leadership of Salar Masud. To further expand the Ghaznavid influence in India, Masud set up his headquarters at Satrikh in the Barabanki area of Uttar Pradesh. From here he dispatched separate forces to capture Bahraich, Gopamau and Benares. The Bahraich expedition was led by Salar Masud's father Salar Sahu, who died at Satrikh in 1032. Salar Masud then himself led the Bahraich expedition in 1033 AD.

Several kingdoms shared their local boundaries with Bahraich. Salar Masud camped at Bahraich. Who isn't familiar with Sultan Mahmud's loot and plunder of the Indian cities and razing of temples to the ground? Mahmud and his followers took women as slaves, raped them, destroyed temples, converted many to Islam, killed those who refused to convert, and their list of atrocities goes on. Mulla Muhammad Ghaznavi in his book *Tawarikh-i-Mahmudi* wrote about Sultan Mahmud, "And in the work of religious war he had planted the banners of Islam and had pulled up the roots of tyrants." Salar Masud exactly followed Sultun Mahmud's footsteps in all of his military expeditions in India.

With an aim to subjugate all of the kingdoms in and around Bahraich, Salar Masud started encountering with the rulers one by one. A year passed by but he was not able to vanquish all of the rulers.

At Bahraich, he saw the ruins of a Hindu temple dedicated to Surya Dev with a sacred reservoir adjacent to it. The site was once an *ashram* where Balark Rishi lived. Masud decided to construct a mosque at the site after his military expedition of Bahraich was complete. According to an account by William Charles Bennet, Salar Masud wished to destroy the shrine and reside there thenceforth.

Meanwhile, Raja Suhaldev invited the rulers of his neighboring kingdoms to his court. The defeated rulers as well as those who were ready to face Salar Masud in battle assembled at Shravasti. As decided, the combined forces of the Hindu rulers led by Suhaldev were to face the Ghaznavid forces at Chittora near Bahraich. Suhaldev strategized on the military formations and other tactics so as to defeat Salar Masud and his forces. The Shravasti king's army consisted of not only infantry but also cavalry, war horses and elephants.

Salar Masud came to know about the plan of Suhaldev. Both parties had entrusted spies to know about the ongoing plans. Masud was well aware that Suhaldev revered cows. Hence, he hatched a plan. He decided to put a huge herd of cows in front of the Hindu army in battlefield. And he knew Suhaldev would not harm cows and hence he and his army would retreat. And then as they would retreat, the Ghaznavid forces would attack and subjugate them. Masud's men captured huge number of cows from the area. Suhaldev came to know about this. A few hours in the night before the great battle was to start, the Raja's men quietly released all the cows.

A fierce battle took place between the combined forces of Suhaldev and Salar Masud at Chiottra near Bahraich on 15 June 1034. The Ghaznavid forces made a dash at the center of the Hindu army lines hoping to dissect the army into two and directly reaching the king. But, the Hindu infantry held on and the resulting melee gave enough time to the cavalry of Suhaldev to outflank the Ghaznavid army. Once flanked, what followed was total carnage as Ghaznavid flanks disintegrated. Confusion prevailed amongst the Mohammedan forces. Salar Masud's army could not withstand the furious charge of the Hindu army. There were major casualties from Masud's side.

Suhaldev himself marched ahead in the battlefield and attacked Salar Masud. The Ghaznavid general was no match to the fierce Hindu king who struck terror amid the Muslim army. In the ensuing fight between the two, Salar Masud was heavily wounded. Before he breathed his last, he asked his followers to bury him near the sacred reservoir in the Surya Dev temple premise.

Hindu kings have a track record of following the rules of Dharma in warfare. They took care of the injured at the end of the day. They never interfered into the religious affairs of the followers of other religion. So did Suhaldev. Salar Masud was allowed to be buried at Bahraich. More than 200 years later, Sultan Firuz Shah Tughlaq turned it into a *dargah*, which emerged as an important pilgrimage site for the Muslims.

Ironically, Hindus in large numbers visit the *dargah* even today to offer prayers to the Ghaznavid Ghazi who once looted and plundered Hindu kingdoms, destroyed temples, killed Hindus, and converted many to Islam. William Henry Sleeman, the British

Resident in Awadh, wrote in his book *Journey through the kingdom of Oude* published in 1850 and later edited by P. D. Reeves in Sleeman in *Oudh: An Abridgement of W. H. Sleeman's A Journey Through the kingdom of Oude*, "Strange to say, Hindoos as well as Mahommedans make offerings to this shrine, and implore the favours of this military ruffian, whose only recorded merit consists of having destroyed a great many Hindoos in a wanton and unprovoked invasion of their territory. They say, that he did what he did against Hindoos in the conscientious discharge of his duties, and could not have done it without God's permission — that God must then have been angry with them for their transgressions, and used this man, and all the other Mahommedan invaders of their country, as instruments of his vengeance, and means to bring about his purposes: that is, the thinking portion of the Hindoos say this. The mass think that the old man must still have a good deal of interest in heaven, which he may be induced to exercise in their favour, by suitable offerings and personal applications to his shrine."

Several historical accounts and architectural additions to the burial place of Salar Masud prove his death in battle to be true. And if his accounts are true and historically proven, the historicity of Suhaldev cannot be questioned, as done by many modern historians and non-believers of the Hindu Raja's saga.

In 1250, Nasir ud din Mahmud, the Sultan of Delhi, constructed an architectural complex around the tomb. Amir Khusro, the 13th century poet, mentioned about Masud's *dargah* in a 1290 AD letter. In 1341, Ibn Battuta and Muhammad bin Tughluq visited the *dargah*; the former wrote about the Ghazi. Ziauddin Barani wrote about Masud in his book *Tarikh-i-Firuz Shahi* mentioning him as one of the heroes of Mahmud's campaigns in India. Mughal court historian Abul Fazl wrote that Salar Masud was connected to Mahmud of Ghazni by blood and that 'he sold his life bravely in battle and left an imperishable name.' Akbar himself visited the *dargah* and made a grant for it. And the list of historical account goes on.

Our reverence and salute to Raja Suhaldev, the forgotten hero of India. Jai Hind!

47

Durgadas Rathore

Protected Jodhpur Prince from Aurangzeb and Kept
Marwar Flag Flying High

He was fiercely loyal to the royal throne of Marwar. He is an
embodiment of the fiercest bravery, valor and loyalty. In real
life, such a selfless man as him is very hard to find. But in
Indian history there was a fierce warrior, a very able strategist and
loyal to the extent that he spent all his life saving the royal family he
served and kept it safe when it was in grave danger of becoming
extinct or converted to another faith. This man never assumed power
although he was revered even more than the king. He was Durgadas
Rathore. He protected and served the royal family of Jodhpur and
kept the Marwar flag flying high when it was in dire straits.

Durgadas Rathore was born in a smaller noble family of Jodhpur
on 13 August 1638. His father Askaran Rathore was a minister in
the royal court of Jodhpur, the then capital of Marwar. Jaswant
Singh was the Maharaja of Marwar. Durgadas had shown his valor
and courage in many battles. He was in the good books of the
Maharaja. By this time, Marwar had accepted the sovereignty of the
Mughals and Jaswant Singh was made the prime commander of the
Mughal army of Aurangzeb. Jaswant Singh was sent by Aurangzeb
to quell the revolt of the Afghans in Kabul, Afghanistan. Here, he
breathed his last in 1678 near Peshawar. At the time of his death,
two of his queens were pregnant.

Aurangzeb was a clever fox who never lost a minute in annexing
a state in such situations. He declared Marwar as a *jagir* of the
Mughal Empire and installed Indra Singh Rathore, a nephew of

Jaswant Singh as its ruler. Aurangzeb personally moved from Delhi to Ajmer to oversee the operation.

Both the pregnant queens of Jaswant Singh gave birth to sons. Now to quell any dispute, Aurangzeb ordered Rathores to send both the queens and sons of Jaswant Singh to Delhi. He assured that he would take care of them and would allot a *jagir* to the elder of the two. The elder son of Jaswant Singh was named Ajit Singh. Pretty soon, the younger brother of Ajit Singh died leaving him as the sole heir of Marwar. Rathores had to reluctantly obey the Mughals as Marwar was under control of Aurangzeb's stooge Indra Singh. Both the queens and infant were brought to Delhi and kept at the Rathore mansion in Shahjanabad (Old Delhi).

Prominent Rathore leaders and noblemen of Jodhpur went in a delegation led by Durgadas Rathore to plead for Ajit Singh to be named as the royal heir and Maharaja of Marwar. Aurangzeb repeated his promise of giving a *jagir* to Ajit Singh with the title of Raja when he attained age. The Rajput nobles persisted their demand of giving the throne of Marwar to Ajit Singh. Now Aurangzeb put forth his next cunning move; he promised he would give the throne of Marwar to Ajit Singh only if he converted to Islam and raised as a proper Muslim in his *harem*.

The Rathores under Durgadas saw through the ploy and retired to their mansion seeking time to think. It was 25th June 1679. Durgadas decided to take both the queens and the child to Jodhpur even at the risk of their lives. A servant girl was left at the mansion with her child disguised as Ajit Singh. Both the queens disguised in male attire and the delegation moved out on the treacherous way to Jodhpur from Delhi. Aurangzeb was quick to react and sent his soldiers to capture Durgadas Rathore and party.

Durgadas quickly took control of the situation and used gunfire to stop them dead in their tracks. With this obstacle removed, the small band of Rathores started on their perilous journey towards Jodhpur. The Mughals were not so easily giving up on them and they soon started following them at a breakneck speed. Durgadas Rathore was in a dilemma as the Mughals were fast catching up on them. Now he had to think fast and act fast. As they were moving towards Jodhpur, Rathores under him devised a scheme to slow down the progress of Mughals chasing them. Few of them stopped and laid an ambush. The Mughals arrived and had to fight their way through this very small party of Rathores. The Rajputs were outnumbered hugely, but this gave the much needed extra time to the fleeing party ahead of them.

The Mughals kept pursuing them; after few miles, the Rathores again followed the same scheme and some of them again sacrificed their lives to keep the heir alive. Several repetitions of this scheme was given shape until the party comprised only of Durgadas, infant Ajit Singh, the queens and three other Rathore nobles. They reached Balunda; here one of the families of the nobles gave shelter to the queens and Ajit Singh at the same time pledging to protect them even at the peril of their lives. Durgadas and the others vanished into the Aravalis to carry on their struggle of placing Ajit Singh on the throne.

A furious Aurangzeb, facing failure, decided to teach the Rathores of Jodhpur a lesson. He captured the boy left behind at the mansion in Shahjanabad and claimed that he had caught Ajit Singh. He converted the boy to Islam. This was done in order to fool people of Marwar that the real Ajit Singh was an impostor.

Aurangzeb ordered his son Muhammad Akbar to occupy Marwar so as to fully integrate it into the Mughal dominion. Akbar moved on to Marwar, commanding a considerable army. Ajit Singh's mother was a Sisodia and from the royal family of Mewar. Through her coercion, Maharana Raj Singh of Mewar decided to help the Rathores. But the combined army of Rathores and Sisodiyas was greatly outnumbered by the Mughal forces. They faced defeat in the open battle field and were forced to retreat to the Aravalis.

Durgadas Rathore was the leader of the Rathore faction. Maharana Raj Singh withdrew his Mewar army towards his own province as he feared a direct assault by Mughals on his kingdom. But, he continued to support the Rathores by actively engaging in guerilla warfare by looting Mughal camps and attacking and disrupting their supply lines. Durgadas Rathore and his followers too continued to do the same.

Aurangzeb was fed up of this and imposed *jaziya* tax on Marwar. He devastated numerous Hindu temples and shrines. For 20 years, Marwar remained under direct Mughal occupation. Meanwhile, Ajit Singh was sent by Durgadas to Sirohi, a remote town on the borders of present Gujarat and Rajasthan. Here he continued to live without Mughal harassment. Durgadas Rathore himself trained the prince on the art of warfare. They waited for the right time to take back the throne of Marwar.

The Mughal Empire was severely affected by the Rathores' guerilla tactics. Durgadas attacked treasuries and looted the Mughals and did not let them rest. It was a time when the Mughals were also being threatened by the Marathas in the Deccan. Aurangzeb decided to send his sons Azam and Muazzam to support Akbar and bring Rathores to their knees.

Durgadas Rathore was quick to understand the gravity of the situation. He secretly started parleys with Muhammad Akbar and incited him to revolt against his father. He promised him full help in his endeavor to become the Mughal emperor. Akbar was told that policies of Aurangzeb were actually harming the Mughal Empire by eroding its support. Akbar on the behest of Durgadas, declared himself emperor in an open rebellion.

Aurangzeb was a wily character; he devised a scheme so as to create discord between Akbar and his Rajput allies. He was successful in this and Akbar had to run away. Akbar later was able to convince Durgadas that the rift caused among them was a scheme of his father Aurangzeb and Durgadas again started supporting him fully.

As Rajput forces were not enough to install him as emperor, Durgadas took him to the Deccan to meet Sambhaji, the Maratha king. Akbar lived there for many years hoping for Maratha aid. His two children, a son and a daughter were under Durgadas's care, who in spite of the schemes and treacheries of the Mughals, arranged for their education and raised them as Musalmans. He could have easily converted them to Hinduism but such was the greatness of Durgadas that he did not do so.

Muhammad Akbar later fled to Persia to garner support for himself but died soon after. After Akbar's death, a peace treaty ensued between Rathores and Aurangzeb. The children of Akbar were handed back to the old emperor who was amazed to find them to be raised in proper Islamic way.

Soon after, Aurangzeb died. This gave perfect opportunity to Durgadas to capture Jodhpur and whole of Marwar. He succeeded! He installed Ajit Singh as the Maharaja of Marwar thus fulfilling his duty and promise as custodian of the Rathore royal family.

Durgadas then left Jodhpur and lived in Sadri, Udaipur, Rampura, and Bhanpura for some time and then left for Ujjain to worship Mahakaal regularly. On 22 November 1718, on the banks of the Shipra at Ujjain, Durgadas finally breathed his last at the age of 81 years. His canopy in red sandstone is still at Chakratirtha, Ujjain, which is a pilgrimage for all those who like the virtues of loyalty and bravery.

So, this was the loyal warrior of Indian history of whom we all never read in our history books. This again brings us to this question as to why such personalities are left out.

The Indian government has issued stamps and coins in honor of Durgadas.

48

Prataprao Gurjar

Defeat of Mughal Army in Salher Battle and Encounter with Bahalol Khan

1672. Battle of Salher, Nashik. It took place between the Marathas and Mughals. This was significant as it was the first open battle where the Mughals faced defeat. This was the battle that reinforced the supremacy of the Maratha Empire. Two brave sons of the soil made this victory possible. They were Prataprao Gurjar, the Maratha Senapati and Morapant Pingle, the first Peshwa, also called Sardar. The Maratha army numbered 20,000 and the Mughals 40,000. The Marathas were less superior to the Mughals in terms of weaponry and war animals. Yet in this fierce battle, the Marathas emerged victorious! Many a war fought in India between Indians and invaders do find a place in our History text books. But is the Salher Battle of 1672 well glorified and well described — a battle that saw the Mughals decimated for the first time in an open battle?

You have heard about the Rakt Talai or the lake of blood pertaining to the Battle of Haldighati, one of the bloodiest of battles in world history that took place in June 1576. In this battle between Rana Pratap's Mewar army and Akbar's Mughal forces, around 18000-4000 from Mewar army and 14000 from Mughal army were killed within four hours leading to the creation of a river of blood that flowed. The Battle of Salher witnessed a similar event on that eventful day of February 1672. In the battle that continued throughout the day, blood of ten thousand men on the two sides that died including that of war animals led to the creation of a stream and a muddy blood pool where soldiers and animals began to sink!

Shivaji had four different Commanders-in-Chief — Mankoji Dahatonde, Netaji Palkar, Prataprao Gurjar, and Hambirrao Mohite. Prataprao Gurjar was the third royal Senapati of Shivaji's army. As commander of the Maratha cavalry, he won the confidence of Shivaji as a trusted military leader after he defeated Mughal armies in Baglan and Bijapur armies near Panhala and helped Shivaji establish Maratha supremacy. He was in charge of the Maratha forces at Aurangabad during the two years of peace between Shivaji and the Mughal Emperor. After Bijapur kings broke the conditions of the treaty with an attack on Maratha territory, Prataprao Gurjar defeated them.

To ensure good administration of his empire, Shivaji created the *Ashta Pradhan*, a council of eight ministers. Morapant Pingle was the first of these ministers, the first Peshwa. A Deshahstha Brahmin, he led battles to victory and won the trust of Shivaji. He participated in several victorious battles against Mughal forces and Bijapur kings — against Adil Shah, capture of Trimbakeshwar Fort, Wani-Dindori, and Shivaji's invasion of Surat. Morapant Pingle was entrusted with the construction and administration of Pratapgad.

On June 11, 1665, the Treaty of Purandar was signed between Shivaji and Rajput ruler Jai Singh I, who represented the Mughals as commander of the Mughal army. Jai Singh had besieged Purandar fort and he agreed to sign a pact and avoid war on certain terms and conditions. Shivaji agreed to save his men and his empire by avoiding a war. According to the treaty, Shivaji ceded 23 strategically important forts including Purandar, Lohagad, Sinhagad, and Karnala to the Mughals. These forts were fortified with garrisons. Salher and Mulher forts of Nashik were already under Mughal siege. Following the terms of the treaty, Shivaji visited Agra to meet Aurangzeb. Shivaji had already built an empire, which proved to be a threat to the Mughals. He knew about Aurangzeb's secret intentions of inviting him to Agra. Soon after Shivaji, his eldest son Sambhaji, and few soldiers reached Aurangzeb's court, they were arrested. After few months, father and son miraculously escaped. Uneasiness between Maratha and Mughal forces followed after this.

Neither party arose for war until following Aurangzeb's orders many temples in Benares were destroyed. Besides, rejuvenation of anti-Hindu policies further hurt the sentiments of Shivaji. And Shivaji declared war against Aurangzeb. In between 1670-1672, Shivaji regained many a territory from the Mughals and retook over a dozen forts. Shivaji's Maratha forces led successive and successful raids into several Mughal territories including Khandesh, Surat, and Baglan. Prataprao Gurjar played an instrumental role in annihilating the Mughal forces at Baglan. Besides, Shivaji also raided territories of the Bijapur Sultanate.

Moropant Pingle led an army of 15000 Maratha soldiers and captured the Mughal forts of Aundha, Patta, and Trimbak. He successfully laid an attack on Salher and Mulher in January 1671. Aurangzeb sent a force of 12000 horsemen under the commandment of Ikhlas Khan and Behlol Khan, two of his generals to reclaim Salher. Mughals captured Salher in October 1671. Shivaji entrusted Moropant Pingle and Prataprao Gurjar to reclaim Salher fort.

Both Prataprao Gurjar and Moropant Pingle marched towards Salher through different directions. The combined army of around 20,000 soldiers met at a plain field near Salher. The Mughal forces under Ikhlas Khan and Behlol Khan were double the Maratha forces. Mughal combination of cavalry, infantry, and artillery were outmatched compared to the light Maratha cavalry. Furthermore, Mughals were superior in arms and ammunitions and the use of war animals. A fierce battle ensued. Part of the Mughal forces fought with artillery-swivels carried on elephants and camels. Soon Maratha forces routed the Mughal army and gave them a crushing defeat.

According to *Sabhasad Bakhar*, a historical narrative in Marathi that chronicles the heroic exploits of Shivaji and his successful wars and raids, the battle of Salher is described such:

"As the fighting began, such a (cloud of) dust arose that for a space of a three-kilometer square, friend and foe could not be distinguished. Elephants were killed. Ten thousand men on the two sides became corpses. The horses, camels, elephants (killed) were beyond counting. A flood of blood streamed (in the battlefield). The blood formed a muddy pool and in it (people) began to sink, so (deep) was the mud."

The Marathas gained hold of 6,000 horses, an equal number of camels, 125 elephants from this battle. Marathas also seized large amount of goods, gold, jewels, treasures, carpets, etc. from the Mughal camps. The two generals were captured along with several Mughal prisoners of war.

After the first Battle of Tarain in 1196, Battle of Salher happens to be the first battle won by a Hindu army against Muslim invaders. The 1196 battle was fought between Prithviraj Chauhan and Ghori. After this victorious battle, Shivaji further reinforced his forces and established Hindu supremacy. His coronation took place two years later, i.e. in 1674.

A few months before Shivaji's coronation, the Sultan of Bijapur Adil Shah sent his general Bahalol Khan with a huge army to attack Maratha territory. Shivaji entrusted Prataprao Gurjar for resistance. The Maratha army under Prataprao Gurjar surrounded Bahalol Khan's camp at Nesari. In a fierce battle that ensued, the Maratha Senapati took Bahalol Khan captive. They captured the Bijapuri forces along with their war material.

Shivaji had warned all of his Senapatis and the Sardars to never trust enemies and never let them go free. When Bahalol Khan repeatedly begged for pardon and promised never to attack Maratha territory again, Prataprao Gurjar gave a second thought. The enemy general's repeat request to let him and his captured army free made him forget Shivaji's warning. His impulsive emotional nature came into play. And he released Bahalol Khan, his troops including the seized war material.

When Shivaji heard about this blunder by Prataprao Gurjar, he sent a letter stating he would not see him until he recaptured Bahalol Khan. Prataprao realized his mistake and he made up his mind to capture Bahlol Khan at any cost.

Meanwhile, days after his release, Bahalol Khan started preparing for a fresh invasion of the Maratha territory. Muslim armies never followed rules of Dharma in warfare. Bahalol Khan did not keep his promise made to the Maratha Senapati. He advanced towards Nesari with a troop of 15,000 soldiers. He camped at Nesari. Prataprao Gurjar had a strength of 1200 soldiers, who were no match to the

15000 Bijapuri army. He felt taking his small army against a huge force would only mean taking them for suicide. At the same time, he remembered Shivaji's letter. His impulsive emotional nature came into play again. He left alone towards Bahalol Khan's camp. Six Maratha sardars joined him when they saw him galloping in his horse towards the enemy all alone. Seven Marathas against 15000 Muslim soldiers! Prataprao Gurjar and the six Maratha sardars fought until death.

Later, the Maratha forces under Anandrao and Hambirao Mohite, defeated Bahalol Khan.

Shivaji was deeply grieved hearing about Prataprao Gurjar's death. He arranged the marriage of the Senapati's daughter Jankibai Gurjari with his younger son Rajaram Bhosale. Jankibai later became the Maharani of the Maratha Empire.

49

Narasimhadeva

Orissa King Who Defeated Turkic Afghan Tughan Khan in 1244 AD

Hindu kings have a track record of following the rules of Dharma in warfare. They avoided fighting with an opponent already engaged in a fight with another. They avoided stabbing from behind or hitting below the navel. They took care of the injured at the end of the day. They considered women, prisoners of war, and farmers as sacred. They never pillaged the land or destroyed standing structures in enemy lands. They were merciful if enemies asked for pardon.

History is full of such examples of Dharma followed by Indian Hindu kings. Prithviraj Chauhan pardoned Mohammad Ghori when he asked for pardon though the latter attacked him several times. At one instance Prithviraj saw Ghori fleeing from the battlefield but he did not attack the running enemy. Had he killed Ghori, History would have been different. King Prithu badly defeated Bhaktiyar Khilji in 1206 AD, but he allowed the Muslim prisoners of war to settle in his kingdom when they sought pardon. That was how Muslim settlement in Assam started.

But Muslim kings did the opposite of these very rules of Dharma followed by Hindu kings in warfare. They followed the tactics of treachery, deception and cruelty. They plundered kingdoms, pillaged land, killed the weak and innocent, raped women and took them as slaves, stabbed warriors from behind, destroyed standing structures and temples, and what not! Converting the defeated people to Islam was one of their key strategies. Akbar, deemed 'the

GREAT' ordered the slaughter of around 40,000 unarmed old men, women and children of Chittorgarh after he captured it on 23 February 1568 as per accounts by Abul Fazl and Badauni, Muslim historians. Rajput women started committing *Jauhar* only to save themselves from disgrace at the hands of Muslim invaders.

Do you know Narasimhadeva I of Orissa followed only a single tactic tagged on by Muslim invaders and defeated the Turkish Muslim Nawab of Bengal? He defeated Tughan Khan in 1244 AD. He did follow the rules of Dharma, but to save his kingdom from being plundered, ransacked, and destroyed by the brutal invaders, he thought it wise to follow it! He was the first king of Orissa to give a strong defence against Muslim invasion during his reign.

Narasimhadeva was one of the greatest rulers of the imperial Ganga family, especially of the Eastern Ganga dynasty, also called Chodaganga dynasty. He was the son of Kasturidevi and Anangabhimadeva III. This dynasty was founded in the 11th century by Anantavarman Chodaganga Deva, whose mother Rajasundari was the daughter of Chola king Virarajendra Chola.

Initially, the territory of this dynasty included the southern part of Kalinga. Later, the empire expanded to include more kingdoms. Narasimhadeva I ascended the Ganga throne in 1238 AD. Under his reign, the Eastern Ganga Empire expanded from up to river Bhagirathi Ganga or Hooghly in the north and Gautami Ganga or river Godavari in the south. Narasimhadeva was also called Langula Narasimhadeva because of some of his bodily deformities.

During the reign of Anangabhimadeva III, his father, the Turkic Afghan Nawabs of Bengal made an unsuccessful attempt to occupy Orissa. The might and power of the Delhi Sultanate and the Nawabs of Bengal during the time of Narasimhadeva could not be underrated. The king realized this and he was certain that they would attack his kingdom in the near future. Hence, he strengthened his military power and decided to launch an offensive against the Muslim Nawabs of Bengal and create terror in their minds. This strategy of setting out to invade Muslim territories and defeating them would help check the enemy's future plans of attacking Orissa.

Malik Izzuddin Tughril-i-Tughan Khan was then the Nawab of Bengal. He established his supremacy, ascending the Bengal throne as Nawab in 1233 AD though he did bow to the supremacy of Razia Sultana.

Narasimhadeva invaded Bengal with a large army in 1243 AD and advanced up to Lakhnor. They seized Katasin fort. The major Muslim army, stationed in Lakhnavati advanced up to Katasin fort, led by Tughan Khan, the Nawab himself on 15th April 1244. The Ganga army retreated without offering a fight and abandoned the fort. They concealed themselves in the thick jungles and bushes surrounding the fort and remained in hiding. It was part of a plan hatched by the Ganga king in line with the war tactics followed by Muslim invaders.

As there was no challenge from the enemy forces and thinking the Ganga army fled, Tughan Khan's army retired for a midday meal and started relaxing. Suddenly, the Ganga forces sprung up from their hideouts and attacked the relaxing Muslim army. Taken by surprise and unprepared for a battle at that moment, the Muslim army could not offer stiff resistance.

Persian historian Minhaj-i-Siraz wrote in his book *Tabaqat-i--Naisiri* how 'a section of the Ganga forces made a sortie from the direction of the fort and simultaneously another detachment of two hundred footmen and fifty horse-men stole their way from behind the cane jungle and fell upon the Muslim forces'. This was followed by heavy casualties from Tughan Khan's army.

Tughan Khan could not continue with the battle. Most of his soldiers were all killed. Defeated, he fled to Lakhanavati, his capital. The Ganga army of Narasimhadeva pursued the Muslim forces far away from Katasin. With this, the Ganga territory expanded up to river Damodar in the north.

In 1245 AD, Narasimhadeva attacked Lakhnor, another principality of the Nawab of Bengal. Fakhor-ul Mulk Karim-ud-din-Laghori was the commandant of Lakhnor fort. The Ganga army easily defeated the commandant and the Muslim forces and captured the fort. Then they advanced up to Lakhnavati fort, laid siege to it at the base, and threatened the Nawab.

Meanwhile, Tughan Khan, who dreaded the Ganga army, sought help from the Sultan of Delhi. He sent Sharf-ul-Mulk-Al-Ashari and Kazi Jalia-ud-din-Kashani to the Imperial court. Following the orders of the Sultan, Malik Qura-quash Khan, the Nawab of Kara Manikpur and Malik Tamur Khan, the Nawab of Oudh advanced towards Lakhnavati with a huge force to help Tughan Khan. They reached Lakhnavati on 30 April, 1245 AD. By then, sensing the arrival of the huge Muslim army, the Ganga forces vacated their siege to the fort and retreated.

Tughan Khan expected that the two forces together would pursue the Ganga army out of the Sultanate territories of Bengal, but in vain. Meanwhile, Tamur Khan developed distrust on Tughan Khan. He seized Lakhnavati and forced Tughan Khan to flee Bengal.

Thus, Narasimhadeva's tactic helped end the supremacy of Tughan Khan and shattered his dreams of him becoming the Sultan of entire Bengal. Besides, the Ganga king snatched back territories in Bengal and Bihar from the Turkic Afghans and established Hindu supremacy.

Narasimhadeva built the famous Konark Temple dedicated to Surya Dev in Orissa. He erected a victory pillar designed as a war chariot. The structure commemorates the victory in the battle against the Muslims.

50

Benoy Badal Dinesh

Bengal Freedom Fighters who Killed Col NS Simpson, British IG of Police

Benoy Badal Dinesh — They are three individuals, three brave freedom fighters from West Bengal, but their names are uttered as one. They are inseparable. Benoy Badal Dinesh together gave shape to a common task — killing brutal British Inspector General of Police, Colonel NS Simpson. They attained martyrdom after this. Benoy Basu was then aged 22 years, Badal Gupta 18 and Dinesh Gupta 19. At such a young age, patriotism ran in their veins. They gave their life for the freedom of the motherland. All three were born in different villages under Munshiganj District, now in Bangladesh. It is a pity that we hardly get to read about the brave warriors of India in our History text books.

Benoy Basu was born on 11 September 1908 at Rohitbhog village. After clearance of his 10th exam, he was enrolled in Mitford Medical School. But he did not clear his medical studies, as he was more concerned about the freedom of India and actively participated in related activities. He joined the Mukti Sangha, a secret group dedicated to similar activities. The words and activities of freedom fighter Hemchandra Ghosh motivated him to join the group. This group was closely connected to the Jugantar Party, a key freedom fighters' group from Bengal. Many members of this group, over time, were arrested, hanged and deported for life to Kaalapani.

Badal Gupta was born in 1912 in Bikrampur village. He belonged to a family of freedom fighters — his paternal uncles

Dharani Nath Gupta and Nagendra Nath Gupta were imprisoned along with Sri Aurobindo Ghosh for their involvement in the Alipore Bomb Case. It was a trial held in Alipore following a conspiracy to kill D.H. Kingford, Chief Presidency Magistrate of Muzaffarpur. Khudiram Bose and Prafulla Chaki threw the bombs on a vehicle coming out of the magistrate's home on April 30, 1908, which they surmised that it carried Kingford. A case was filed against many freedom fighters on their 'conspiracy' for 'waging war against the King'. While in school, Badal Gupta was influenced by his teacher Nikunja Sen. And he joined the Bengal Volunteers, a secret group started by Subhash Chandra Bose in 1928.

Dinesh Gupta was born on 6 December 1911 in Josholong village. He joined Subhash Chandra Bose's Bengal Volunteers, while studying in Dhaka College. Dinesh Gupta translated a short story written by Anton Chekhov; it was published in a magazine called *Prabasi*. The key activities of Bengal Volunteers were directed towards action against police repression in different jails in Bengal. Members planned to execute infamous British police officers. Dinesh Gupta went to Midnapore, which was a secret centre of training freedom fighters in the use of firearms. Himself an expert in the use of the firearm, Dinesh Gupta trained young freedom fighters in Midnapore.

In August 1930, Bengal Volunteers planned to kill Mr. F.J. Lowman, the Inspector General of Police of Dhaka. He was famed for notoriety, especially of brutally punishing freedom fighters who were arrested. Benoy Basu was entrusted with the task of assassinating him. Lowman was scheduled to visit Medical School Hospital in Dhaka to see an ailing senior police official undergoing treatment. Hodson, the Superintendent of Police, would accompany him. Benoy Basu was then a student of Medical School Hospital. It was 29th August 1930. Benoy Basu dressed in traditional Bengali attire, breached the security. He fired at Lowman from close range. He also fired at Hudson. Benoy immediately managed to escape from there and then to Kolkata. While Lowman died instantly, Hodson was grievously injured. Benoy was never caught or convicted for this.

The next in target in the list was Col N.S. Simpson, the Inspector General of Prisons. He brutally oppressed the prisoners in jails. Members of Bengal Volunteers also decided to launch an attack in the Writers' Building in the Dalhousie square in Kolkata. A successful attack would help infuse terror in the minds of the British in the official circle. Benoy Basu, Badal Gupta, and Dinesh Gupta were entrusted with the task.

Members of Bengal Volunteers often disguised themselves when giving shape to their tasks so that no one recognized them. On 8 December 1930, Benoy Badal Dinesh dressed themselves in European costume and entered the Writers' Building. They shot Simpson from close quarters. The Inspector General of Prisons died on the spot. The sound of gunshots alarmed the police force. British police retaliated; they started firing at Benoy Badal Dinesh.

A fierce gunfight ensued between the British police and the three freedom fighters. While the three were wounded, they were able to injure several British officers. Worth mentioning are Twynam, Prentice, and Nelson. The British police were superior in numbers. Soon they overpowered the trio.

To avoid arrest, Badal Gupta consumed potassium cyanide. He had brought it along so that if caught he would consume it. He died on the spot. Benoy and Dinesh shot themselves with their own revolvers. While Benoy was seriously wounded, Dinesh's wound was minor.

Benoy was taken to the hospital. Though his wound was treated, he infected it by repeatedly putting in his finger into it. He died of infection of the wound 5 days later, i.e. on 13 December 1930.

Dinesh Gupta was taken to Alipore Jail where he was jailed during the trial. While in Alipore Jail, he wrote letters to his sister. These letters were later compiled into a book titled *Ami Shubhash Bolchhi*. He was convicted and sentenced to death by hanging. Mr. Gerlick was the judge who gave the verdict. Dinesh was hanged on 7 July 1931 at Alipore Jail.

Do you know Kanailal Bhattacharya, another member of Bengal Volunteers, took revenge of Dinesh Gupta's conviction just twenty days later? He killed Mr. Gerlick, the judge on 27 July, 1931. Such was the level of patriotism in the young minds of Bengal during the freedom movement!

Later, few of Dinesh Gupta's students in the use of firearms training in Midnapore were successful in the assassination of three District Magistrates in succession — James Peddy, Robert Douglas, and D.E. Burge in 1931, 1932, and 1933 respectively.

James Peddy was notorious for beating freedom fighters to unconsciousness. He would take the women Satyagrahis to the open streets, strip them and leave them there. He was shot at close range by Jyoti Jeevan Ghosh and Vimal Dasgupta. He succumbed to his injuries the next day. Robert Douglas had killed two unarmed young freedom fighters at Hijli Detention Camp. Two brothers successfully carried out the task of killing Douglas. The younger Pradyot Bhattacharya, famed to be very handsome, was arrested and hanged to death. D.E. Burge was also renowned for his atrocities meted out to the Satyagrahis. He was killed by Anath Panja and Mrigen Datta; while escaping, Mrigen was caught and shot to death. Chaos prevailed in Bengal for sometime after these leading to arrest of many. Brojo Kishore Roy Choudhary, Ram Krishna Roy and Nava Jeevan were arrested, tried, and awarded death sentence pertaining to the case. They were hanged at Midnapore Jail, which had 3000 inmates. At the time of their execution, the inmates chanted slogans of 'Vande Mataram' that echoed in the Midnapore sky.

The last words of the martyrs were:

"We are going and leaving the unfinished task in your hands to finish."

Benoy Badal Dinesh inspired many freedom fighters hereafter so did the others who sacrificed their lives for the motherland. Arrest, executions, and deportations did not deter the spirit of the members of Bengal Volunteers. They continued with their activities until India gained Independence.

After independence of India, the Dalhousie Square in Kolkata was named B.B.D. Bagh in memory of Benoy Badal Dinesh. A plate in the name of the trio was also engraved in the wall of Writers' Building on the first floor.

Salute to Benoy Badal Dinesh! Salute to all freedom fighters who sacrificed their lives for the freedom of Bharat! Jai Hind!

51

Nag Bhat I

This Gurjar Pratihar King Badly Defeated Arab Forces

As soon as a child goes to school and starts learning Indian history, all he/she learns is defeats faced by Indian kings at the hands of invaders. From my childhood to teenage, I went through the same ordeal. History, especially military history being my favorite subject, I was often left wondering: were we always defeated? Were we on the losing side always? So I started reading whatever I could find anywhere beyond the pathetic NCERT books.

Yes, NCERT books are indeed pathetic because as a young mind I, like countless others, was influenced much by the defeats and routs. Such portrayal creates a feeling that we were inferior to the invaders, thus sowing the seeds of inferiority complex. This happens to such an extent that one robotically tends to think that all that is from foreign lands is better than what we have here.

Here is a battle of a period which has been more or less ignored by history books taught in schools. Today's battle we are going to delve into was fought between the Arab forces and an alliance of Indian dynasties i.e. the Gurjar Pratihars, Chalukyas, Rashtrakuta, Guhil, etc. This was actually a series of engagements fought between Arabs and Hindus and it finally culminated in utter destruction and defeat of the Arab forces.

The final engagement of this bloody series was fought in 738 AD. The Arabs had previously attacked and ransacked cities up to Ujjain but could not hold on to their outposts. This was due to two reasons: problems in maintaining a long supply line and revolts by locals.

The Arab governor of Sindh, Emir Junaid led a large army consisting of infantry and cavalry numbering to a total of 50,000 to 60,000 men. As news of this oncoming foe reached the Indian kings, they decided to forge an alliance to face the enemy. The Arab force consisted of cavalry from Syria and Iraq, aided by men from Sindh along with mercenaries.

Nag Bhat I, king of the Gurjar Pratihar Empire, was chosen as the leader of the Indian alliance comprising of Rashtrakuta, Guhil, Chalukya, and Gurjar armies to face the enemy. This alliance was between North Indian and South Indian rulers. Vikramaditya II was then the king of the Chalukya dynasty and Bappa Rawal of the Guhils.

Nag Bhat I led an army of 30,000-40,000 men mostly consisting of cavalry and infantry. He was a great military commander and organised his army by dividing his cavalry in parts on the flanks. The battle hardened infantry was positioned in the center with reserve cavalry and possibly war elephants in the back as a rearguard.

The battle was fought somewhere on the borders of modern day Rajasthan and Sindh.

The Arabs advanced, ravaging the countryside and destroying many temples along the way besides forcefully converting many to Islam.

Arabs made a dash at the center of Hindu lines hoping to dissect the army into two and directly reaching the king. But, the infantry held on and the resulting melee gave enough time to the cavalry of Nag Bhat I to outflank the Arab army. Once flanked, what followed was total carnage as Arab flanks disintegrated and total confusion prevailed.

The Arab cavalry could not withstand the furious charge of the Indian cavalry and a rout started. Emir Junaid tried his best to motivate his forces and stop the rout but the charge was too strong to hold on and in the ensuing melee, Junaid was killed. Without a leader, the Arab army disintegrated.

In the words of Suleiman, an Arab chronicler, the Arab forces were scattered like hay by the hoofs of the horses of the Gurjar king and his alliances.

A battered Arab army reached the other bank of the Indus. They later constructed a new city in Sindh named Mansurah and abandoned all dreams of capturing India. The annihilation was so complete that even Arab chroniclers described the Gurjar king in their history records as the biggest enemy of Islam in the whole world.

Inscriptions about this great victory have been found at various places including Gwalior in Madhya Pradesh. Now, why this important battle has been omitted from Indian History is anyone's guess.

52

Santi Ghosh and Suniti Choudhury
How the Two Teenage Freedom Fighters Assassinated British Magistrate

Fight and perish — this was the spirit of patriotism that was conspicuous in every freedom fighter across India during British rule. Santi Ghosh was only 15 years old and Suniti Choudhury 14 when they jointly assassinated Charles Geoffrey Buckland Stevens, a British bureaucrat and the District Magistrate of Comilla. It was 14 December 1931. Both their families negatively suffered the brunt of their heroic deed.

Santi Ghosh was born on 22 November 1916 in Calcutta. She grew up in a patriotic environment. Her father Debendranath Ghosh was a freedom fighter and a professor of philosophy at Victoria College, Comilla. At the age of 15, Santi Ghosh co-founded the Chhatri Sangha (Girl Students Association) and served as its Secretary. She was not only inspired by her family to be a part of the freedom struggle but also by Prafullanandini Brahma, who was older to her by two years. Brahma was a member of the Jugantar Party, a group that believed in the use of arms to drive the British out of India. It was a secret group that masterminded the assassination of many British officers.

Many members of Jugantar Party caught by British were arrested, hanged, or deported for life to Kaalapani, the Cellular Jail in the Andaman Islands. Santi Ghosh joined the Jugantar Party. Just imagine the level of patriotism of these young girls — Brahma aged 17 and Ghosh 15 who were ready for armed rebellion against the British without fearing the consequences! After joining the Jugantar

Party, Santi Ghosh trained herself in self-defense and the use of arms, especially using swords, clubs, and firearms. She looked slightly older than her age, as she dressed herself to look older - her hair gathered in a knot at the nape and often draped in a white cotton sari.

Suniti Choudhury was born in Comilla on 22 May 1917. Comilla is currently a city in the Chittagong division of Bangladesh. From a very young age, Suniti hated the British. She belonged to a family of freedom fighters. Two of her elder brothers were already actively involved in the freedom movement. She mixed up with friends who nurtured similar ideologies — of being participants in India's struggle for independence and drive the British out of India through armed rebellion. During her school days, she met Santi Ghosh and Prafullanandini Brahma and was inspired by their patriotic zeal. She was deeply influenced by the activities of Ullaskar Dutta, who manufactured bombs intended for use against British colonial officials.

Prafullanalini Brahma recruited Suniti Choudhury as member of the Jugantar Party. She also became a member of Tripura Zilla Chhatri Sangha and then as the Sangha's captain of its Women's Volunteer Corps wing. She became popular as Meera Devi. 14 year old Suniti became an expert in the use of the dagger, sword, and *lathi*. She was thus recruited as the in-charge of training female members of the Chhatri Sangha in the use of *lathi*, sword and dagger. She was also selected as the 'custodian of firearms'.

Till this time, it was men who took the lead role in giving shape to bombings and assassinations pertaining to British officers. Women freedom fighters worked in the background. Considering their valor and courage at such a young age, Santi Ghosh and Suniti Choudhury were chosen for direct action — of assassinating Charles Geoffrey Buckland Stevens, the District Magistrate of Comilla.

During this time, the freedom movement had taken a serious turn in Bengal. Many freedom fighters openly revolted, leading to their arrest. A group of patriots under the banner of a secret group started assassinating infamous British police officers who were notorious for committing atrocities on arrested freedom fighters such as beating them to unconsciousness, inflicting them various forms of torture, and of undressing women Satyagrahis in the streets. There were also rumors about British police raping women Satyagrahis. Santi Ghosh and Suniti Choudhury were all the more determined to take action.

Freeman Thomas, the Earl of Willingdon was then the 22nd Viceroy and Governor-General of British India. He passed an ordinance in India that suppressed the civil rights of Indians, including that of free speech. British district magistrates and police officers misbehaved with the Indians, especially those who were arrested and tried. These magistrates and police officers also raped Indian women.

Meanwhile, news about the hanging of Bhagat Singh, Rajguru, and Sukhdev on March 23, 1931 shook the nation. This cruelty and heartlessness of the British Raj was directed towards instilling fear in the hearts of other freedom fighters, but in vain. A thousand Bhagat Singh, Rajguru and Sukhdev sprang up from across the country. So did resentment in Bengal increase! Santi Ghosh and Suniti Choudhury and other young freedoms were all the more ready to attack and kill British officers. And they waited for an opportune time.

Santi Ghosh and Suniti Choudhury sought permission to meet Comilla District Magistrate, Charles Geoffrey Buckland Stevens. Their request for permission was granted against presenting a petition of arranging a swimming competition amongst their classmates in school. They entered the Magistrate's office room where he was seated. They carried automatic pistols hidden under their shawls. As they were school girls, British police did not suspect them and avoided searching them. They facilitated their easy entry.

While Stevens looked at the document, Santi Ghosh and Suniti Choudhury took out their pistols and shot at Stevens, killing him on the spot. The sound of gunshots alerted the British police. Soon they were overpowered and arrested. It was 14 December 1931 — near to nine months past the martyrdom of Bhagat Singh, Rajguru, and Sukhdev.

The two girls were mercilessly beaten. But they maintained their calmness all the while. They didn't panic. They expected to die a martyr's death. As they were minors, they were sentenced with life-imprisonment. The first bullet had pierced from Suniti Choudhury's gun, which immediately caused the British officer's death. The next round of bullets by both the teenage girls left no scope for the Magistrate to survive. Hence, Suniti was given a harsher punishment. She was segregated from all other political prisoners.

Periodicals in the West portrayed the assassination of Buckland Stevens as a sign of outrage against the ordinance passed by Freeman Thomas. After the verdict was announced, a flyer praising Santi Ghosh and Suniti Choudhury as nationalist heroines was found by the intelligence branch of Rajshahi district police. The poster read, 'THOU ART FREEDOM'S NOW, AND FAME'S', displaying photographs of the two brave teenage freedom fighters with the following lines from a poem composed by Robert Burns, a Scottish poet:

> "Tyrants fall in every foe!
> Liberty's in every blow!"

The British stopped Suniti's old father's pension. They detained her two brothers without trial and tortured them. Her family members in no time were on the brink of starvation. Later, her younger brother died due to years of malnutrition.

Later, their life imprisonment tenure was reduced to 10 years.

Salute to nationalist heroines Santi Ghosh and Suniti Choudhury. Jai Hind!

To be continued in next part of this series on unsung warriors....

Bibliography

(Besides the sources mentioned below, the authors have also relied upon oral narrations, folklore, ballads, site visits, narration by locals and guides at few historical sites, and more.)

Chapter 1 - Rampyari Gurjar

1. Singh, Nau Nihal, *The Royal Gurjars: Their Contribution to India*, Anmol Publications, 2003.

2. Russell Jesse, Cohn Ronald, *Ram Pyari Gurjar*, Book on Demand, 2012.

3. अहलावत, कैप्टन दलीप सिंह, *जाट वीरों का इतिहास*, Dalip Singh Ahlawat, 1989, 1992.

4. 'Jograj Singh Gurjar and Timur Lang Battle', *Patrika,* Jan 2017.

Chapter 2 – Prithu

1. Barua, B.K., *A Cultural History o f Assam*, Vol l, K.K. Barooah; Assam; 1951.

2. Barpujari, H. K., *The Comprehensive History of Assam*, Publication Board, Assam, 1990).

3. Gait, Edward Albert, *History of Assam*, Thacker, Spink & Company, 1906.

4. Dutta, Debabrata, *History of Assam*, Sribhumi, 1982.

5. Siraj, Minhajuddin, *Tabaqat - 1 - Nasiri*, (English Translation by Raverty), 1881, London.

Chapter 3 – Saraswathi Rajamani

1. 'An INA veteran lives in penury', *The Hindu,* Jan 2005.

2. 'Voice of an Independent Indian', YouTube.

3. 'The forgotten spy', reddif.com, August 2005.

4. 'Jaya dole for Netaji spy', *The Telegraph,* June 2005

Chapter 4 – Jhalkaribai

1. Naimisharay, Mohandas, *Veerangana Jhalkari Bai*, Radhakrishna Paperworks, 2016.

2. Narayan, Badri, *Women Heroes and Dalit Assertion in North India: Culture, Identity and Politics*, Sage India, 2006.

Chapter 5 – Bajiprabhu Deshpande

1. Gokhale, Balkrishna Govind, *Poona in the Eighteenth Century: An Urban History*, OUP India, 1988.

2. 'Baji Prabhu Deshpande : The Hero of Pawankhind', Hindu Janajagruti Samiti.

Chapter 6 – Rani Karnavati

1. Rawat, Ajay S (2002), *Garhwal Himalayas: A Study in Historical Perspective*, Indus Publishing Company.

Chapter 7 – Rana Sanga

1. Sen, Sailendra, *A Textbook of Medieval Indian History*, Primus Books, 2013.

2. Chandra, Satish, *Medieval India: From Sultanat to the Mughals,* Har Anand Publications, Second Reprint, 2006.

Chapter 8 – Haldighati Battle

1. Sarkar, Jadunath, *Military History of India*, Orient BlackSwan, 1960.

2. *Medieval India (Part Two): From Sultanat to the Mughals*, Satish Chandra Har-Anand Publications, Second Reprint, 2006.

Chapter 9 – Tonkham Borpatra Gohain

1. Barpujari, H. K., *The Comprehensive History of Assam*, Publication Board, Assam, 1990).

2. Ingty, P.W., *War Drums of Eagle King,* Partridge India, 2015.

3. Shakespear, Leslie, *History of Upper Assam, Upper Burmah and North-Eastern Frontier,* Andesite Press, 2017.

Chapter 10 – Veer Savarkar

1. Savarkar, Veer, *Essentials of Hindutva*, Kindle Edition, 2016.

2. Keer, Dhananjay, *Veer Savarkar*, Popular Prakashan, 1966.

3. 'Hindutva a way of life and not a religion: Supreme Court to continue hearing of 1995 verdict', *Zee News* (zeenews.india.com), Jan 2017.

Chapter 11 – Rani Chennamma of Keladi

1. Malwad Shantadevi, *Keladi Chennamma*, Translated by Susheela Padiyar, Litent ePublishing, 2010.

1. 'Biography of Queen Keladi Chennamma', yousigma.com.

Chapter 12 – Kuyili

1. Kumar, Madhan, *Thamizh Is Not Just A Language: The Valour*, Educreation Publishing, 2017.

2. *Legendary Leaders*, Book 3, Z. Madhur, Aakar Books, 2018.

Chapter 13 – Unknown Hindu Yogi

1. Mitchell, William Forbes, *The Project Gutenberg EBook of Reminiscences of the Great Mutiny 1857-59*, Macmillan and Co Ltd., 1910 (First Edition 1893).

Chapter 14 – 1824 Hundreds of Gurjars Martyred

1. Grant, James, *Cassell's Illustrated History of India*, Oxford University, 1879 (Digitized 2006).

Chapter 15 – Naiki Devi

1. Majumdar, Asoke Kumar, *Chaulukyas of Gujarat: A Survey of the History and Culture of Gujarat from the Middle of the Tenth to the End of the Thirteenth Century*, Bharatiya Vidya Bhavan, 1956.

2. Majumdar, Ramesh Chandra, *Ancient India*, Motilal Banarsidass, 2017 (10 edition).

3. Sharma, Dasharatha, *Early Chauhan Dynasties: A Study of Chauhan Political History, Chauhan Political Institutions and Life in the Chauhan Dominions from 800 to 1316 A. D.*, Motilal Banarsidass Publ, 2002.

Chapter 16 – Tarabai Bhosale

1. Eaton, Richard M, *A Social History of the Deccan, 1300–1761: Eight Indian Lives*, (The New Cambridge History of India), 2008.

2. Majumder, RC, *The Mughul Empire*, Bharatiya Vidya Bhavan, 1974.

3. Mehta, JL, *Advanced Study in the History of Medieval India*, Sterling Publishers Private Limited, 1996 (2nd edition).

Chapter 17 – Baji Rout

1. Rautray, Sachidananda, *Baji Raut*, Grantha Mandir.

Chapter 18 – Tirot Sing

1. May, Andrew, *Homo in Nubibus: Altitude, Colonisation and Political Order in the Khasi Hills of Northeast India*, Article in *The Journal of Imperial and Commonwealth History* 42(1), January 2014.
2. The Eastern Panaroma (www.easternpanorama.in), August 2009.
3. 'Tirot Sing was the brave hero of the hills', *DNA India*, December 2016.

Chapter 19 – Bishnois

1. Jain, Pankaj, *Dharma and Ecology of Hindu Communities: Sustenance and Sustainability*, Routledge, 2016 (Ashgate Publishing, 2011).
2. Collins, Brian H, 'Review of Dharma and Ecology of Hindu Communities: Sustenance and Sustainability' in Journal *Philosophy East and West*, Volume 63, No. 1, January 2013.
3. Edugreen (edugreen.teri.res.in).

Chapter 20 – Kanaklata Barua

1. Pathak, Guptajit, *Assamese Women in Indian Independence Movement*, Mittal Publications, 2008.

Chapter 21 – Uda Devi

1. Mitchell, William Forbes, *The Project Gutenberg EBook of Reminiscences of the Great Mutiny 1857-59*, Macmillan and Co Ltd., 1910 (First Edition 1893).
2. 'Uda Devi: Dalit Freedom Fighter In The 1857 Uprising', *feminisminindia.com*, October 2017.

Chapter 22 – Roipulliani

1. Lalthangliana, B, *Culture and Folklore of Mizoram*, Publications Division, 2005.

Chapter 23 – Kartar Singh Sarabha

1. *Echoes of Freedom: South Asian pioneers in California 1899-1965*, University of California, Berkeley, Bancroft Library, 2018.
2. sikh-history.com.

Chapter 24 – Bhagat, Rajguru, Sukhdev

1. Nayar, Kuldip, *The Martyr Bhagat Singh: Experiments in Revolution*, Har Anand Publications, 2000.

2. Gupta, Amit Kumar, 'Defying Death: Nationalist Revolutionism in India, 1897–1938' in Journal *Social Scientist*, Vol. 25, No. 9/10, Sep. - Oct. 1997.

3. Rana, Dr. Bhawan Singh, *Shahid Bhagat Singh* (Hindi), Diamond Pocket Books.

4. Verma, Anil, *Rajguru - The Invincible Revolutionary*, Publications Division, M/O Information & Broadcasting, Govt. of India, 2010.

5. Mande, Pramod Maruti, *Sacred Offerings into the Flames of Freedom*, Vande Mataram Foundation, 2005.

Chapter 25 – Chandrasekhar Azad

1. Rana, Dr. Bhawan Singh, *Chandra Shekhar Azad (An Immortal Revolutionary of India)*, Diamond Books, 2005.

2. Bhattacherje, SB, *Encyclopaedia of Indian Events & Dates*, Sterling Publishers, 2009.

3. chandrashekharazad.org.

Chapter 26 – Khudiram Bose

1. Agarwal, SK, *Khudiram Bose*, Prabhat Prakashan, 2017.

2. Patel, Hitendra, *Khudiram Bose: Revolutionary Extraordinaire*, Publications Division, 2016.

3. midnapore.in

4. Gupta, Manmathnath, *History of the Indian Revolutionary Movement*, Somaiya Publications, 1972.

Chapter 27 – Paona Brajabashi

1. Kabui, Professor Gangmumei, *History of Modern Manipur (1826-1949)*, Edited by Dr. Lal Dena, Orbit Publishers-Distributors, 1991.

2. Singh, N. Khelchandra, *Battle of Khongjom*, N. Khelchandra Singh, 1983.

3. e-pao.net.

Chapter 28 – Shivdevi Tomar

1. David, Saul, *The Indian Mutiny: 1857*, Gardners Books, 2003.

2. जाखड़, महावीर सिंह, *जाटों के विश्व साम्राज्य और उनके युग पुरुष*, मरुधरा प्रकाशन, 2004.

Chapter 29 – Veerapandiya

1. Yang, Anand A, 'Bandits and Kings: Moral Authority and Resistance in Early Colonial India' in Journal *The Journal of Asian Studies*, October 2007.

2. Mukund, Kanakalatha, *The View from Below: Indigenous Society, Temples, and the Early Colonial State in Tamilnadu, 1700–1835*, Orient BlackSwan, 2004.

3. Karunakarapandian, K, 'A Political History of Ettayapuram of Thirunelvelli District, Tamil Nadu' (Chapter 19), in *History of People and Their Environs: Essays in Honour of Prof. B.S. Chandrababu*, Edited by S Ganeshram and C Bhavani, Indian University Press, 2011.

Chapter 30 – Kanhoji Angre

1. Nairne, Alexander Kyd, *History of Konkan*, JJetley, for Asian Educational Services, 1988.

2. Sen, SN, *Military System of the Marathas*, Orient Longmans, 1928 (Digital publication, 2010).

3. Sardesai, GS, *The New History of the Marathas*, Vol.II, Munshiram Manoharlal Publishers, 1986.

4. Hindu Janajagruti Samiti (hindujagruti.org).

Chapter 31 – Pasaltha Khuangchera

1. Lalthangliana, B, *Culture and Folklore of Mizoram*, Publications Division, 2005.

Chapter 32 – Rani Lakhsmi Bai

1. Blair Brysac, Shareen and Meyer, Karl E, *Tournament of Shadows*, Basic Books, 2006.

2. Jones, David E, *Women Warriors: A History*, Potomac Books, 2005.

3. Lebra, Joyce, *Women Against the Raj: The Rani of Jhansi Regiment*, Institute of Southeast Asian Studies, 2008.

4. Edwardes, Michael, *Red Year: The Indian Rebellion of 1857*, Cardinal, 1975.

Chapter 33 – Hemchandra Vikramaditya

1. Chandra, Satish, *Medieval India: From Sultanate to The Mughals, Part II: Mughal Empire (1526–1748)*, Har Anand Publications, 2007.

2. Bhardwaj, Kanwal Kishore, *Hemu: Napoleon of Medieval India*, Mittal Publications, 2000.

Chapter 34 – Alluri Sitarama Raju

1. Balakrishna G, V, *Freedom Movement in Andhra Pradesh*, Government of India Press Information Bureau (web.archive.org), 2002, 2011.

2. Rao, P. Rajeswar, *The Great Indian Patriots*, Mittal Publications, 1991.

3. Singh, M.K., *Encyclopaedia Of Indian War Of Independence (1857-1947)*, Anmol Publisher, 2009.

4. Rao, Bandlamudi Nageswara, *Mapping the Tribal Economy: A Case Study from a South-Indian State*, Cambridge Scholars Publishing, 2013.

Chapter 35 – Rana Hammir Singh

5. Sen, Sailendra, *A Textbook of Medieval Indian History*, Primus Books, 2013.

6. Hunter, William, *A Brief History of the Indian Peoples*, Clarendon Press, 1892.

7. Barani, Ziauddin, *Tarikh-I Firoz Shahi*, Translated by Ishtiaq Ahmed Zilli, Primus Books, 2015.

Chapter 36 – Kapaya Nayaka

1. Talbot, Cynthia, *Precolonial India in Practice: Society, Region, and Identity in Medieval Andhra*, Oxford University Press, 2001.

2. Eaton, Richard M, *A Social History of the Deccan, 1300–1761: Eight Indian Lives*, (The New Cambridge History of India), 2008.

3. Sastry, PV Parabhrama, *The Kākatiyas of Warangal*, Govt. of Andhra Pradesh, Hyderabad, 1978.

Chapter 37 – Matmur Jamoh

1. Chaudhuri, Sucheta Sen, 'Pasighat: Post-colonial Geography and History in Interface' in *Glocal Colloquies*, 1(1), ISSN No 2454-2423, 2015.

2. pasighat.wordpress.com.

Chapter 38 – Kalyan Singh Gurjar

1. Grant, James, *Cassell's Illustrated History of India*, Oxford University, 1879 (Digitized 2006).

2. ashokharsana.proboards.com, October 2008.

Chapter 39 – Sambhudhan Phonglo

1. Barpujari, SK, *History of the Dimasas: from the Earliest Times to 1896 AD*, Autonomous Council, N.C. Hills District (Assam), 1997.

2. Bezbaruah, Indrajit, *Dimasa Nationality Question* submitted in Faculty of Arts, Gauhati University, 2010 and referenced in Shodhganga (shodhganga.inflibnet.ac.in).

Chapter 40 – Banda Singh Bahadur

1. Sagoo, Harbans Kaur, *Banda Singh Bahadur and Sikh Sovereignty*, Deep & Deep Publications, 2001.

2. Pletcher, Kenneth, *The History of India*, Rosen Education Service, 2010.

3. Singh, Ganda and Singh, Teja, *A Short History of the Sikhs: 1469-1765*, Publication Bureau, Punjabi University, 1989.

4. The Encyclopaedia of Sikhism (sikhiwiki.org).

Chapter 41 – Mula Gabharu

1. Datta, Amaresh, *Encyclopedia of Indian Literature: Devraj to Jyoti*, Volume 2, Sahitya Akademi, 1988

2. Barpujari, H. K., *The Comprehensive History of Assam*, Publication Board, Assam, 1990).

3. Ingty, P.W., *War Drums of Eagle King*, Partridge India, 2015.

4. Shakespear, Leslie, *History of Upper Assam, Upper Burmah and North-Eastern Frontier*, Andesite Press, 2017.

Chapter 42 – Chain Singh

1. Sarala, Srikrshna, *Indian Revolutionaries A Comprehensive Study, 1757-1961*, Volume 1, Ocean, 1999.

2. Grant, James, *Cassell's Illustrated History of India*, Oxford University, 1879 (Digitized 2006).

Chapter 43 – Kaneganti Hanumanthu

1. 'History of AIKS' in Guntur pages (aiksc2010atguntur.tripod.com).

Chapter 44 – Avantibai

1. Rag, Pankaj, *Relics of 1857, Madhya Pradesh*, Directorate of Archaeology, Archives, and Museums, Madhya Pradesh, 2007.

2. Mitchell, William Forbes, *The Project Gutenberg EBook of Reminiscences of the Great Mutiny 1857-59*, Macmillan and Co Ltd., 1910 (First Edition 1893).

Chapter 45 – Mahabiri Devi

1. Bates, Crispin and Major, Andrea, *Mutiny at the Margins: New Perspectives on the Indian Uprising of 1857*, Edited, Sage India, 2013.

2. Gupta, Charu, 'Dalit Viranganas and Reinvention of 1857' in Journal *Economic and Political Weekly*, Vol. 42, No. 19 (May 12-18, 2007) (sgtbkhalsadu.ac.in), May 2007.

Chapter 46 – Suhaldev

1. Narayan, Badri, *Fascinating Hindutva: Saffron Politics and Dalit Mobilisation*, SAGE India, 2008.

2. Reeves, PD, *Sleeman in Oudh: An Abridgement of W. H. Sleeman's A Journey Through the kingdom of Oude*, Edited, Cambridge University Press, 1971.

3. Suvorova, Anna, *Muslim Saints of South Asia: The Eleventh to Fifteenth Centuries*, Routledge, 2011.

4. Amin, Shahid, *Conquest and Community: The Afterlife of Warrior Saint Ghazi Miyan*, Orient Blackswan, 2015.

Chapter 47 – Durgadas Rathore

1. Sen, Sailendra, *A Textbook of Medieval Indian History*, Primus Books, 2013.

2. Rapson, Edward James; Haig, Wolseley; Burn, Richard *The Cambridge History of India*, CUP Archive, 1962.

Chapter 48 – Prataprao Gurjar

1. Ranade, Mahadeo Govind, *Rise of Maratha Power*, Publications Division, M/O Information & Broadcasting, Govt. of India, 2012.

2. Sen, Surendra Nath, *Siva Chhatrapati, Being a Translation of Sabhasad Bakhar with Extracts from Chitnis and Sivadigvijaya, with Notes*, Wentworth Press, 2016.

3. Sardesai, HS, *Shivaji, the Great Maratha*, Volume1, 2, Genesis Publishing Pvt Ltd, 2002.

4. Deopujari, Murlidhar Balkrishna, *Maratha Art of War*, Vidarbha Samshodhan Mandal, 1973.

Chapter 49 – Narasimhadeva I

1. Mitra, Debala, *Konarak*, Archaeological Survey of India,1976.
1. Haq, MA, *Muslim Administration in Orissa*, Punthi Pustak, 1980.
2. Siraj, Minhaj-I *Tabaqat-i-Nasiri*, Edited by W.Nassau Lees, College Press, 1864 (digitized at archive.org)
3. Sarkar, JN, *History of Bengal*, BR Publishing Corporation, 2011.
4. 'Narasimhadeva I', (PDF), Shodhganga (shodhganga.inflibnet.ac.in), August 2017.

Chapter 50 – Benoy Badal Dinesh

1. Mazumdar, RC, *History of the Freedom Movement in India*, III, Firma K.L. Mukhopadhyay, 1963 (Digital Library of India, 2006).
2. Dasgupta, Hemendranath, *Bharater Biplab Kahini*, II & III, New Madan Press, 1948 (Digital Library of India, 2013).
3. en.banglapedia.org.

Chapter 51 – Nag Bhat I

1. Puri, Baij Nath, *The History of the Gurjara-Pratihāras*, Oriental Publishers & Distributors, 1957.
2. Sen, Sailendra Nath, *Ancient Indian History and Civilization*, New Age International, 1999.
3. 'First Battle of Rajasthan – Where Arab lost to Indians', defence.pk, January 2013.
4. Gwalior inscription of Gurjar Pratihar king Mihira Bhoja.
5. Somani, Ramavallabha, *History of Mewar, from Earliest Times to 1751 A.D.*, Mateshwari Publications, 1976.
6. Tripathi, Rama Shankar, *History of Kanauj: To the Moslem Conquest*, Motilal Banarsidass, 1959.

Chapter 52 – Santi Ghosh and Suniti Choudhury

1. Guhathakurta, Meghna and Schendel, Willem van, *The Bangladesh Reader: History, Culture, Politics*, Duke University Press Books, 2013.
2. Forbes, Geraldine Hancock, *Indian Women and the Freedom Movement: A Historian's Perspective*, Research Centre for Women's Studies, S.N.D.T. Women's University, 1997.
3. Smith, Bonnie G., *The Oxford Encyclopedia of Women in World History*, Volume 1, Bonnie G. Smith, Oxford University Press, 2008.

❑❑❑